The Book of Genesis
Part I

Professor Gary A. Rendsburg

THE TEACHING COMPANY ®

PUBLISHED BY:

THE TEACHING COMPANY
4151 Lafayette Center Drive, Suite 100
Chantilly, Virginia 20151-1232
1-800-TEACH-12
Fax—703-378-3819
www.teach12.com

ISBN 1-59803-192-9

Gary A. Rendsburg, Ph.D.

Professor of Jewish Studies, Rutgers University

Gary Rendsburg holds the Blanche and Irving Laurie Chair in Jewish History at Rutgers University in New Brunswick, NJ. He serves as chair of the Department of Jewish Studies and holds an appointment in the History Department.

Dr. Rendsburg majored in English and journalism as an undergraduate at the University of North Carolina and graduated in 1975. He then pursued graduate work in Hebrew Studies at New York University and received his Ph.D. in 1980.

He previously taught at Canisius College in Buffalo, NY (1980–1986), and at Cornell University in Ithaca, NY (1986–2004).

Professor Rendsburg's areas of special interest include literary approaches to the Bible, the history of the Hebrew language, the history of ancient Israel, and the literature and culture of ancient Egypt.

Dr. Rendsburg has held a National Endowment for the Humanities fellowship and has taught as a visiting professor at the University of Pennsylvania, at Colgate University, and at the State University of New York at Binghamton.

Professor Rendsburg is a frequent guest of the Hebrew University of Jerusalem, where twice he has served as visiting research professor and twice he has held the position of visiting fellow at the Institute for Advanced Studies.

Dr. Rendsburg is the author of five books and more than 100 scholarly articles. His most popular book is a general survey of the biblical world entitled *The Bible and the Ancient Near East*, co-authored with the late Cyrus H. Gordon (1997).

He has visited all the major archaeological sites in Israel, Egypt, and Jordan and has participated in excavations at Tel Dor and Caesarea. In addition, he has lectured around the world, including Europe, Japan, and Australia.

For more information, go to:
http://jewishstudies.rutgers.edu/faculty/grendsburg/.

Table of Contents
The Book of Genesis
Part I

The Book of Genesis

Scope:

This course of 24 lectures focuses on the first book of the Bible (in both the Jewish and Christian canons), the book of Genesis. This particular book is an extremely rich text that can be approached from a variety of perspectives, including literary, historical, theological, and archaeological. Most of the stories in Genesis (creation, flood, Abraham, Jacob, Joseph, and so on) are well known, but many crucial issues in the study of the book are less familiar to general audiences. We will present these issues in a detailed fashion; the 24 lectures afford us plenty of time to work through the 50 chapters of the book of Genesis.

The course will speak to the different perspectives listed above. First and foremost, we will approach the text as a piece of literature, highlighting the many literary devices and techniques employed by the ancient author(s) of the book. In so doing, we will demonstrate that what on the surface may look like rather simple tales are, in fact, the products of great literary sophistication. This finding bespeaks not only a remarkably gifted author but also an ancient Israelite audience that could appreciate and understand literature of such high quality and brilliance. We are led to conclude that literature played a central role in the life of ancient Israel, thus establishing at a very early time the notion that the Jews are the people of the book.

We will talk about the history that lies behind the book of Genesis. We will address such questions as when Abraham lived, where his birthplace of Ur was located, under which pharaoh did Joseph serve, and so on. We will also raise even more fundamental questions, such as did Abraham and Jacob and Joseph and so on exist at all, or were they simply literary creations of ancient Israelite literati? To answer these questions, we will need to look at other ancient Near Eastern sources from the three main regions: Egypt, Canaan, and Mesopotamia. Thus, this course also will provide an introduction to these neighboring cultures, especially as they affect our understanding of the Bible.

We will delve into theological issues. What can we learn about the religion of ancient Israel from reading these stories? Did the ancient Israelites believe in one God? Or did they only worship one God without denying the existence of other deities? And what was the nature of the God of Israel? Was he similar to the other deities of the ancient Near East? Or was he uniquely different? Was he, in fact, even a he? Religion is more than the conception of the deity, however; it also includes the relationship between God and man, and this, too, embodied in the covenant concept of the Bible, will be a topic of exploration in this course.

As intimated above in the paragraph about history, this course will use a vast array of archaeological evidence to illuminate issues in the book of Genesis. The evidence, both textual and artifactual, will come from across the ancient Near Eastern landscape, from Mesopotamia in the northeast, from Canaan most proximate to Israel, and from Egypt in the southwest. We are required to retain such broad horizons because the book of Genesis itself does so. Abraham is born in Mesopotamia; he migrates to the land of Canaan; his grandson Jacob returns to Mesopotamia, where he lives for 20 years; and at the end of the book, Joseph and his brothers are resident in Egypt.

Most importantly, we will deal with questions of authorship. Is the book of Genesis the result of a haphazard compilation of disparate sources? Or does it present itself as a unified literary whole, suggesting a single author? And in either case, when might the book have been written and/or achieved its final written form?

Finally, we will explore various other issues that emanate from our reading of Genesis. Often, these topics will be of interest to biblical studies in a wider scope. For example, we will explore the question of women in the Bible: Why does the Bible include so many female characters, especially in comparison to other ancient Near Eastern literature, and why are these women often portrayed in unexpectedly heroic fashion, often at the expense of the male characters? We will discuss different translations of the Bible: Why are there so many different versions? How are they different? How are they similar? And we will take time to consider the way later generations of Jews and Christians understood the Bible, especially given that these later readings are often quite different from the original authorial intent.

In sum, the multifaceted book of Genesis allows for numerous avenues of inquiry: We will do our utmost in this course to tackle all of them.

Lecture One
On Reading the Book of Genesis

Scope:

We begin with a basic overview of the course, touching on a number of crucial issues at the outset, creating almost a set of ground rules, as it were, for reading the book of Genesis. We will approach the text as literature, as history, and as theological treatise—all at once! Most importantly, we will attempt to understand the text in its original setting, reading it with the knowledge and worldview that an ancient Israelite would have brought to his or her reading of Genesis. Finally, in contrast to those scholars who carve up the text into separate sources, we will take a holistic approach to the text of Genesis.

Outline

I. This course is, first and foremost, a course on the book of Genesis, the first book of the Bible in both the Jewish and Christian canons. We will perforce need to look at other biblical material at times, but we will keep our focus on Genesis throughout. Because both the Bible in general and Genesis in particular are so wide-ranging, I will need to use a variety of approaches while presenting the material.

A. Most importantly, we must recall that we are reading ancient literature; thus, we will most frequently use literary analysis—that is to say, the course will look and sound like a literature course.

B. Second, much of the material in the book of Genesis, especially from chapter 12 onward, to the end of the book in chapter 50, needs to be situated in a historical context. Thus, we will bring historical analysis to the material, as we seek to uncover the history of ancient Israel and the surrounding cultures in the ancient Near East—that is to say, at times, the course will look and sound like a history course.

C. Third, we must recall that the text that we are reading presents some of the most basic concepts of ancient Israelite religion, such as the worship of a single deity; thus, we will need to discuss aspects of ancient religion, cult, and theology—in such instances, the course will look and sound like a religion course.

II. There are three questions that one may ask while reading the Bible:

    A. What was the author's original intent, and how did his or her original audience understand the text? This will be our main emphasis throughout the course. To successfully answer this question, we must immerse ourselves in the world of ancient Israel by attempting to live and think, as well as we can, like an ancient Israelite in, say, c. 1000 B.C.E.

    B. How has the text been interpreted by the two faith communities who hold the Bible to be sacred, namely, Judaism and Christianity, throughout the ages? This subject requires a different approach, as we will illustrate with a few examples. Before moving to these illustrations, however, note that the formative periods of Jewish and Christian interpretation largely coincided: Jewish midrashic writings from the rabbis and early patristic writing from the church fathers both date to the late Roman or Byzantine period (4th through 6th centuries B.C.E.).

        1. Later Jews and Christians developed a belief in creation *ex nihilo*, that is, "out of nothing," and therefore, read this belief into their reading of Genesis 1. As we shall see, however, Genesis 1 states exactly the opposite.

        2. The wording of Genesis 1:26, "Let us make a human in our image, by our likeness," may suggest a belief in the Trinity, but this is a later Christian theological development not to be found in the Jewish Bible.

    C. What does the text mean to me today? For this question, one turns to one's personal clergy for religious guidance, but this is not a matter into which we will enter during this course.

III. The book of Genesis is a book about origins. It presents ancient Israel's understanding of two beginnings.

    A. The first 11 chapters of Genesis discuss the origins of the world, since those stories are of a universal nature.

B. Chapters 12–50 in Genesis present the origins of the people of Israel. Actually, Israel is not quite a people yet but, rather, a family, namely, Abraham and his descendants.

C. These two origins reflect Israel's theology, their belief in a God who is at once the God of the world in general and the God of the people of Israel in particular.

IV. Many scholars have proposed reading Genesis as a composite of three separate sources that were put together more or less haphazardly by a redactor or compiler. We will explore this theory further in Lecture Six, but for now, we note simply that we will take a different tack. We will approach the story as a unified literary whole. We will not sweep minor contradictions and divergences under the rug, but we are much more impressed with a unified reading than one that places the text under a microscope and divides it into tiny component parts. Again, as noted, we will return to this issue in much more detail in Lecture Six.

V. Next, there is the question of what translation to use. We will devote all of Lecture Sixteen to the issue of Bible translations, but for now, let me simply recommend a few of the standards.

A. The most widely used Bible in college classrooms is the Revised Standard Version, which comes in a variety of editions, such as the *New Oxford Annotated Bible*. This translation adheres closely to the Hebrew original, word for word.

B. The Jewish Publication Society Version (technically the New Jewish Publication Society Version, because an older one was produced in 1916) is the standard among Jewish readers of the Bible. Note that it is a more idiomatic rendering and frequently departs from the Hebrew text literally. A fine recent edition, which includes this translation, is *The Jewish Study Bible*.

C. Robert Alter, a professor at the University of California at Berkeley, produced a translation of the book of Genesis alone in 1996, replete with superb notes of a literary nature; he then completed the task for the entire Torah, published in 2004.

D. The most literal translation of the Torah, which of course, includes the book of Genesis, is that of Everett Fox, professor at Clark University in Worcester, MA. For those readers who wish to get as close to the Hebrew text as possible, with the result that the English is often a bit odd-sounding, this is the text for you.

VI. Finally, let me say a word about the overall structure of the lectures that follow. Generally, I go back and forth between and among different kinds of presentations: close readings of selected texts, broader readings of larger swaths of material in Genesis, and contextual material providing background information not only for Genesis but for the Bible in general.

A. We cannot read all of Genesis in the same detail; thus, I have chosen a representative sampling of stories to examine closely, including, for example, the two creation accounts and selected episodes from the lives of Abraham, Jacob, Joseph, and Judah.

B. I admit that my rationale for selecting these particular texts is sometimes subjective: I simply enjoy the episode in Genesis 29, for example, better than the story that precedes it or the one that follows it.

    1. One point that attracts me to this story is the very human quality of this episode—the interplay between the human characters is front and center at all times, and God is not mentioned in the text at all.

    2. Yet, as we shall see in Lecture Eighteen, when Jacob is deceived by Laban, the reader has no doubt that the hand of God is present and that this is Jacob's punishment for having deceived his father, Isaac, two chapters earlier.

C. Furthermore, the individual stories that I have chosen to examine in fine detail provide us with a sampling of the literary devices utilized by the ancient Israelite literati. To take Genesis 29 again as our example, when we reach that story in Lecture Eighteen, we will see such devices as the typescene, wordplay, alliteration, and change in perspective—all present in a single chapter of the book of Genesis.

D. Here, in a more detailed fashion, is how the course will proceed.

1. We will look at the first two stories of Genesis—the two stories of Creation.

2. We will do an overview of the history of ancient Israel from the very beginning through the end of the biblical period, a period of about a thousand years.

3. Then, we will talk about the ancient Near East (Egypt, Canaan, and Mesopotamia) and regions beyond the Near East that will have some play in our course, including Greece and Persia.

4. We will devote a lecture to the theory that holds that the book of Genesis derived from three sources.

5. We will look at the Flood story and the Mesopotamian literary tradition, especially the Gilgamesh epic.

6. We will talk about the two covenants—the one with Noah, which is representative of all of humanity, in Genesis 9, and the one with Abraham, which is representative of God's relationship with the people of Israel and described in Genesis 15 and 17.

7. We will then look at the Abraham story, with a special emphasis on the story of the binding of Isaac, known as the *Aqedah*.

8. We will look at women in the Bible.

   a. We will look at Sarah and Hagar, and we'll talk about why the Bible, especially in contrast with other ancient Near Eastern material, spends so much time talking about female characters.

   b. We will talk about Isaac getting a bride—Rebekah.

   c. We will consider "the barren woman" motif (Sarah, Rebekah, and Rachel all have trouble conceiving) and "the younger son" motif (think of Isaac, Jacob, and Joseph).

9. We will compare the Abraham and Jacob cycles.

10. We will devote a lecture to different Bible translations.

11. We will do close readings of the story of Jacob and Esau, and the story of Jacob and Rachel.

12. We will investigate the date of the book of Genesis.

13. Next, we will turn to the story of Joseph, which commences in Genesis 37.

    a. All of a sudden in Genesis 38, Joseph is actually not in the story, which instead is about his brother Judah and Judah's daughter-in-law, Tamar.

    b. We will also read closely the next chapter where Joseph returns, engaged in work for Potiphar, whose wife tries to seduce Joseph.

    c. Joseph is living in Egypt, so we will also talk about the Egyptian background of the story of Joseph.

14. We will sum it all up as we will complete our journey through the remarkable book of Genesis.

Essential Reading:

Robert Alter, *Genesis*, pp. xi–xlvii.

Supplementary Reading:

Elliot Rabin, *Understanding the Hebrew Bible: A Reader's Guide*, pp. 1–47.

Questions to Consider:

1. How are the three questions that one may legitimately ask when reading the Bible different from each other? Why do we choose to focus on the first of the three during our course?

2. Why are there so many different translations of the Bible available?

Lecture One—Transcript
On Reading the Book of Genesis

Welcome, everyone, to our course on the book of Genesis. Hello, I'm Professor Gary Rendsburg of Rutgers University in New Brunswick, New Jersey, where I hold positions in two departments, the Department of Jewish Studies and the Department of History. I have been engaged with the study of the Bible in general, and the book of Genesis in particular, for most of my adult life, and I invite you to join me as we journey through this remarkable book, the first book of the Bible in both the Jewish canon and the Christian canon. We will, perforce, need to look at other biblical material at times, but we will need to keep our focus on the book of Genesis throughout with all of those very well known stories that most people are familiar with—the story of the Creation of the world, Noah and the Flood, stories about Abraham, and Jacob and Joseph.

Now, because the Bible in general and the book of Genesis in particular are so wide ranging, I will need to use a variety of approaches while presenting the material in this course, three approaches in particular. First and most importantly, we must recall that we are reading ancient literature. We are reading a literary text, and so very frequently and in fact, most frequently, we will use a literary analysis when approaching the book of Geneses. That is to say, this course will look and sound like a literature course. I myself was an English major as an undergraduate, and I've always loved literature, so I am naturally attracted to reading a book such as Genesis as a piece of great literature.

Second, much of the material in the book of Genesis, especially from chapter 12 onward, to the end of the book in chapter 50, needs to be situated in a historical context. Thus, we will bring an historical analysis to the material, as we seek to uncover the history of Ancient Israel and the surrounding cultures in the ancient Near East. We will attempt to place individual characters in Genesis, such as Abraham and Joseph, in a specific chronological setting on the historical timeline. As such, at other times this course will look and sound like a history course and I've always had a love of history, as well, so I very much enjoy bringing this aspect to our course.

Third, we must recall that the text that we are reading presents some of the most basic concepts of the religion of Ancient Israel, such as the worship of a single deity, and thus, we will need to discuss aspects of ancient religion, cult, and theology. In such instances, this course will look and sound like a religion course, a course offered in a Department of Religion or Religious Studies at any North American university. I must note here that the book of Genesis and the Bible in general never present a theology of Ancient Israel in a systematic fashion. Keep in mind that nobody sat down to write the theology of Ancient Israel in ancient times. Efforts to write true theological treatises would not arise until centuries later in late antiquity. Accordingly, we need to extract that theology from reading the stories, and that is exactly what we will do during this course.

Now, we will move back and forth between and among these three approaches throughout our course. That is to say, we'll do a literary reading, then we'll talk about some historical material, and then we'll talk about the theology that is forthcoming from the text, at times all in the same lecture. Not only these three approaches, I should add, but on occasion other academic disciplines will inform our course—including, for example, archaeology, anthropology, linguistics, and the history of law. This back-and-forth procedure will, I hope, give our course certain vibrancy, allowing us to go with the flow as required.

There are three questions that one may ask while reading the Bible, and they are all legitimate questions. Let's talk about these. First question: What was the author's original intent, and how did his or her original audience understand the text? Those are two sides of the same question; let me repeat them. What was the author's original intent? And, how did the original audience in Ancient Israel understand the text? This will be our main emphasis throughout this course. Now, to successfully answer this question, one must immerse oneself in the world of Ancient Israel by attempting to live and to think, as best as possible, like an Ancient Israelite in, say, 1000 B.C.E. or 800 B.C.E., sometime almost 3,000 years ago. I, for one, feel very comfortable in that world—indeed, my kids often accuse me of living in the year 1000 B.C.E. Thus, our first and main question: What was the author's original intent and how did his or her audience understand the text?

The second question one could ask: How has the text been interpreted by the two faith communities who hold the Bible to be sacred—namely, Judaism and Christianity—throughout the ages since the Bible's composition down to our present day? Now, this subject will require a different approach, and I can illustrate this with a few examples. Before moving to these illustrations, however, note that the formative periods of Jewish and Christian interpretation largely coincided. Jewish Midrashic writing from the rabbis and early patristic writing from the Church Fathers both date to the late Roman or Byzantine Period, about the fourth through the sixth centuries C.E. The canon was closed by that point and both Judaism and Christianity moved into the period of the interpretation of the biblical text.

Now, here are a couple of those illustrations to bring out this point. Later, Jews and Christians—by "later," I mean not during the biblical period, but during the post-biblical period, about 2,000 or 1500 years ago—these "later" Jews and Christians developed a belief in Creation *ex nihilo*. That is, creation "out of nothing." They, therefore, read this belief into their reading of Genesis 1, the story of Creation. As we shall see, however, Genesis 1, the test of Genesis, states exactly the opposite. The text states very clearly that there was preexistent matter and that God created the world out of that preexistent matter. He did not create the world *ex nihilo*, out of nothing. So, we have a difference here between what the text stated in its original context and the way later interpreters interpreted the biblical material.

Another example: The wording of Genesis 1:26, "Let us make a human in our image, by our likeness," and I emphasize here the three first-person plural forms. "Let us make a human in our image, by our likeness." This is God speaking. This may suggest, for example, a belief in the Trinity, but this is a later Christian theological development not to be found in the Jewish Bible, and accordingly, again, we need to make a distinction between the way the text would have been understood at the time of its composition and its reception in Ancient Israel and the way it was interpreted later on in a Jewish, or in this particular case, Christian context. So, these are the first two questions that one can ask when looking at the biblical material.

The third one is: What does the text mean to me today? For this question, one turns to one's personal clergy for religious guidance. Generally, this is not a matter for our consideration during this course. It brings us into denominational settings, into a particular church or synagogue setting. This is the way the Bible might be studied in seminaries or in Christian-affiliated or Jewish-affiliated schools and universities. These are all very legitimate approaches, I add, but it is not something we will do in this course. I'm very much interested in theological issues, as I've already indicated, but we will focus on the theology of Ancient Israel and not necessarily the theology of later-day Judaism or Christianity into the 21st century.

So, there you have the three different questions, all equally legitimate. These are, again, first, the original intent of the author and how the text was understood in Ancient Israel. That's question number one, which will be the main focus of our course. Question number two, which we will delve into from time to time, the way the text was understood in later Jewish and Christian interpretation. And third, as I noted, what does the text mean to me today?

At this point in our introductory lecture, we probably should ask the question: What is the book of Genesis? The book of Genesis is a book, as the title indicates, about origins. It discusses the origin of the world in its first 11 chapters—chapters 1–11 of Genesis—and then it moves to talking about the origins of the people of Israel, which at this point, is not quite a people yet, but more a family. There were four generations—Abraham, Isaac, Jacob, and then the 12 sons of Jacob, of whom the most famous is Joseph. The stories of these four generations comprise chapters 12–50 of the book of Genesis. The book, accordingly, is divided into two parts of unequal length—chapters 1–11, the origins of the world, and chapters 12–50, the origins of the people of Israel, represented by the family of Abraham and the succeeding generations.

The point that I have just made about the two parts of the book of Genesis tells us a lot about the theology of Ancient Israel. Here is an example of how we extract theological perspective from the stories, discovering what the people of Ancient Israel believed, in particular, how they understood God and God's relationship to mankind. That is to say, as the first eleven chapters indicate, God is the God of the entire world, and therefore the Bible begins by talking about the world in general. At the same time, God is the God specifically of the people of Israel, and that is why the book of Genesis moves its focus very quickly to the people of Israel from Abraham onward; thus, the book of Genesis, and we'll keep that point in mind as we proceed through our course.

The next issue I want to address is the word book, as in the title of our course *The Book of Genesis,* with the focus on the word "book." The word "book" in our culture, suggests an individual volume with pages between two covers that was created, more or less, in a single stroke, by a single author. Many scholars have proposed reading Genesis not in that light, but rather as a composite of three separate sources, which were put together, more or less, haphazardly, by a redactor or compiler. "Redactor" is a fancy word, a scholarly term for an editor or a compiler. In a later lecture we will explore this theory, that the book of Genesis is the product of more than one author, three in particular, in detail. At this juncture in Lecture One, though, we will simply note that in this course we will take a different tack.

We will approach the story as a unified literary whole. We will not sweep away the minor contradictions and divergences under the rug, because these are the little issues that have led to the theory that the book of Genesis is, in fact, the compilation of different sources. But I personally am much more impressed with the unified reading of the book of Genesis, one which sees it as a literary whole, that's "whole" with a 'w'—w–h–o–l-e. Using the unified approach we will look at the book as a whole, as a single piece of literature, treating the book of Genesis as it appears in its final form, the form in which it has reached us from antiquity. Yes, at times, we will place the text under the microscope, and yes, we will see contradictions from time to time. But when we pull back the lens, we will see how the book of Genesis works in a macroscopic fashion. Again, as noted, we will return to this issue in much more detail in a later lecture. But here at the outset of our course I want to stress how my reading of the book of Genesis, as a literary whole, differs from the way most scholars approach the text. They see it as a compilation of different sources; I see it as a literary unit.

Another question we need to address is the question of what translation to use. We will devote a full lecture down the road to the issue of Bible translations, and we will make comments now and then about this interesting topic in other lectures as well. For now, though, let me simply say a few words about translation and recommend a few of the standards. To some extent, it matters not which translation of the Bible you use. The oldest English translation still in use by people today is the *King James Version* and it is a perfectly acceptable translation, although its English is very archaic filled with forms such as thou, thee, and thy. The most widely used Bible in college classrooms today is the *Revised Standard Version*, which comes in a variety of editions, such as the *Oxford Study Bible*. Both of these translations adhere closely to the Hebrew original, rendering each Hebrew word with a corresponding English equivalent word.

There are other options, however. *The Jewish Publication Society Version*—which, technically, is the *New Jewish Publication Society Version*, since an older one was produced in 1916; this is the standard among Jewish readers of the Bible. It is a more idiomatic rendering of the Bible; it frequently departs from the Hebrew text literally and prefers instead to capture the Hebrew text with an idiomatic English style. A fine recent edition, which includes this translation, is a volume called the *Jewish Study Bible*, also published by Oxford University Press.

In addition, there are two translations of the book of Genesis that have been produced by individual scholars. The first three that I have mentioned, the *King James Version*, the *Revised Standard Version*, and the *Jewish Publication Society Version*—all of these were produced by committees of scholars working together. But then, there are two volumes, as I've just noted, produced by individual scholars here in the United States. Robert Alter, professor at the University of California at Berkeley, produced a translation of the book of Genesis as a stand-alone volume in 1996, replete with superb notes of a literary nature. He then completed the task of translating the entire Torah, which was published in 2004. So, one could have a look at Robert Alter's translation, and use it and read it with great profit—either the single volume on Genesis, or the entire Torah. Indeed, given the heavy literary analysis that we will utilize in this course, I commend to you Alter's work even more so.

As an aside, let me provide a definition of the word "Torah," which I just used. "Torah" is the Hebrew word for "Pentateuch," and it refers to the first five books of the Bible from Genesis through Deuteronomy. Literally the word means "Teaching" in Hebrew, because the basic teachings of Ancient Israel are found in these five books. "Pentateuch" is the equivalent term in ancient Greek, meaning "five books," or more literally "five scrolls," since each of the five books was written on an individual scroll in ancient times.

A second translation done by an individual scholar—and it is the most literal translation of the Torah that exists today in English, and therefore, of course, includes the book of Genesis—is that of Everett Fox, professor of biblical studies at Clark University in Worcester, Massachusetts. For those readers who wish to be as close to the Hebrew text as possible, with the result that the English is often a bit odd sounding, this is the text for you. Professor Fox tries to capture the rhythms, sounds, syntax, and, frequently, the alliterations, as well, of the Hebrew in his very excellent English text.

I can recommend all of these volumes to you and there are a host of other volumes that you should feel welcome to use as well. The *New International Version* is another example of a widely used English Bible translation here in America, especially among evangelicals. *The New American Bible* is also a fine work, it was produced by Catholic scholars and it, as one might expect, used mainly by Catholic readers. What I ask you not to do is to use a paraphrase of the Bible, and there are certain English versions, which paraphrase more than others. I ask that your translation be a translation of the Hebrew text. Whether it takes the more idiomatic route or whether it utilizes the word-for-word approach more, it is important to have a text that actually translates the Hebrew, because we will be talking about various specific passages and verses in the Bible that will demand an accurate translation.

Of course, I should mention the obvious here that the Bible as a whole—the Jewish Bible or the Hebrew Bible, the Christian Old Testament, including the book of Genesis of course, is written in Hebrew, ancient Hebrew. Hebrew is a Semitic language and we know the language very, very well. There is an unbroken tradition from antiquity down to the present day—certainly among Jews and to some extent among Christians aw well in the reading of the Bible in Hebrew—and so when we read an English translation, it is important to keep in mind that indeed we are reading a translation and that the original text was written in Hebrew thousands of years ago. On all of these topics we will have more to say on as we proceed through the course.

I want to say a word here about the overall structure of the lectures that follow. Generally, I move back and forth between and among different kinds of presentations. We will do what I call "close readings" of selected texts. In these cases, we will look at individual verses, even individual words. These are close readings. We will look at how one verse flows into the next and the kind of meaning that we can extract from reading very closely a particular chapter in the book of Genesis. At other times, we will do broader readings. We will look at large swaths of material. We will, for example, look at the entire story of Abraham in overview fashion to have the large picture in one lecture, and we will do likewise for other chunks of the book of Genesis. At other times, as I said, we'll be looking at the smaller component parts of that larger picture. So, we'll have close readings of selected texts, and we'll have these broader readings as well.

We also need to have lectures on the contextual material. We need to provide background information not only for Genesis, but also for the Bible as a whole. We'll talk about the history of Ancient Israel, not only the period covered in the book of Genesis, but the entire trajectory of Ancient Israelite history. We'll talk about how the Bible became canonical, how the different books of the Bible were canonized, that is, accepted as sacred scripture. We will situate the book of Genesis in the ancient Near East as a whole. The ancient Near East includes Egypt and Canaan and Mesopotamia, and within Mesopotamia, we can subdivide the region into Babylonia and Assyria and other areas as well. We will need to situate the book of Genesis in these larger settings of a historical nature. So, our lectures will go back and forth between close readings, the larger swaths of material, and what I call "the contextual material," giving us background information about the history and culture of the ancient world, the world from which the Bible sprung.

Even with the twenty-four lectures at our disposal in this course, we cannot read all of Genesis in the same detail, and thus I have chosen a representative sampling of stories to examine closely, including, for example, the two Creation accounts and selected episodes from the lives of Abraham, Jacob, and Joseph. Having just mentioned the two Creation accounts, that may come as a surprise to some of you, for the Bible begins not with a single story of Creation, but with two individual accounts of the origin of the world and we'll be looking at both of those.

I admit that my rationale for selecting a particular text here and there is sometimes very subjective. For example, I simply enjoy the episode in Genesis 29. It's the story of Jacob meeting Rachel at the well and Jacob's relationship with his uncle and soon-to-be father-in-law, Laban. I like that story. I like it better than the one that precedes it, and I like it better than the one that follows it, and so, it's one of the stories I have elected to read with you. One point that attracts me to this story, in fact, is the very human quality of this episode in the book of Genesis—the interplay between the human characters is front and center at all times, and, in fact, God is not mentioned in this text at all. Yet, as we shall see when we deal with this chapter in a future lecture, when Jacob is deceived by Laban, the reader has no doubt that the hand of God is present and that Jacob is punished here for his having deceived his father Isaac two chapters earlier. It is the interplay between the human and the divine in that story that attracts me to it very much. Indeed, not only in that story, but in the book of Genesis as a whole, as we will see time and again in this course.

Furthermore, the individual stories that I have chosen to examine in fine detail, our close readings, provide us with examples of the many literary devices utilized by the Ancient Israelite authors. You'll hear me refer to these individuals as the Ancient Israelite literati. I love that term. It actually has alliteration unto itself, "the Ancient Israelite literati." These are the individuals who wrote the Bible, who used the panoply of literary devices at their disposal, never missing an opportunity to treat their audience of readers to a dazzling display of language. To take Genesis 29 again as our example, we will see that in that one chapter alone, one finds the following literary devices—typescene, although that term may not mean much to you now, we will talk about typescene when we reach that story; wordplay, where single words may have more than one meaning; allusion, where a particular phrase used in the story refers to the same phrase used in an earlier story and thereby invites the reader to connect the two episodes. Then there's the literary device, which is called a change in perspective, a change in camera angle, as it were. All of these are present in a single chapter of the book of Genesis. Genesis 29 truly is an amazing chapter, and its finely crafted language is another quality that attracts me to this story. We have a lot more ground to cover before we are there, so at this point I am giving you but a sampling and a taste of what's to come.

I invite you to join me on our journey through this first book of the Bible, a text which is almost 3,000 years old, and that, too, is a topic for future discussion, the date of the book of Genesis. Our text has been interpreted through the ages by both Jews and Christians, as we've noted, and yet it is still very much alive and vibrant in our own day. Now, let me illustrate for you how the course will proceed in a more detailed fashion, which will give you an understanding and some idea of where we are headed.

As I noted, we will look at the first two stories of Genesis, the two accounts of Creation. We'll talk about the differences between these two stories, but we also will look at these two stories as a literary unit.

We then will present three of the contextual lectures that I described. We will do an overview of the history of Ancient Israel from the very beginning through the end of the biblical period, a course of about a thousand years. We then will talk about the ancient Near East, focusing our attention on Egypt, Canaan, and Mesopotamia. We'll devote a lecture to the composition of Genesis, including the dominant scholarly approach which holds that the book is comprised of three sources.

Next, we'll go back and look at specific chapters in Genesis once more, starting with the flood story. We will, in addition, compare the biblical account with the very similar account that appears in the Gilgamesh epic, the great literary classic of the ancient Near East. We'll talk about the concept of "covenant," a subject that appears in Genesis 9 and again in chapters 15 and 17. The first of these covenants is with Noah, representative of all of humanity, and the second of these is with Abraham, the ancestor of the people of Israel. This harks back to something we mentioned a few moments ago, that the origins of the world and the origins of the people of Israel are both found in Genesis—two origins, two covenants.

We'll then look at the Abraham story, using both a literary approach and an historical approach, as we will seek to answer such questions as where did Abraham live, and when did Abraham live? We'll look in particular at Genesis 22, one of the most famous stories in the Bible—the binding of Isaac, the near sacrifice of Isaac by his father Abraham.

We'll treat the subject of women in the Bible, with a focus on characters such as Sarah and Hagar and Tamar. We'll read the story about Abraham's servant obtaining a bride for Isaac, the longest narrative text in the Bible. There are two motifs that repeat throughout Genesis—the barren woman motif and the younger son motif, and we'll discuss both of these topics.

As I mentioned, we'll devote a lecture to different Bible translations, and then we'll go back and do some more close readings. We'll look at the story of Jacob and Esau, and we'll read the story of Jacob and Rachel, which I already have illustrated for you.

In the last section of our course, we will read the final major unit of the book of Genesis, the story of Joseph in Egypt. We'll talk about the Egyptian background of the story; after all, Joseph was living in Egypt by then; thus the narrative transports the reader to the land of Egypt, with a host of Egyptian words and personal names included in the text and various Egyptian customs, such as mummification, reflected in the closing chapters of Genesis. Finally, we will sum up everything as we will complete our journey through the book of Genesis, which in my opinion, and I hope that by the end of this course you will concur with my view, is the most brilliant literary composition from the ancient world.

Lecture Two
Genesis 1, The First Creation Story

Scope:

We begin at the beginning, by reading the first creation story (Genesis 1:1–2:4a). We delay the usual introductory material until Lectures Four through Six, opting instead to plunge right into the biblical text, with the goal of learning how to read the literature of ancient Israel, which is greatly removed from our world in both time and place. We will discuss both the literary aspects of the text and the theology that lies behind it. We will pay close attention to the description of the world as preexistent, with matter symbolic of evil (noting that the belief in creation *ex nihilo* is a later theological development), and we further will note how God's actions bring goodness into the world. Finally, we will demonstrate how the literary form of the story parallels its content, with order out of chaos as the prevailing theme.

Outline

I. The first thing we notice about Genesis 1 is that, contrary to what most people might assume or believe, the world is not created *ex nihilo*, that is, "out of nothing." Instead, the earth begins as a mass of preexistent matter, with four of the five key words listed in verse 2 (*unformed, void, darkness, deep*) symbolic of chaos and evil (only the wind is not of that ilk).

   A. God's role is to bring order and goodness into this chaotic and evil world.

   B. He does so by creating light, which he sees as good, in verses 3–4 (henceforth, everything that God creates will be good, as the refrain repeats throughout chapter 1), and by separating the light from the darkness, that is, the good from the evil, in verse 4 (the first of several separations that occur in the creation story).

   C. As such, the beginning of the story seeks to explain the question of evil in the world. This is a theological issue that all religions must answer.

      1. For the polytheisms of the ancient world, there was a simple answer because there were plenty of gods to go

around, and some of these were evil gods capable of inflicting great harm on humans.

2. For Israel, by contrast, this was a major problem, because only one God is worshipped, and that god, by definition, is a good God. Thus, this story gets God "off the hook," as it were, for the existence of evil in the world. He cannot be blamed, because evil is preexistent. God brought only goodness into the world.

3. We hasten to add that this is the answer to the problem of evil forthcoming from the pen of the author of Genesis 1. Other biblical authors, such as the prophet Second Isaiah, will have different answers.

II. Days 2 and 3 continue the story of creation, with the sky created on day 2, and the dry land and the vegetation created on day 3, in two separate stages.

III. An important point to be noticed is the presence of demythologizing, that is, the conscious avoidance of words that can be associated with pagan deities.

A. This is seen especially on day 4, where the words *sun* (*shemesh*) and *moon* (*yareah*) are consciously avoided.

B. Even the singular form *sea* (*yam*), which was also the word for the sea god of the ancient Canaanites, is studiously avoided in favor of the plural *seas* (*yamim*).

C. The author does not want the reader to think for a moment that God is responsible for the existence of pagan deities.

IV. The living creatures are created on days 5 and 6. Fish and fowl are created on day 5, and the land animals and the first human couple are created on day 6, again via two stages of creation.

V. A major problem in the story is the threefold use of first-person plural pronouns in Genesis 1:26: "Let us make a human in our image, by our likeness."

A. This could be an echo of an earlier polytheism lurking behind or beneath our text, but that seems most unlikely for a text that goes out of its way to demythologize at every turn.

B. We may see here a reference to the angels, but the belief in angels developed in the later biblical period, and there is no hint of angels anywhere else in this chapter.

C. The most likely explanation appears to be the royal *we*, as well known from English style, except to note that nowhere is this usage attested in all of ancient Near Eastern literature.

VI. The six days of creation are aligned according to a pattern, with the first three days paralleled by the second three days.

A. Light in day 1 is paralleled by the lights in day 4.

B. The waters and the sky in day 2 are paralleled by the fish and the birds in day 5.

C. There are two stages of creation in day 3—first, the dry land, then, the vegetation—corresponding to two stages of creation in day 6—first, the land animals, then mankind, both of whom inhabit the dry land and eat the vegetation.

D. This pattern acts as a blueprint and establishes the overall theme of Genesis 1, namely, creation of the world according to an order, representative of goodness, continuing the theme of order out of a chaos, or good out of evil, expressed above. As such, our text is an example of "form follows content."

VII. Literary refrains appear throughout the text, bolstering the orderly pattern just noted:

A. "And God said, 'Let [such and such happen].'"

B. "And God saw that it was good."

C. "And it was evening and it was morning."

D. We note, however, that the second of these is lacking in day 2. The reason for this is that the second day deals with the separation of the waters into the waters above and the waters below. Because the watery mass is symbolic of evil, as noted above, the refrain must be omitted. That is to say, the author sacrificed literary perfection here in order to make the theological point.

Essential Reading:

Nahum Sarna, *Understanding Genesis*, pp. 1–23.

Robert Alter, *Genesis*, pp. 3–6 = Robert Alter, *The Five Books of Moses*, pp. 17–19.

Supplementary Reading:

Michael Fishbane, *Text and Texture: Close Readings of Selected Biblical Texts*, pp. 3–16.

Pamela T. Reis, *Reading the Lines: A Fresh Look at the Hebrew Bible*, pp. 15–26.

Questions to Consider:

1. Why does the author use the first-person plural pronouns in the passage "Let us make a human in our image, by our likeness" in Genesis 1:26?

2. How would you explain the creation of light on day 1 before the creation of the sun and the moon on day 4? Similarly, how would you explain the reference to "and there was evening and there was morning" on days 1, 2, and 3 before the creation of the sun and the moon on day 4?

Lecture Two—Transcript
Genesis 1, The First Creation Story

As we noted in Lecture One, we will spend a considerable amount of time discussing the two stories of Creation with which the book of Genesis begins. So, let's plunge into our biblical text here at the beginning of Lecture Two by reading the first Creation account.

First and foremost I want to discuss the literary aspects of this text with the goal of learning how to read the literature of Ancient Israel. We'll use this first story to illustrate the process. Genesis is part of a literature that is greatly removed from our world, both in time and in place. Then, we'll look at the theology that lies behind this text. We will pay close attention to the description of the world as preexistent with matter symbolic of evil. Further, we'll note how God's actions bring goodness into the world. Finally, we will demonstrate how the literary form of this story parallels its content, and you'll hear me use the phrase "order out of chaos." That's one of the prevailing themes in this story and we'll talk about all of this, but let's begin with our reading.

Let me read for you the first three verses of Genesis 1, using the *Jewish Publication Society Version*. I'll sometimes call that, for short, the JPS, the Jewish Publication Society translation. The text goes like this: "When God began to create heaven and earth, the earth being unformed and void with darkness over the surface of the deep and a wind from God sweeping over the water, God said, 'Let there be light.' And there was light." Now, that is three verses. Older translations of the Bible render each of those three verses as an independent sentence—verse 1, verse 2 and verse 3. In this translation, however, which I believe adheres more closely to the syntax of the original Hebrew, the first verse is a dependent clause, instead of the traditional English rendering, "In the beginning, God created the heaven and the earth," which is an independent sentence unto itself. In the text that I just read, the first verse is a dependent clause: "When God began to create heaven and earth," comma, and then the sentence continues into verses 2 and 3. In actuality, we don't reach the independent sentence until verse 3 because verse 2 is interposed; it actually is set off with dashes in the JPS version, which gives us the state of the Earth, the state of the Earth before God does any creative work.

Therefore, as we noted earlier, contrary to what most people might assume or believe, the world is not created *ex nihilo*, "out of nothing," according to the biblical account at the beginning of Genesis 1. Instead, the Earth begins as a mass of preexistent matter, with five elements or five key words—I don't mean "elements" in the chemical sense of the word, but rather five key items—five key words, key elements, that are present at the beginning of Creation. They're all mentioned in verse 2. Four out of those five key words are symbolic of chaos and evil. What are they? The Earth was "unformed and void." If something is unformed and void, we have a negative attitude towards it, and that is the way the Earth is described here. Darkness is mentioned. Darkness is a symbol of evil in many religious traditions, including those from the ancient Near East. Then, we have the phrase, "the deep." "The deep" refers to the great waters of the oceans, the great salt water. This too is symbolic of evil in the ancient Near East. Why? Because of the destructive nature of the oceans, with their great sea storms—wrecking ships and destroying coastlines—not to mention the inability to use the salt water in the ocean. The deep, therefore, is symbolic of evil. Then, we have the word "water" itself at the end of verse 2, with the "wind from God sweeping over the water…" This water represents the salt water that I just referred to.

The only item in this list that is not symbolic of chaos or evil is the wind, described here as a "wind from God." Some of the older translations, including the *King James Version* say, "The spirit of God," but "spirit" and "wind" are the same word in Hebrew and most recent translations go with the word "wind." So, four out of these five elements are symbolic of chaos, and together represent the evil nature of the world at its beginning before God accomplished any creative activity.

Now, when I say that these are symbols of chaos and evil in the ancient Near East, it's because we actually have texts from Mesopotamia and Canaan—and from Egypt, to some extent as well, from across the Near East—which indicate that these items are symbols of evil: the darkness, the deep, the salt water, and so on. In short, we have before us our biblical text, but underneath that text, beneath the biblical text, as it were, lies an entire world of the ancient Near East. The people of Ancient Israel who were reading the book of Genesis, and who were part and parcel of that ancient Near

Eastern world, would have recognized the point very clearly, that the preexistent matter in this story is symbolic of evil.

God's role is to bring order and goodness into this chaotic and evil world, and that is why when we come to verse 3, we finally have an independent clause, as the final part of the Bible's first sentence: "God said, 'Let there be light,' and there was light." Light is a symbol of good. It's the antithesis of the darkness. It is even described as being good because in verse 4 we read, "God saw that the light was good." That is a refrain that will repeat throughout our story. Almost everything that God creates will have this refrain, that it was good. Then, continuing in verse 4, we read "he separated the light from the darkness," that is, he separated the good from the evil. This is the first of several separations that occurs in the Creation story. We'll see that one of the things that continues to happen in this story is the separation of X and Y. What is going on with these separations? Well, if the earth started out in an "unformed and void" fashion, as we noted—in a chaotic fashion—what God is doing is separating things out, organizing things. The Earth was in a chaotic state and God is putting things into their separate categories. Light from darkness is the first of these; we'll see other examples.

Perhaps I can illustrate this by suggesting the following analogy. If you walked into my office and you saw papers everywhere all over my desk, you would gain a relatively negative impression about me or the way I keep my office, because things would be scattered in every direction. My office, or my desk, would be unformed and void. If you came in the next day and saw that all my papers were in nice piles and files and so on, you would have a much more positive impression. Why? You'd have a more positive impression because I've separated things out. So, that is what's happening in the Genesis account. The Earth, which begins with that "unformed and void" mass, is now being separated out into its component parts, the first being light from darkness.

As such, with God creating light, which is good, and separating it from the darkness, the beginning of this story seeks to explain the question of evil in the world. This is a theological issue that all religions must answer. They all must deal with it in some fashion, the problem of evil. Now, for the polytheisms of the ancient world—and remember, that except for Israel, everybody in antiquity was polytheistic. The peoples that I have mentioned—the Egyptians, the

Babylonians, and so on—believed in many gods. For them, there was a very simple answer to the problem of evil. There were plenty of gods to go around, and some of these were evil gods who were capable of inflicting great harm on human beings.

For Israel, by contrast, there was a major problem since only one god is worshipped, and that God, by definition, is a good God. So, what this story does—Genesis 1—is it lets God "off the hook," as it were, for the existence of evil in the world. He cannot be blamed since evil is preexistent. That was the whole purpose of verse 2 with all of those items: the darkness, the deep, the salt water, and so on. God only brings goodness into a world preexistent of evil. Now, I hasten to add that this is the answer to the problem of evil forthcoming from the pen of the author of Genesis 1. Other biblical authors, such as the prophet Second Isaiah, who lived, according to my dating, centuries after the author of Genesis, have a different answer to the problem of evil in the world. What I am doing in the present instance is focusing only on the theology of Israel as presented by the author of Genesis 1.

If it surprises you to find one theological approach in Genesis 1 that lets God off the hook for the existence of evil, and a different theological answer given elsewhere in the Bible—and I mentioned the prophet, Second Isaiah—who specifically states that if there is only one god in the universe, then that single God must be responsible for both good and evil. That's the opposite approach from the one taken by the author of the book of Genesis. If this surprises you, let me explain that it is okay to find divergent opinions in the Bible. In fact, for almost any particular issue that one might wish to raise, one finds different answers provided in the Bible. Why? It's because the Bible is an anthology. We're only talking about the book of Genesis, the focus of our course, but the Bible is a collection of different books by different authors in different places and at different times. Most of them in Israel, most of them during a period of several centuries, but nevertheless, one encounters differences of opinion with different theological perspectives and with different theological answers presented. So, keep that in mind that we are dealing here with an anthology. The author of Genesis 1 lets God off the hook, to repeat that point, he lets God off the hook for the existence of evil; it is preexistent. God creates the good; he creates light, which is specifically identified as good in our opening verses.

Then, the first day continues in the following way, as I now read from verse 5: "God called the light 'day' and the darkness he called 'night.' And there was evening, and there was morning, a first day." Now we come to day two and, again, let me read from the JPS translation in verses 6–8:

> God said, 'Let there be an expanse in the midst of the water that it may separate water from water.' God made the expanse and it separated the water, which was below the expanse from the water, which was above the expanse. And it was so. God called the expanse 'sky.' And there was evening, and there was morning, a second day.

Now, the older translations use the word "firmament." In this translation, you'll notice you've heard several times the word "expanse." What it is, is the sky because it is named "the sky" in this description of day two of creation. What has happened again in this day is once more a separation, a separating out. Did you notice the word that the expanse separates the waters above from the waters below? So, if the world begins as a watery mass and that's how it's been described in day one, you now have this sky, the expanse—the firmament—being placed in the middle, separating the waters above from the waters below. This is how the people of Ancient Israel described and understood the cosmos. That is, they knew about the waters below—that's all the water that's here on earth, the rivers, and the seas, and so on—and they believed that above the sky, there were the waters above. That is the storehouse of water, which brings the rainfall, so, this story seeks to explain how water was separated into waters below and waters above. That is day two.

Then, in day three, which I won't read in total, but it goes from verse 9 down to verse 13. In verses 9 and 10 there's a further separation. In this case, the waters below are gathered into a single place and what is revealed, then, is the dry land, or the "Earth." And so, we have a further separation. We began with that chaotic mass of earth back in verse 2, and we've seen a series of separations. The text is describing the process of creating order out of chaos. You heard me use that expression at the outset—we have "order out of chaos"—happening throughout this story. This is what God is doing—good out of evil, order out of chaos. On the surface, this may look like a very simple story just talking about the development or the origins of the Earth, but as you can see, it is a highly sophisticated theological statement made here by the author of our text in Genesis Chapter One.

Now, returning to day three. Day three, unlike the first two days of creation, actually has two stages of creation. The first stage is the one I just referred to, which is the separation of the sea, the water, from the dry land. There's a second stage of creation in day three, namely, God's statement that the earth should sprout forth vegetation, which it does. The importance of this point is not readily seen at this moment, but we'll come back to that point and so I ask you to just register in your minds the fact that day three has two stages to creation.

Next, we move to day four and, again, let me read. In verse 14: "God said, 'Let there be lights in the expanse of sky to separate day from night and they shall serve as signs for the set times, the days and the years. And they shall serve as lights in the expanse of the sky to shine upon the earth' and it was so." verse 16: "God made the two great lights. The greater light to dominate the day and the lesser light to dominate the night and the stars." And then, it goes on through verses 18 and 19 and again we have the usual refrain, "that God saw that this was good. And there was evening and there was morning, and there was a fourth day."

Now, did you notice while I was reading this passage that the words "sun" and "moon" are not mentioned? There is no doubt in anyone's mind that it is the Sun and the Moon and the stars, as well, that are being created here, but I want to read again verse 16: "God made the two great lights. The greater light to dominate the day and the lesser light to dominate the night and the stars." Again, notice no use of the words "sun" and "moon." No doubt in anyone's mind that the greater light that dominates the day is the Sun and the lesser light that dominates the night is the Moon, but those terms, themselves, are not used. This is what we call "demythologizing," that is, the conscious avoidance of particular words that refer to pagan deities known from the mythologies of the ancient world. The author does not want the reader to think for a moment that God is responsible for the creation, for the very existence of pagan deities. For while the Israelites may have worshipped only one God, the peoples around them were polytheistic, that is, they worshipped many gods.

I need to point out, at this point, and we'll return to this in a future lecture, that the Israelites at this stage were not pure monotheists yet, with the belief in a single god. They worshipped one God and if you've listened carefully, I've used only that expression, "the worship of one God" because they had not yet moved to the belief in one God, a pure monotheism. Therefore, the Israelites could recognize, at least tacitly, the existence of these other gods worshipped by other peoples, their neighbors in Canaan and places further afield—Egypt, Babylonia, Assyria, Greece, etc. Thus, the author of our story does not want you to think, less the innocent reader to think, that God is somehow responsible for these pagan deities. Therefore, the words "sun" and "moon" are not used, and why is that the case? It is because the words in Hebrew for "sun" and "moon" are the names of the Sun deity and Moon deity in Canaanite.

A word about the Hebrew language, which we mentioned in Lecture One; it is an ancient Semitic language, or to be more exact, a dialect of the Canaanite language. The land of Canaan was shared by the Israelites or Hebrews or Jews, and the people of Canaan, whom we call the Canaanites. But, they spoke the same language, different dialects, not differing any more than the various dialects of English—British English from American English from Australian English or within America, Boston English from Texas English, for example. They could all speak to one another and understand each other and; therefore, I'm going to give you here, for example, the Hebrew word—*Shemesh*, which means "sun". This word would have been the name of the Sun god in the Canaanite pantheon, and so the author consciously avoids using that word. This would have been the same, by the way, in almost all the pantheons of the ancient world. So, for example, Ra, the Sun god in Egypt, is also the basic word for "sun" in Egypt and Helios in Greece is the Greek word for "sun." Although the deity is sometimes called Apollo, Helios is the basic word for "sun" and the name of the Sun deity. In short, our text is characterized by demythologizing, with the author of Genesis 1 consciously avoiding the use of these terms.

In fact, once we understand that that is the case here with the Sun and Moon, I also should mention that if you go back to verse 10 in day three, you will notice that the waters are called "seas" in the plural. Did it strike you as somewhat odd that the word "seas" was used in the plural and not the word "sea" in the singular? That is because the word "sea" in the singular, which in Hebrew is *yam*, is the name of the sea god of the ancient Canaanites, and so the author studiously avoids using that term. It's okay to use the plural form, which in Hebrew is *yamim*, but he abstains from using the singular form *yam*. I trust that you have an idea here of the kind of thought that goes into the production of an ancient text, with great attention to detail, and how the literary and theological interface in our text. Thus far that was day four.

We now move to day five. In day five, we have the creation of the fowl—the birds—and the fish. These two categories of animal life, these two components of the animal kingdom, are created on day five. We then move to day six. I want to point out, as we did with day three, that also in day six, we have two stages to creation: "six-A," we may call it, the creation of the land animals, and "six-B" the creation of the human couple, male and female; 1:26-27 is the creation of mankind. Therefore, we have two stages of creation in day six; we also previously noted two stages to creation in day three and, again, we'll come back and talk about why this point is significant.

Now, a major problem that arises in our story in the threefold use of the first-person plural forms of Genesis 1:26, as we noted already in Lecture One. Let's read it again: "God said, 'Let us make man in our image, after our likeness'." How do we explain this usage here? Now, a couple of thoughts come to mind. This could be an echo of an earlier polytheism lurking behind or beneath our text. I just referred to the fact that the Israelites were not pure monotheists. They tacitly recognized the existence of other gods among the other peoples of the ancient world, although these deities were off limits for the Israelites to worship. But, this seems a most unlikely explanation for our text, because the prose of Genesis 1 goes out of its way to demythologize at every turn. If the author refused to use the words "sea" and "sun" and "moon," it is highly unlikely that our author would have slipped up, as it were, and used the plural forms here for God.

A second possibility comes to mind. We may see here a reference to the angels; however, the belief in angels developed only in the later biblical period, at least angels as later understood in Judaism and Christianity as part of God's entourage in heaven. And, there is no hint of angels anywhere else in Genesis Chapter 1. Yes, it's true that the word "angel" or "angels" in the plural occurs earlier in the Bible, including in the book of Genesis, but those angels are manifestations of God. That's the way we should understand the word "angel" when we encounter it in the books of Genesis and Exodus and the other earlier books of the Bible. As an example, I would note that the burning bush in Exodus 3 is, in fact, called an angel. It's a manifestation of God, and that's not quite the same as the later angels who are in Heaven as part of God's entourage, so that is probably not the explanation for the first-person plural forms here in Chapter 1:26.

A third possibility comes to mind and that is the most likely explanation. That is, we are encountering here what we call the royal "we." Something well-known from English style, for example, in Shakespeare's King Lear, where the title character speaks as an individual but uses the first-person plural forms, pronouns such as "we" and "our." Note, that this is the first time in our text where God refers to himself. He's spoken numerous times up until now, each time commanding that something happen, but it was always a third person reference—"Let there be light" or "Let this happen" or "Let the earth spring forth vegetation." He has not referred to himself yet. This is the first time where God refers to himself and therefore, the royal "we" is used. I rather like this explanation; I think it's the best explanation to our crux. By the way, most of the times that God refers to himself, he uses singular forms, but in this particular case, plural forms are used. I rather like that explanation, because it suggests that we are to understand, which we clearly are, that God is the King of the Universe, King of the World, the Ruling Sovereign and therefore, the author places the royal 'we' into God's mouth at the first possible instance, so that we the readers can learn this point about God's majesty very quickly. Obviously, the sovereignty of God is implied everywhere in the Bible; but nevertheless, the author of Genesis 1 makes the point here in a more explicit way.

But, I have to issue a caveat, and that is the following: Nowhere in all of Near Eastern literature is the royal "we" attested—not anywhere in Egypt, nor in Babylonia—never do kings use this style of speaking. So, while Shakespeare may place the royal 'we' into the mouth of King Lear and we know of this usage from elsewhere in English, we do not know of this usage from anywhere else in the ancient Near East. So, it seems to work, but we have to remember that it may not be the answer because of this point that I have just mentioned. Perhaps a future archeological discovery will reveal an example from an ancient text where, in fact, the royal we is used that way, but up until now we have none.

Some of me, part of me, is content to say we simply don't know the answer to the question we are pondering here, why the first-person plural forms in Geneses 1:26, "Let us make man" and so on. The other part of me would prefer to go with the royal "we" explanation at least for the time being. But, I'm happy at times just to raise these issues with you, without necessarily presenting definitive answers.

That's how the six days of creation come to an end with man, with man or the human couple, male and female, as the last thing created in this first Creation story. Now, the six days of creation are aligned according to a pattern, with the first three days paralleling the second three days. Let me show you what I mean. Days one, two and three parallel days four, five, and six. How and in what way? Day one, the creation of light, the first thing God created; on day four, the creation of the lights in the sky. In fact, I will give you another reason not to use the words "sun" and "moon" in the description of day four, because it allows the author to use the word "lights," a slightly different form of the word "light" that we heard in day one, thus driving home the connection between days one and four though this lexical link.

Days two and five are parallel. In what way are they parallel? In day two, the waters were not created because remember they were preexistent, but the waters were the subject of day two, or perhaps better to say, they were the object of God's creation. What he did create on day two was the sky, which separated the waters, so water and sky are central to day two. In day five, God created the fish and the fowl—the fish, which inhabit the waters, and the birds, which inhabit the sky, and so, these two days and their respective items match up.

Now remember what I said about day three and day six both having two stages of creation, and thus they form a match. It's not just the fact that they have two stages of creation, but that they also correspond to each other in the following way: In day three, you have the creation of the dry land and the vegetation, and in day six, you have the creation of the land animals and mankind, both of whom inhabit the dry land and eat the vegetation. We didn't look at the passage, we didn't read it aloud, but I invite you to consider

Chapter 1:29 through 30 where God commands that man and the animals, as well, can eat the vegetation. In fact, that's part of the Creation story, as well; the harmonious world is created with no killing. Neither man nor the animals is given permission to eat meat here, instead the intention, God's design, is for a vegetarian diet only. We'll come back and talk about this point in a future lecture, the permission to eat meat, which is granted in Genesis Chapter 9.

Now, the pattern that I have presented for you acts as a blueprint and establishes the overall theme of the story that we have before us, the creation of the world is an orderly creation. You have the three days—in column one, days one, two, and three and in column two, days four, five, and six, which parallel each other. This is a stellar instance of form following content. You will hear me use that expression a number of times during our course—"form follows content." Creation was order out of chaos, or good out of evil, you'll remember, and the Creation itself was done in an orderly fashion. When you begin to construct anything—let's talk about a building—what do you begin with? What's the first thing you have, the first thing you need? It is a blueprint, and that's what the genius of constructing a building is all about, the architect's creativity as visualized in the blueprint. And, to take nothing away from the hard work that is required by engineers and construction workers to build a building—you need builders and electricians and masons and plumbers and so on—we always state "so-and-so built this building," meaning he or she was the architect, the one who created the blueprint. That's what you have here as well in Genesis Chapter 1. The pattern that I have shown is the blueprint by which God created the world and that is where the genius in this story is to be found.

I also want to note that there are literary refrains that appear throughout the text, which bolster the orderly pattern that we have noted. There are three refrains. First, each day or each creative act begins with "God said, 'Let such and such happen'." We then have the refrain, "God saw that it was good." And finally at the end of each day appears the refrain, "And it was evening and it was morning," for all six days. These refrains add to the literary pattern. Together they support the notion of "form following content," the order out of chaos, as the refrains repeat in an orderly fashion.

We note, however, that the second of these refrains, "And God saw that it was good," is lacking in one of the days; it is lacking in day two. The reason for this is that the second day of creation deals with the separation of the waters into the waters above and the waters below. Since the watery mass is symbolic of evil, as we noted, the refrain must be omitted. That is to say, the author sacrificed literary perfection here in order to make the theological point, an intentional omission. The brilliance that lies behind the crafting of these narratives in the book of Genesis is something that we all can marvel at. Thank you.

Lecture Three
Genesis 2–3, The Second Creation Story

Scope:

The second creation story begins properly in the middle of a verse, at 2:4b, and continues through the end of chapter 3. It comprises both a different account of how the world came to be and the story of Adam and Eve in the Garden of Eden. This lecture will highlight the four major differences between the two creation accounts, and it will discuss the main reason why the book of Genesis, and hence, the Bible as a whole, begins with two divergent narratives. We will note that the first story is cosmocentric in its focus, including the sky, sun, moon, stars, and so on, while the second story is anthropocentric in its focus, with an emphasis on man and his activities. Both foci are required in Israel's approach to religion: God and man in their separate realms yet inextricably interlinked.

Outline

I. We begin by completing our reading of the first creation story, which continues into Genesis 2.

   A. We first present a quick note on the history of the chapter and verse divisions—a new chapter does not always mean a new story begins at that point. The chapter and verse divisions in use today were accomplished by Stephen Langton (c. 1150–1228), the Archbishop of Canterbury in England.

   B. The Sabbath serves as the culmination of the first creation story, prompting comparison with the Babylonian creation story, *Enuma Elish* (which means "when on high").

      1. The Babylonian story begins with a conflict among the gods—in particular, the deity Tiamat, who is the goddess of salt water and is symbolic of evil, and the god Marduk, who is the heaven god or storm god and symbolizes good.

      2. Marduk kills Tiamat, and he creates the world out of her body, using the upper part of her body to create the vault of heaven and the lower part of her body to create the earth. The story continues with the creation of the sun,

the moon, and the stars, and it finishes with the creation of man.

3. The Babylonian story ends with the construction of the temple to Marduk in Babylon—holiness in physical space—as is typical of the polytheistic world.

C. The biblical story ends with the establishment of the Sabbath—holiness in time—a unique contribution of ancient Israel to world religion.

II. We now turn to our reading of Genesis 2:4b–25, the second creation story. We note the segue between the two stories in verse 4, whose first half has the wording "heaven and earth" and whose second half has the wording "earth and heaven." There are four major differences between the two stories.

A. Different names for the deity are used: Elohim ("God") in the first story and Yahweh ("LORD") in the second story, though actually in a combined form, Yahweh Elohim ("LORD God").

B. The method of creation is different: creation by fiat (the spoken word) in the first story versus creation by physical means in the second story (for example, God plants a garden).

C. The order of creation is different: The first story progresses from vegetation to animals to humans, while the second story begins with humankind (only male, though), then comes the vegetation (in the form of the Garden of Eden), and finally, comes the animal kingdom.

D. In the first story, male and female are created at once (1:26), while in the second story, male alone is created first, with female following later.

III. The two stories of creation are to be read in tandem, with the cosmocentric approach provided by Genesis 1 and the anthropocentric approach presented in Genesis 2. This is the essence of ancient Israelite religion: the two working in sync together, the melding of the world of God and the world of man, in unique relationship with each other.

A. Elsewhere in the ancient Near East, deities were associated with nature, and thus, there was a distance between the gods and humankind.

B. In Israel, by contrast, God was seen in close relationship with humankind, as illustrated in the mind of the Israelites by the covenant concept, to which we shall return in Lecture Eight.

IV. We add a few brief comments on Genesis 3, the Garden of Eden account, which is an extension of the second creation account. (Note that the divine name "LORD God" continues to be used in this chapter, as does the theme of the prohibition of eating from the Tree of Knowledge.)

A. "Good and evil" may be a merism, a literary device, in which one takes two opposites, such as good and evil, and combines them to express the totality of something, in this case the totality of all knowledge.

B. The main point of the story is how man gained knowledge, or the ability to obtain knowledge, and that is a trait which distinguishes man from the animal kingdom. Far from being the fall of man, one could argue that we are dealing here with the rise of man.

C. However, man still violated God's command.

    1. This may be the author's attempt to present an alternative answer to the problem of evil, which Genesis 1, as we saw in our previous lecture, explained as a preexistent feature of the world.

    2. By so doing, the author of Genesis 2–3 introduces us to the concept of free will, a dominant motif in the Bible and in Judaism in general.

    3. Note one further instance of later interpretation that is not present in a surface reading of the chapter. I refer to the (mainly) Christian interpretation that understands the snake in Genesis 3 ("the shrewdest of all the wild beasts") to be Satan. There is no hint of this in the biblical text, and in any case, the belief in the Satan figure is a very late development in Jewish theology, from which it passed into Christian belief.

D. The biblical narrative begins with a journey—Adam and Eve expelled from the Garden of Eden—paralleling both Israel's journey in a physical sense (beginning with Abraham) and the metaphorical journey of all humankind ("the game of life" we may call it).

Essential Reading:

Robert Alter, *Genesis*, pp. 7–15 = Robert Alter, *The Five Books of Moses*, pp. 20–28.

Supplementary Reading:

Everett Fox, *The Five Books of Moses*, pp. 16–23.

Questions to Consider:

1. How does the presence of two creation accounts in Genesis 1–2 relate to the theology of ancient Israel?

2. What other interpretations for the Garden of Eden story might be forthcoming?

Lecture Three—Transcript
Genesis 2–3, The Second Creation Story

Welcome back. In fact, welcome once more to the first Creation story. We ended the previous lecture with the assumption, perhaps, that we had completed our reading of the first creation account because we did, in fact, reach the end of chapter 1 of Genesis. But, the first Creation account continues into the beginning of chapter 2. Certainly, it goes into the first three verses of chapter 2, and probably the first half-verse of verse 4 of chapter 2; yes, it is that fine and detailed. So, we'll come to the second Creation account, which dominates chapter 2 in Genesis, but first we need to say more about the first Creation story, and in fact, the ending of the first Creation story. Before we do that, however, let's take a moment to talk about why the account continues into chapter 2 and, in fact, let's take a moment to talk about the chapter and verse divisions in general.

First to point out that our ancient Hebrew manuscripts do not have chapter or verse divisions. There are no little numbers to tell you that you are moving into a new chapter or a new verse. The only thing the ancient manuscripts have is white space from time to time, which gives us an idea of where the scribes saw units beginning and ending, a type of paragraphing in effect, although they had much larger blocks of material than one finds in the typical English prose paragraphing. Now, if there were no numbers accompanying the text, how did anybody refer to a biblical text at any given time in antiquity? They simply quoted it and, presumably, the assumption was that the person to whom you were speaking would say, "Oh, that's from Psalms," or "That's from Isaiah," or "That's from Job." Or, you may have said, "As it says from the book of Isaiah," and that would be your lead in, but you wouldn't quote chapter and verse by number because those numbers didn't exist. How did all this change? Our chapter and verse divisions, which we use today in all English translations and, in fact, in all Hebrew editions of the Bible as well, are a relatively recent development in the history of the transmission of the biblical texts. They originate in the early 13th century C.E., that is to say, about 800 years ago.

There was a remarkable individual named Stephen Langton, who was born in 1150 and died in 1228. He was the Archbishop of Canterbury in England. Now, you have to remember, we're still in the Middle Ages and so while today that position, the Archbishop of

Canterbury is head of the Church of England, obviously there was no Church of England, yet before the time of the Reformation and Henry VIII. We're talking about the Roman Catholic head of the Church in England. He is most well known in history for having supported the landed barons of England in their efforts—eventually successful efforts—to have King John end the tyranny in England and to sign the Magna Carta. That's how most people know the name of Stephen Langton, a major player in the events leading up to the signing of that remarkable document, the Magna Carta, in the early 13th century in medieval England.

For biblical scholars, however, Stephen Langton had a much more important role to play in world history, as we often like to joke amongst ourselves. Anybody could have King John to do this or that and have an instrumental role in the signing of the Magna Carta, but it takes somebody of truly special nature to create the chapter and verse divisions of the Bible. Langton devoted considerable energies in going through the entire Bible, the Christian canon. That is to say, the Jewish Bible or Old Testament, and the New Testament as well—and chapter by chapter, verse by verse, he numbered the individual passages or verses and the larger units called chapters. Ever since then, from the early 13th century down to our day, we now can say, "Genesis 2:1" or "Deuteronomy 12:8," and we can turn right to it without having to quote it and expect people to know from memory exactly where the passage is to be found. So, that's the work of Stephen Langton, therefore, we have a new chapter here based on Langton's divisions, Genesis 2:1.

Now, in almost all cases, the chapter divisions accord with new stories. In this particular case, however, and it's simply just a coincidence at this point, the first Creation story we now know actually continues into chapter 2. I don't want to say, having just built up Langton as a great hero of mine, that indeed he made a mistake at this particular juncture, but it is important to note that the first Creation story flows into chapter 2. We'll see where the segue from the first story into the second story is to be found. So, yes, generally chapter divisions are new stories, but not always. Why Langton divided a particular story here or there, we do not necessarily know, although from time to time we can assume what his guiding principle was. Having said that, let's look at Genesis

2:1–3, along with the first half of Verse 4, and I'll read this, again, using the Jewish Publication Society Version:

> The heaven and the earth were finished and all their array. On the seventh day, God finished the work that he had been doing and he ceased on the seventh day from all the work that he had done. And God blessed the seventh day and declared it holy because on it, God ceased from all the work of creation that he had done. Such is the story of heaven and earth when they were created.

Now, what is being described here at the beginning of Chapter 2? Clearly, the seventh day is being described, the seventh day of the week, the Sabbath. The Hebrew word, by the way, is *Shabbat* from which our English word, Sabbath, derives. It serves as the culmination of the first Creation story. The presence of the Sabbath at the end of the creation account prompts for us a comparison with the most well known Creation story from the ancient world and that is the Babylonian creation story called the *Enuma Elish*. Those two words, "*Enuma Elish*," are in the Babylonian language. That's how the ancient Babylonians themselves referred to the story. They are the opening words of the text and the phrase means, "when on high." And the myth goes on, "When on high, the gods did such and such and so and so," and that, by the way, is how a number of ancient compositions were known to the readers of those texts in antiquity. They did not have titles, per se; they simply used the opening word or words to refer to those texts. So, this is the Babylonian Creation story called the *Enuma Elish*.

Let me tell you a little bit about that story. It actually begins with a conflict among the gods—in particular, the deity Tiamat, who is the goddess of salt water and is symbolic of evil, and the god Marduk, who is the heaven god or storm god and symbolizes good. It is an ongoing battle between the two of them. Actually, much of that is underneath our text in Genesis 1, as we described in the last lecture without going into detail at that time, that the ancient Israelite reader of this story would have known much about the Babylonian text. Notice, though, that in Genesis there is no conflict and there's no struggle. There's none of that happening in the story of Genesis 1. Our biblical text is a totally harmonious story, one based on a single God creating the world; but the Babylonian story because of their mythological world, has these gods in conflict with one another.

More important for our present concern is the way the Babylonian story ends. Marduk kills Tiamat and out of her body, he creates the world, using the upper part of her body to create the vault of heaven and the lower part of her body to create the earth. The story continues with the creation of the sun, the moon, and the stars, and finally with the creation of man. It actually follows quite nicely the story in Genesis 1, or perhaps we should word that the other way around, that Genesis 1 follows quite nicely the order of creation in the Enuma Elish myth.

The culmination of the Babylonian story, the actual end of the story after the creation of man, is the appointment of Marduk as king of the gods, crowned as the head of the Pantheon, and then, the very last item narrated in the myth, is the construction of a temple to Marduk in the city of Babylon.

That's how the *Enuma Elish* ends. This is what we call "holiness in physical space" or "holiness in a physical place," and this is what typifies the religions of the ancient world. This is how the polytheists understood where holiness was to be found. It could be in natural places such as mountains. We're all familiar with the Mount Olympus tradition from Greece, and there are similar traditions of sacred mountains in the ancient Near East. Or, it could be a holy river as we have in various religions of the world, as well. Or, it could be in a manmade place, a temple in a city. That's what you have in this story. The temple built in the city of Babylon for the god, Marduk—holiness in physical space.

In like fashion, the biblical story of creation also concludes with the establishment of holiness—the Sabbath day, narrated for us in Genesis 2:1–3. But notice the crucial difference, for holiness in the Genesis account is not situated "in physical space," but rather, it is in time. The institution of the Sabbath is what we call "holiness in time," and it is a unique contribution of ancient Israel to world religion. So, as we read through that text, and I want to emphasize those words again, in verse 3, "God blessed the seventh day and he declared it holy." There's that word, "holy;" the seventh day, the Sabbath, becomes holy.

The similarity, accordingly, between the two stories is that they both end with the creation of holiness. In both the Babylonian story and the biblical story, after the various phases of creation ending with the creation of man, we read of the establishment of holiness. The difference, however, is crucial. Holiness for the polytheistic world was to be found in physical space, for Israel, by contrast, holiness was to be found mainly in time—not only the Sabbath, but eventually the holy days or festival days of the calendar, as well. This point reverberates in a much larger way, and this point is quite significant, for the gods of antiquity among the polytheists were associated with nature and the various natural places that we referred to, such as mountains and rivers, whereas the God of ancient Israel was associated with history. This is the topic for a future lecture, where we will explore this important point in greater detail. For our present purposes, note the main point—holiness in ancient Israel was identified with the Sabbath, with time.

I want to point out here, by the way, that the word "Shabbat," the Hebrew word from which we have our English word, Sabbath, is not used in Genesis 2:1–3; it's continually referred to as "the seventh day." This is another example of the demythologizing that we talked about in the previous lecture, because not only do you have the words "sun" and "moon" not mentioned as we saw during the days of creation, the word "Sabbath," or "Shabbat" in Hebrew, is not used here either. Why? Because it happens to be the Hebrew word for the planet Saturn, and, as you know, the planets were seen as deities in the ancient world. In fact, we still call our seventh day of the week "Saturday" after the planet Saturn, who of course, was a major deity in the Roman pantheon. So for the author of this story, although the word "Shabbat" will be used elsewhere in the Bible, obviously when the word "Sabbath" needs to be described or the concept of Sabbath needs to be talked about, this author in Genesis chapter 2 continues the demythologizing trend that we saw in chapter 1 into the first several verses of chapter 2. Thus, in our story the word "Sabbath" is not used, and yet everyone who reads the story knows very clearly what is involved here with the description of the seventh day.

Let's segue at this point from the first account of Creation to the second account of Creation, which begins in Genesis 2:4, actually in the second half of verse 4, what we scholars call 2:4b. That is to say, 2:4a is the first half of the verse; 2:4b is the second half of the verse. Now, it may come as a surprise to learn that there are two different Creation stories in the book of Genesis at the beginning of this book. If you look at the larger world of the ancient Near East, however, as we are doing in this course, one quickly realizes that multiple creation stories in a single culture are quite expected. I've mentioned the most important of the Babylonian stories, the *Enuma Elish*, but there are other creation traditions in Babylonia as well. In Egypt, there are four or five main creation stories, each one involving a different deity or several deities. In like fashion, in ancient Israel, there are two Creation stories, and both of them are included at the beginning of the book of Genesis.

Now, the first story ends in Genesis 2:4a and I want you to notice very carefully the different wording. Genesis 2:4a reads, as we quoted earlier, "Such is the story of heaven and earth when they were created." Notice that pair of words—heaven and earth. Genesis 2:4b begins: "When the Lord God made earth and heaven..." The pair of words, the noun pair, is switched. It's now earth and heaven. This change marks the distinction between the first story, which begins in Genesis 1:1 with the expression "heaven and earth"—"When God began to create heaven and earth," and ends with the same wording "heaven and earth" in Genesis 2:4a. In Genesis 2:4b, by contrast, the words appear in reverse order, now the phrase is "earth and heaven." This change, I submit, is a sign for us, as readers, that we are entering a new story. I'll actually say a little bit more about this point in just a few moments.

Now, the two stories have major differences. I want to emphasize that point and I want to look at these differences with you. We will talk about four of them in particular, especially where we can actually contrast something from one story with something in the other story. First point, different names for the deity are used, different names for God. In the first story, the word "God" is used in English translations, and this is the Hebrew word "Elohim." In the second story, and it's already in the half verse that I just read, the beginning of Genesis 2:4b, "When the LORD God made earth and heaven." Here you have two names for God, "LORD God," and that is the term that is used for God throughout Genesis 2, the second Creation account. Now, the English word "Lord" translates into the Hebrew word "Yahweh." It's a word that was written with four consonants corresponding to our English letters, Y-H-W-H. Scholars are not absolutely certain as to how the word might have been pronounced in antiquity, but Yahweh is the best scholarly guess and it is a convention that we use. So, the first story uses "Elohim" and the second story uses a compound name, "Yahweh Elohim." That's already an indication of some difference, and thus we take note of it here.

Second, the method of creation in the two stories is different. In the first story, the method of creation is creation by fiat. That's not a term I used previously, let's talk about what that means. It means creation by the spoken word. God says let something happen and it happens. That occurs over and over again in the first Creation account—simply by speaking, simply by fiat, the spoken word, things come into existence. That is the first Creation account. What do we have in the second Creation story? We have creation by physical means. God actually physically has to do things. For example, God forms man in verse 7, note the verb, form, out of clay, using, in fact, the same Hebrew verb that appears elsewhere to describe the action of a potter forming a vessel out of clay. In verse 8, God plants a garden in Eden. Note the verb, plants. In verse 19, again the verb 'form' used for the creation of the animals, which are also from the earth, and finally in verse 22, the creation of woman out of the rib, or side, of man, here we encounter the word 'build'. In short, the verbs that are predicated of God in this story are those characteristic of typical human activity—form, plant and build, as if these were things that human beings could do. So, the method of creation in the two stories is also different.

Third item to note, the order of creation is different. Now, of the living things—and that's the only thing we can compare or contrast in these two stories—of the living things, the story progresses in the first account from vegetation on day three to the animal kingdom on days five and six, and then to mankind as the second stage of creation on day six. In the second Creation story, the order is different. Man is created first and it's only the male, as we'll see in a moment. Then comes the vegetation, in the form of the Garden of Eden, and finally comes the animal kingdom. So, the order of creation is our third different point in these two stories.

Fourth, as I just noted, in the first story male and female are created at once. This is narrated for us in Genesis 1:26–27, which we discussed in the previous lecture. In the second story, as I've already intimated, the male alone is created first, with the female following later, created out of the rib, or side, of the man. I have not used the words "Adam and Eve" yet. They actually don't have their names fully until chapter 3. They're basically still called "the man" and "the woman" at this point; although I should note that the Hebrew word "Adam," our English "Adam", in fact, is the basic word for man and so since it bears the definite article in our text, we render the word as "the man." Eventually, as you read on in Genesis, it segues simply into the proper noun—Hebrew, "Adam"; English, "Adam."

Thus we have four major differences between the two stories. Let's review them. Different names of God, different methods of creation, different order of creation, and the question of male and female created either at once or separately. Now, according to those scholars who read the book of Genesis as the compilation of different sources, these two stories are evidence for different authors. No single person could possibly have written story "A" and story "B" with these kinds of differences. In fact, there are still other differences between the two stories. I've highlighted the four main ones that we can really contrast, but I guess we also should comment here that the first story gives us the creation of items that are not mentioned in the second story. So, for example, the first story includes the creation of the sun, and the moon, and the stars, while none of this is referred to in the second Creation story, which actually leads to another discussion.

I prefer to read the two stories together, in tandem. The first story presents what I call the "cosmocentric" approach. The second story presents the "anthropocentric" approach. Those are some complicated words. Let's talk about what they mean. Cosmocentric means focusing on the cosmos. That's why you have the sky, the waters, the seas, the dry land, the sun, the moon, the stars—all of that—in the first Creation story, the cosmos. The second story is anthropocentric, focusing on man. That is why man is created first and that is why things will happen only here on earth without a reference to the things that are associated with heaven or the sky— the sun, the moon, the stars, the sky, and so on. In addition, as we've seen, the verbs are words like form, plant, and build, which can equally be used of human actions. Moreover, the man in the second story actually does something. He names the animals when they are created in verse 20 and he even speaks in verse 23.

Now, the two stories, in my opinion, should be read together—the cosmocentric approach in chapter 1 and the anthropocentric approach in chapter 2. This is the essence—and this is why I like to read these two stories together—this is the essence of ancient Israelite religion. It is the two components working together, in sync, the melding of the world of God and the world of man. The first story we may call "The World of God," where God is in charge of the entire cosmos. The second story is "The World of man," focusing our attention here on Earth. Reading the two stories together allows us to see how the two realms, the divine and the human, operate in unique relationship with one another.

Now, elsewhere in the ancient Near East, and I alluded to this earlier, deities were associated with nature, and thus there was a distance between the gods and humankind. In Israel, by contrast, God was seen in close relationship with humankind, as illustrated in the mind of the Israelites by the concept of the covenant, and we'll return to that topic in a future lecture in much greater detail. So, while other scholars highlight the differences between story one and story two, and see that as evidence, if not proof, of two separate authors, I take a different tack, as I mentioned at the outset of our course, preferring to read the two stories as a single unit. The two accounts of creation were juxtaposed by an author, redactor, compiler, editor, somebody; they were juxtaposed in the final form of our text and, and notwithstanding their differences, I believe that they should and can be read together. By reading them in this fashion, we gain an important insight into the mind of ancient Israel and into their theology, in particular. You have to have both—a religion centered on God and an appreciation of man, with the constant interaction between the two, in close relationship with one another. The stories, when read together, provide us with this vision.

I want to point out here—and this is an important point, which will serve us throughout this course—I want to point out that nowhere does the text tell us this. It doesn't state, "We need two stories of creation because we have to have a cosmocentric view and an anthropocentric view, because that's the way our religion operates with a focus on both and the relationship between the two." That's not the way the biblical material operates. As I said in our opening lecture, what you don't have in the Bible or anywhere in ancient Israel or in the ancient world is a systematic presentation of theology. "We believe x, y, z. We believe a, b, c. These are the five points or the ten points that we hold to be central." That would be a systematic presentation of the religion. You don't have that. What we have are stories. What we need to do is to extract the theology out of those stories, and that's what I have attempted to do here, by bringing forth, out of the juxtaposition of the two stories and their inclusion at the beginning of the book of Genesis, the theology of ancient Israel.

Before leaving this topic, let me return quickly to a point made earlier. Recall that 2:4a uses the phrase "heaven and earth," while 2:4b uses the expression "earth and heaven." We now realize why the change. The first story, with its focus on the cosmos, places 'heaven' first in this word pair. The second story, with its greater focus on man, places 'earth' first in this word pair. Life is in the details, or shall we say, literature is in the details, and this intentional change, a very slight one, but a significant one, points the way, guiding the reader to perceive and comprehend the interrelationship between the two creation accounts.

Now, let's talk about Genesis 3, the story of the Garden of Eden. It is an extension of the second Creation account. There are connections between chapters 2 and 3. Thus, for example, the garden is planted in chapter 2, and it becomes a much more important component, an element in chapter 3. Also, note that the divine name or the compound divine name, "Lord God" used in chapter 2, continues into chapter 3. In addition, we read of the prohibition in chapter 2 of the eating from the Tree of Knowledge, and this becomes the major point in chapter 3, when Adam and Eve do not abide by God's word.

The main point of chapter 3, accordingly, is that humankind cannot live up to the simplest of God's commands. God told Adam—we're going to call our characters Adam and Eve at this point, as we segue into chapter 3—God told Adam back in chapter 2 not to eat from the Tree of Knowledge. He could eat from the trees of the garden, but not from the Tree of Knowledge. This information, apparently, must have been transmitted from Adam to Eve at some point, although we're not given that scene in our story, but obviously Eve must have learned of it as well. The human couple was unable to live up to this single command, because they violated God's word by eating the fruit of the Tree of Knowledge.

That tree is called, more fully, the Tree of Knowledge of Good and Evil. Now, some people think that that somehow the reference here is to these two individual words, good on the one hand and evil on the other, with a greater emphasis on the latter. An alternative interpretation of this phrase, one that I prefer, is that we are dealing here with the knowledge of everything, all knowledge. Good and evil are what we call, in literary study, "merism." Merism is a literary device, by which you take two opposites, such as good and evil, and combine them to express the totality of something. If I said in English, "They came, young and old alike," that does not mean that just the toddlers and the senior citizens came, it refers to everybody in between as well. So, the Tree of Knowledge of Good and Evil would be the "Tree of All Knowledge." I want to decrease our emphasis, on the word "evil," and suggest that the main point of the story is how man gained knowledge, or the ability to obtain knowledge, and that is a trait which distinguishes man from the animal kingdom. Far from being the fall of man, one could argue, according to this view we are dealing here with the rise of man.

It comes at a cost, however, for man still violated God's command, and to some extent this story does deal with evil. Most likely it represents an attempt by the author of our second account to present an alternative answer to the problem of evil. Genesis 1, as we saw in our previous lecture, explains evil as a preexistent feature of the world, thereby letting God off the hook for the presence of evil. This story, by contrast, puts the focus on man, as it casts the responsibility for evil in the world onto mankind for having not followed God's command. By so doing, if that is in fact the intention here, the author of Genesis 2-3 introduces us to the concept of free will. Again, it's not a phrase that is used in the text, but it is something that we can gain by our reading of the text. This is a dominant motif in the Bible and in Judaism, in general. To some extent, it appears among Christian theologians as well, although Christianity typically takes a different route on this issue. Man has free will—our author wants us to know—and therefore may eat of the Tree, may make his own decision. In this case, it was the human couple's decision to eat of that fruit and to violate God's command. That may be, very subtly, how the author of our second Creation story explains evil in the world.

These texts, I repeat, are very sophisticated literary and theological statements, and we understand the points that these stories are making by the juncture of literature and theology. Now, I want to take this opportunity to note one further instance of a later interpretation that developed in post-biblical times, but which is not present in a surface reading of the story. I refer to the interpretation—and it is mainly a Christian one, more than a Jewish one—which understands the snake to be Satan. There is no hint of this in the biblical text. The snake is described in Genesis 3:1, as "the shrewdest of all the wild beasts," but he is not identified with evil. There is no hint that the snake is Satan in our text and in any case the belief in a Satan figure is a very late development in Jewish theology from which it passed into Christian belief.

The biblical narrative begins with a journey. Adam and Eve are expelled at the end of this chapter from the Garden of Eden. This, itself, is quite remarkable. This journey parallels Israel's journey in a physical sense—beginning with Abraham who has to journey from his home to a new land, as we shall see when we come to Genesis 12—and it parallels the metaphorical journey of all of humankind, "the game of life" we may call it. It is a point that the Israelites understood well. Life is a journey, the fate of all mankind.

Lecture Four
An Overview of Ancient Israelite History

Scope:

With this lecture, we turn to a presentation of the basic introductory material necessary for any study of the Bible. This lecture traces the history of ancient Israel from Abraham c. 1400 B.C.E. to the conquest of Alexander the Great in 333 B.C.E. Our study of Genesis will focus on the earlier period only, but an overview of the entire 1,000-year period is necessary for other questions that we will address in this course. We also will discuss the development of the biblical canon, that is, how and when the books of the Bible came to be considered sacred.

Outline

I.   We present here a basic outline of Israelite history.

   A.   The first major period is the pre-monarchic period (1400–1020 B.C.E.).

   1.   The biblical tradition begins with the three patriarchs—Abraham, Isaac, and Jacob.

   2.   We then read of the experience in Egypt, with the highlights being Joseph, the Slavery, Moses, and the Exodus.

   3.   This, in turn, is followed by what we call the emergence of Israel as a nation. Three shorter periods fit here: the wandering through Sinai, the settlement in Canaan, and the period of the Judges.

   B.   The next major epoch is the monarchic period.

   1.   Israel moves to a monarchy c. 1020 B.C.E., with Saul as the first king (1020–1000 B.C.E.).

   2.   The united monarchy, marked by the reigns of David and Solomon (1000–930 B.C.E.), is Israel's glory period.

   3.   On the death of Solomon, Israel splits into two kingdoms, what we call the period of the divided monarchy, with the kingdom of Israel in the north comprised of nine tribes (930–721 B.C.E.) and the

kingdom in Judah in the south comprised of three tribes (930–586 B.C.E.).

4. In the year 721 B.C.E., Assyria destroyed the northern kingdom of Israel, including its capital city of Samaria, and exiled the population to Mesopotamia to work in Assyria and surrounding regions.

C. Finally, there is the late period, closing out the era of biblical history.

1. The Babylonian Exile (586–538 B.C.E.) resulted from the Babylonian destruction of Jerusalem and the deportation of the people to Mesopotamia.

2. The Persian period (538–333 B.C.E.) commenced with the Persian conquest of the Babylonians and the decree by their king, Cyrus the Great, to allow the Jews to return to Jerusalem and rebuild the Temple, which was dedicated in the city of Jerusalem in the year 516 B.C.E.

3. During the Babylonian Exile and the decades right after the Exile, Israel transitioned from a monolatry to a pure monotheism.

4. The conquest of Alexander the Great (333 B.C.E.) brought an end to the era of biblical history. The period that follows is called either late antiquity or the post-biblical period.

II. The implication of this outline is that the Bible is essentially historically accurate, but the picture is more complicated than that. In recent decades, two competing schools of scholarship have developed.

A. The maximalists believe that, because so much of the Bible has been demonstrated to be historically accurate, even when there is no confirming evidence from elsewhere in the ancient world, we should accept the Bible as essentially reflecting history.

1. Maximalists do not believe that every single statement in the Bible is true—for example, one would have a problem accepting that Abraham fathered a child at 100 and lived to 175, or that there were 600,000 adult Israelite males leaving Egypt during the Exodus—but that the basic story line is historically accurate.

> **2.** One excludes from this view, however, the first 11 chapters of Genesis, because everyone, with the exception of some fundamentalist Jews and Christians, recognizes that the pre-Abraham material is in the world of myth and legend.

B. The minimalists believe that only where there is confirming evidence from elsewhere in the ancient world can we assume that the Bible is historically accurate. Thus, because there is no confirmation for any of the characters from Abraham through the early kings, including David and Solomon, the large narrative of the Torah, Joshua, Judges, Samuel, and much of Kings must be seen as a pious fiction, created by later Jewish authors to give a glory to ancient Israel that never existed.

C. I personally place myself in the maximalist camp, and thus, I will speak of the events in the Bible as essentially historical. At the same, though, I recognize that the stories in Genesis about Abraham, Isaac, Jacob, and Joseph are literary creations, with more literary quality to them than historical reality per se. We will return to this issue in Lecture Nineteen.

III. We now turn to surveying the development of the biblical canon from the time of authorship to the final canonization of the books.

A. The writing of the biblical books took place over the course of 1,000 years.

    1. A small amount of the Bible is archaic poetry (1150–1000 B.C.E.), representing the earliest preserved literature from ancient Israel. Examples include Exodus 15, some snippets in Numbers 21, and Judges 5.

    2. The flowering of ancient Hebrew literature occurred during the 600-year period commencing with the United Kingdom in 1000–B.C.E. and continuing into and beyond the Babylonian Exile.

        a. The most important representative of this literary productivity, especially for our course, is the great narrative from Genesis through Kings.

    b. A second category in this period is that of the classical prophets (Isaiah, Jeremiah, Ezekiel, and so on).

    c. A number of other important biblical books date to this period, too, including Psalms, Proverbs, Ruth, Lamentations, and Ezra-Nehemiah.

  3. Finally, a few biblical books were written at a later stage (400–150 B.C.E.), including such works as Qohelet (Ecclesiastes), Esther, Chronicles, and Daniel (authored in 164 B.C.E.).

B. The canonization of the biblical books is another matter. The books did not become holy or sacred or canonized overnight. Much time passed between the authorship of these books and the establishment of a *canon*, or collection of sacred writings.

  1. The Jewish canon is a tripartite one: Torah, Prophets, Writings. The first letters of the three Hebrew words for these texts (Torah, Nevi'im, Ketuvim) form the Hebrew word *Tanakh*, meaning "the Bible."

  2. The Christian canon, by contrast, is a four-part one: Pentateuch, Histories, Wisdom, Prophets. Christians call this the Old Testament, to which were added additional books, known as the Apocrypha (though these are not canonical in the Protestant tradition), and of course, the New Testament books.

Essential Reading:

Hershel Shanks, ed., *Ancient Israel*, 2nd ed.

Cyrus H. Gordon and Gary A. Rendsburg, *The Bible and the Ancient Near East*, pp. 109–314.

Supplementary Reading:

Marc Z. Brettler, "The Canonization of the Bible," in A. Berlin and M. Brettler, eds., *The Jewish Study Bible*, pp. 2072–2077.

Questions to Consider:

1. In the debate between the maximalists and the minimalists, with which group would you side?

2. Of all the peoples of the ancient Near East, why did only Israel create a canon of its sacred writings?

Lecture Four—Transcript
An Overview of Ancient Israelite History

Welcome to our lecture on ancient Israelite history. The last two lectures were devoted to reading biblical chapters, specifically the Creation accounts, which begin the book of Genesis. In this lecture and the next two lectures, we're going to depart from that reading of the biblical text to introduce some of the broad pictures, some of the background information that's necessary for the study of the Bible in general and of course, for the topic of our course, the book of Genesis in particular. In this lecture, I'm going to present the history of ancient Israel from its origins, which are traced back to the person named Abraham, through the end of the biblical period, which usually is marked with the conquest of Alexander the Great, the king of Greece, in 333 B.C.E. Our study of Genesis will naturally focus only on the earlier period because, obviously, Genesis is the first book of the Bible. But, we need an overview of this entire period of biblical history—about a thousand years are covered in that history—to answer some of the questions that we will address in this course. I also want to, in this lecture toward the end, talk about the biblical canon, the writing of the biblical books and the formation of the canon, those books of the Bible that came to be considered sacred both in Judaism and in Christianity.

Now, let's start with the presentation of the history of ancient Israel. We divide that thousand years—it might even be more than a thousand years, we'll talk about that in just a moment—into three large epochs: the pre-Monarchic period, the Monarchic period, and the post-Monarchic period. Now, we date Abraham to about 1400 B.C.E. and that's where we begin with the pre-Monarchic period, which takes us down to about 1020 B.C.E. when Israel shifts to a monarchy with the person of Saul becoming the first king. Let's talk about our term "B.C.E." for a moment. The usual English usage is "B.C." and "A.D." Now, those two terms, which stand for "before Christ" and "*anno domini,*" present a Christian view of the world—that is to say, the person of Jesus who is seen as the Christ or "Messiah" and "*anno domini*" is Latin for "year of our Lord" and therefore, that also suggests a Christian theology. Biblical scholars, especially in the very ecumenical world in which we live today, have decided to use more commonly the terms "B.C.E." and "C.E." B.C.E. stands for "before the common era" or "before the Christian era," and C.E. is used for the "common era" or "Christian era," and that is the era in which we are today, almost more than 2,000 years later.

Now, in our course, we will be almost always using the B.C.E. dates. So, if I occasionally mention a date and don't append anything to it, you can be sure that it's the B.C.E. period. You may ask, "Why don't we just come up with some theologically neutral system of dating? Why do we continue to use the years even if they are B.C.E. and C.E.?" A change in our dating system would naturally create a chaotic system if we had to start all over again and find some other points in the timeline for which to begin our counting of the years. Furthermore, regardless of whether one is Christian or not, everybody recognizes that the life of Jesus changed world history forever and, therefore, it remains a convenient marker; so we continue to use the years, but we shifted, as noted, from B.C. and A.D. to B.C.E. and C.E.

Let's go back to our biblical history, which I have just begun to outline for you. As I stated, we date Abraham to about 1400 B.C.E. Now, the picture is not that simple. That is the date I prefer, but there is actually a wide debate amongst scholars as to when Abraham actually lived. Some would date him centuries earlier—1600, 1800 or even as far back as 2000 B.C.E. So there is about a 600-year spread in the scholarly debate as to when Abraham lived. I prefer to place him at the end of that 600-year spread, as late as possible, 1400 B.C.E. We'll return in a future lecture to discuss that problem in detail. How do we date the life of Abraham? Abraham is the first of the three patriarchs with which the biblical tradition begins. The other two are Isaac, his son, and Jacob, his grandson. Those three individuals would fit into the 14th century, or the 1300s B.C.E., according to the dating scheme that I present here.

The next small division, a minor division, within the pre-monarchic period is the experience in Egypt. The highlights there are the life of Joseph, which is recorded at the end of the book of Genesis. Then, there are the elements of Israelite history that are related in the book of Exodus. I refer specifically to the slavery in Egypt, the life of Moses, and the exodus itself from the land of Egypt. That exodus occurred, according to most scholars, around the year 1200 B.C.E., give or take 20 or 25 years, perhaps. After the Israelites leave Egypt, we move into a period that we call the emergence of Israel as a nation. That is to say, when you read the book of Genesis, Abraham, Isaac, Jacob and Jacob's sons—the most famous of whom is Joseph—they are really talking about a family more than about a nation somewhere in the land of Egypt. As they emerged from the land of Egypt, the Israelites were then a nation divided into twelve tribes. Those tribes wandered through the Sinai Desert. Eventually they settled in Canaan, and that's related in the book of Joshua.

Then, we move into the period called the time of the Judges. The word "Judges," incidentally, is a misnomer because the individual Judges—people such as Deborah and Gideon and Samson—are not judicial leaders necessarily but are social and military leaders who had great charisma and who led the people of Israel during this period of their formation, still in the pre-Monarchic epoch. We're stuck with the term "Judges," however, and we continue to use it, even though, as I've indicated, it really means something quite different. Rarely are these individuals ever seen judging legal cases as that English term might apply.

Somewhere around 1020 B.C.E., we move to the next major epoch, which we call the monarchic period. At that time, slightly more than 3,000 years ago, the tribes solidify into a single political entity. During the period before the monarchy, between the time of Genesis and the family structure and a monarchy, the period of Israel as a tribal league, is a loose confederation of tribes. One particular tribe did not necessarily have anything in common with another particular tribe other than, of course, the devotion to the single God that united all the tribes of Israel. They didn't have a political unity, that is to say, but around 1020 B.C.E. a variety of factors, most importantly, military and political, led the Israelites to come together, all the tribes under a single king. That individual was King Saul.

Roughly 1020 B.C.E. to 1000 B.C.E. are the approximate years of the 20-year reign of Israel's first king. Saul is actually a transitory figure. That is to say, he has the title of king, but he doesn't necessarily have the trappings of kingship. For example, he doesn't build a palace and he doesn't have a capital city. He continues to live in his family home, he continues to live in his village or town—it wasn't even much of a city where Saul came from. He doesn't have the kind of government bureaucracy that we usually associate with a monarchy or a kingship or any government of any sort, and in fact, in one scene, he's continually working on his farm. He's actually out there making furrows and working in his fields when somebody comes to tell him that war has broken out. That's an indication of what I mean when I say he has the title of king, but not necessarily the trappings of kingship.

This will change with the next two kings of Israel, and they are David and Solomon. David was the son-in-law of Saul who succeeded him on the throne and Solomon was the son of David who succeeded him as the king of Israel. Now, the reign of these two kings, David and Solomon, is known as the time of the united monarchy. This is true of Saul as well, but it's even more so true of David and Solomon who solidified the union of the 12 tribes under one monarchy. This is Israel's "Golden Age," 1000 B.C.E to 930 B.C.E. It's Israel's glory period, when they reached the heights of their military, political, and economic power in the world of the ancient Near East. Among David's several accomplishments was the conquest of Jerusalem and the establishment of that city as the capital of ancient Israel and, of course, it has remained central to the Jewish and Christian traditions for the last 3,000 years, ever since David's conquest and establishment of Jerusalem as the capital city. His son, Solomon, would build the Temple in Jerusalem and this, of course, establishes Jerusalem as the religious center for ancient Israel, as well as the worship of God comes to be solidified in that important city in the land of Israel.

This glory period of Israel, however, was short lived because when Solomon died in 930 B.C.E., the kingdom split into two. We move into what we call the period of the divided monarchy. We're still in that middle epoch, that second of the three great epochs of ancient Israelite history, the monarchic period, but at this point, the monarchy divides into two. It was for political reasons that this occurred and what happened was, the three southern tribes remained loyal to the dynasty that David and Solomon had established and their descendents continued to rule on the throne in Jerusalem in what we called the Kingdom of Judah because out of those three tribes in the south, Judah was the most powerful.

The nine northern tribes, however, did not remain loyal to the dynasty of David and Solomon, and they established their own kingship, their own kingdom in the north. There was no single royal family that held sway over those nine tribes for the course of its two centuries of history but never did those northern tribes reunite with the southern kingdom and follow the leadership of the Davidic/Solomonic Dynasty. And, that northern kingdom continues to use the name "Israel." That's the kingdom of Israel. There are two kingdoms— the kingdom of Israel in the north comprised of nine tribes and the kingdom of Judah in the south comprised of three tribes. That begins in the year 930 B.C.E. and, again, we call that the divided monarchy.

The history of those two kingdoms is as follows. The northern kingdom of Israel existed for a bit more than two centuries and it came to an end in the year 721 B.C.E. The great world power at that time was Assyria, located in Mesopotamia, modern-day Northern Iraq, along the Tigris River. Assyria created the world's first great empire. They marched westward from their homeland across what is today known as Syria, Lebanon, Jordan, and Israel, reaching the Mediterranean, and they brought to an end the kingdom of Israel. They destroyed it, destroyed its capital city of Samaria and exiled the population back to Mesopotamia to work in Assyria itself and surrounding regions. The kingdom of Judah continued on. Those three southern tribes that comprised the kingdom of Judah were able to exist independently for more than another century, down to the year 586 B.C.E., about 140 years or so beyond the end of the kingdom of Israel.

They too, however would meet a similar fate. What happened in 586 B.C.E. was that the empire of Babylonia, which was now the great power in the world, came westward and destroyed the kingdom of Judah. Babylonia had succeeded Assyria as the great world power only a few decades before their conquest of Judah. They defeated Assyria, inherited that great empire that I described, and then were the rulers of most of the Near East. They expanded the boundaries of the Assyrian empire in their own new Babylonian empire and that included the incorporation of Judah into their empire and the destruction of Jerusalem, the capital city. This, of course, would mean the end of the Davidic/Solomonic Dynasty, which had lasted for 400-plus years. It would bring an end to the Temple, which was destroyed as well, which had lasted for almost 400 years since Solomon built it, and it meant the deportation of the people of Judah to Mesopotamia as well. This is the end of our second epoch because this brings an end to monarchy in ancient Israel. Never again would Israel, during the biblical period, have kings ruling on the throne.

The people would live within the larger empires, subservient to the kings of those empires—first Assyria and then Babylonia.

That brings us to the late period, or the late epoch, the last of the three major periods, which closes out the era of biblical history. Now, when the people of Judah go off into Mesopotamia in 586 B.C.E., we call that period "The Babylonian Exile" and that's an important period in biblical studies. Everybody divides the biblical period not only into the three epochs that I've just done, but we speak about the pre-Exilic, Exilic, and post-Exilic. The Exile lasted for less than 50 years from 586 B.C.E. to 538 B.C.E. What brought it to an end? Why such a short period? Within a few decades of Babylonia having conquered Judah, the new world power on the horizon was Persia. It wasn't long before Persia was able to conquer Babylon and succeed it as the rulers of the entire Near East. In fact, Persia expanded its own empire to horizons and boundaries that had never been seen before, so large was its empire. It reached east to the Indus Valley in India and it reached west southwest to the southern part of modern-day Egypt, down toward the border of the Sudan.

The Persians were led by their king, Cyrus the Great, and the Persians had the opposite policy of the previous empires, the Assyrians and Babylonians. You'll recall that I mentioned that those two powers had exiled the peoples that they had conquered; Assyria had exiled Israel and Babylonia had exiled Judah. Persia, led by Cyrus the Great, issued a decree that allowed the peoples who had been exiled to return to their homelands and to establish their lives once more in those homelands. They would not be independent, but they would have some autonomy and be allowed to live freely in the countries in which they originated. That meant that the Jews who were now living in Babylonia and surrounding regions were allowed to return to the land of Judah, to the city of Jerusalem, and to rebuild the Temple. They did that. It didn't happen overnight. It took time for the people to start moving back, and of course, it took even longer for the Temple to be rebuilt. But, in the year 516 B.C.E., 22 years after Cyrus's decree, the Second Temple, as we call it, was dedicated in the city of Jerusalem and the worship of God was reestablished in that very important city.

You'll notice a moment ago I used the word "Jews." Now, typically when we refer to the people of ancient Israel, we call them the Israelites, and sometimes we call them the Hebrews because those are the terms that the Bible itself uses. As we move into this late biblical period, however, the term "Jews" comes to be used more and more by the biblical books in that period, and therefore, scholars adopt that term as well. It is one continuum from ancient Israel to the religion of Judaism and the people called the Israelites and the Jews are one and the same. But, we use this Babylonian Exile and the period right after the Exile as a convenient marker to change our terminology and we do so for a couple of reasons.

First, and most important to my mind, is a change in the religion of ancient Israel. You'll recall from our previous lectures that we mentioned that Israel was not quite a pure monotheism. They worshiped only one God, but they continued to have a tacit recognition of the existence of other gods. This changed during the Babylonian Exile and the decades right after the Exile. Israel switched or changed, transitioned into monotheism. Their religion now was pure monotheism, only one God. They believed only in the existence of one God and they no longer recognized, tacitly or otherwise, the existence of other gods—pure monotheism. We mark that change by changing our terminology from the religion of ancient Israel, which is after all, a rather cumbersome term, to the simple one-word expression, Judaism, and the people about whom we are speaking, we no longer call the Israelites necessarily, but we now begin to call them Jews, a word which develops in English from the first syllable of Judaism. Where does that word "Judaism" come from? It's the "ism" of Judah because the only kingdom that continued on was the kingdom of Judah. We actually lose sight of the nine tribes of the northern kingdom of Israel once they were exiled by Assyria. But, the biblical record continues to talk about the people of Judah as they go off into exile and as they return from exile to Jerusalem, to their homeland of Judah. Therefore, we have Judaism, the "ism" of Judah.

In 333 B.C.E., after two centuries of Persian rule and after about a century of battles between the Persians and the Greeks, the biblical period comes to an end with the conquest of Alexander the Great, king of Macedon and Greece. He defeats Persia, once and for all after a century of battles, and thereby inherits that great empire and now creates what is now the world's largest empire. Again, it stretched as far east as Western India, and of course, incorporated much of the eastern Mediterranean, the Aegean region, the area of modern-day Greece. This brings an end to the biblical period for a couple of reasons. The books that would eventually make it into the Jewish canon, more or less, cease at this time. Jews would continue to write books, but most of the books written after this period would no longer be incorporated into the biblical canon. We'll talk about the formation of that canon in just a few moments. Furthermore, this is the first time that the people of Israel, the Jews and the people of the Near East in general, are ruled by truly foreign rulers. That is to say, the Assyrians, the Babylonians, and the Persians were all rooted in the area of the Near East. Now, the rule from Greece means that rule was coming from across the Mediterranean Sea. It's a very different kind of rule. It's a very foreign rule and this brings an end to our era of biblical history. So if we date Abraham to 1400 B.C.E., and we take our biblical period down through the Alexander the Great Conquest in 333 B.C.E., you can see how we arrive at a 1,000-year span of time.

Now, the implication of the outline that I have just presented is that the Bible presents an essentially historical picture, that it is, essentially, historically accurate. But the picture is more complicated than that. In recent decades, two competing schools of scholarship have developed. They are the maximalists and the minimalists. Let's describe them. The maximalists believe that, since so much of the Bible has been demonstrated to be historically accurate, then even when there is no confirming evidence from elsewhere in the ancient world, we should accept the Bible as reflecting history. Let me give you some examples. We know, from Persian records, that Persia ruled the entire Near East and that Cyrus issued a decree, as I described, allowing peoples to return to their homelands. We know, from Babylonian records, that Babylon indeed destroyed Jerusalem in 586 B.C.E. We know, from Assyrian records, that indeed Assyria destroyed the Northern kingdom of Israel in 1721 B.C.E. That's what I mean when I say we have confirming evidence from elsewhere in the ancient world that demonstrates that the Bible is essentially historical. Therefore, the maximalists believe that even where we don't have confirming evidence, we can assume it to be historical. It's true that the material, which we don't have confirmation of, is the earlier material, but we can assume, according to this view, that even then the Bible's picture is historical. So we move back to people such as Solomon and David, and move even further back in time to Moses and eventually back to Abraham, none of whom is mentioned in contemporary text but, according to the maximalist view, are to be seen as historical.

Not if every single statement in the Bible were to be accepted as true, one would have a problem, for example, accepting that Abraham fathered a child at the age of 100, or that he lived to 175, or that Sarah gave birth at the age of 90. One would raise an eyebrow with the statement in the book of Exodus 12 that 600,000 adult Israelite males left Egypt during the Exodus. That would imply a total population of two million people or more. But, one would not throw out the baby with the bathwater just because the datum here or there may raise an eyebrow. The basic story line is historically accurate. One excludes from this view, by the way, the first 11 chapters of Genesis—the ones that we've been reading—since everyone, with the exception of some fundamentalist Jews and Christians, recognizes that the pre-Abraham material in Genesis 1–11 lies in the world of legend, and that individuals such as Adam and Eve and Cain and Abel and Noah and so on cannot be placed in an historical context or on an historical timeline.

The minimalists, by contrast—that's the second school of thought— believed that only where there is confirming evidence from elsewhere in the ancient world can we assume that the Bible is historically accurate. Therefore, since there is no confirmation for any of the characters from Abraham through the early kings, including David and Solomon, the larger narrative of such biblical books as the Torah, Genesis through Deuteronomy, Joshua, Judges, Samuel, and much of Kings, must be seen as fictional literature created by later Jewish authors to give a glory to ancient Israel that never existed, a glory that can be seen in the reigns of David and Solomon, a glory that can be seen in the person of Abraham who originated the tradition. That's the minimalist view. I personally place myself in the maximalist camp and thus, I will speak of the events in the Bible as essentially historical during this course. At the same time, though, I recognize that these stories in Genesis about Abraham and Isaac and Jacob and Joseph are literary creations, with more literary quality to them than historical reality per se. This is a topic that we'll address in a future lecture, but nevertheless, I still see the biblical picture as essentially historical.

Let's now take a look at the biblical canon, from the time of the authorship of the books to the final canonization of the biblical books. Just as the history of Israel takes up about a thousand years of history, the writing of the biblical books takes place over the course of about 1,000 years. It's not the same thousand years, however. It stretches from around 1150 B.C.E. down to 150 B.C.E, and here, too, it's convenient to divide the period of biblical book authorship into three smaller units. The first is the archaic material—archaic poetry from around 1150 B.C.E. down to around 1000 B.C.E. We have snippets of such poetry preserved in Exodus 15 and in Judges 5 and in a few other places such as Numbers 21.

The flowering of ancient Hebrew literature occurs from 1000 B.C.E. onward down to around 400 B.C.E. It's a 600-year period commencing with the United Kingdom and the vast majority of biblical books were written during this period. Most importantly for our course, I include here the great narrative that stretches from Genesis through Kings. This was written during this period of the monarchy and the Exile from around 1000 B.C.E. down to 400 B.C.E. The third unit here would be the late-biblical books, those books written after 400 B.C.E. Here we have such books as Ecclesiastes, known in Hebrew as *Qohelet*, Song of Songs, the book of Esther, the book of Chronicles and the book of Daniel. These books are written in the late-biblical period and the last of these books is the book of Daniel, authored about 150 B.C.E. That's the last book to be written. So, there's our 1,000-year span of time.

That's the authorship of the biblical books. What about the canonization? How and when and under what circumstances did the canon arise? Now, first of all, the term "canon" is a tough term to define. It means, basically, the books that came to be considered sacred. A canon is a collection of sacred writings. True, we do use it in other contexts. We can speak of the Shakespearean canon, which would be all the plays and poems of Shakespeare, but here we're talking about a collection of sacred writings when we're talking about the biblical canon. Let's also note that the concept of a canon was something specific to ancient Israel, to Judaism. No other people in the ancient Near East took their writings and created a canon like the people of Israel did, and we can talk about why they did this. With the destruction of the Temple in Jerusalem and with the dispersion of the Jews, not only into the Exile in Babylonia, but in other directions as well—for some fled into the opposite direction, into Egypt—Judaism was no longer a single religion practiced in a single land. Jews were living in a variety of places in the ancient world. The creation of a canon would unite those people no matter where they were living because if they were living outside the land of Israel, they could not participate necessarily in the worship of God in Jerusalem in the proper fashion as defined and described in the authoritative texts. But, they could all have this union together with Jews everywhere by holding on to one sacred text.

Therefore, the Torah arose as the first part of the canon. The first biblical books to be canonized were the Torah. This forms the basis of the Jewish canon, which would eventually develop into a tripartite canon, three parts. The Torah, the first to be canonized took place in around the year 450 B.C.E. exactly what I referred to. Yes, the Temple had been rebuilt but there were Jews living outside the land of Israel and they used the Torah to unite them in this canon that emerged at this time. The Prophets was the second book to be canonized, and that happened about 250 B.C.E. The third group was the Writings. It's a miscellaneous category. It means all those books that were not in the Torah or the Prophets, and that included books such as Psalms, Proverbs, Job, Esther, the Song of Songs and a few others. That's the "catch-all" category and that material was canonized around 100 C.E. or maybe even later, 150 C.E. That brought an end to the biblical canon in the Jewish tradition. The three parts—Torah, Prophets, and the Writings—now comprise the Bible in Judaism.

The Christian canon, by contrast, is a four-part one. Christians take the biblical books and put them in a slightly different order and arrange them differently—the Pentateuch, the Histories, the Wisdom books, and the Prophets, in that order. The Pentateuch is the same as the Torah. The Histories is all the material that is historical in nature. Wisdom includes books such as Psalms and Proverbs, and Prophets, of course, are the great biblical prophets—Isaiah, Jeremiah, Ezekiel and others. Christianity accepted the canon of Judaism and just rearranged the books in the manner that I have just described. Christians call this material the Old Testament, to which was added additional books, known as the Apocrypha, though those are not canonical in the Protestant tradition. Of course, finally, Christianity added the New Testament books, detailing the life of Jesus and the early Church, the work of Saint Paul and the other disciples. The Christian canon came to a close in about the 2nd or 3rd century C.E.

We've placed Genesis into the larger picture of ancient Israelite history and the formation of the biblical canon. Thank you.

Lecture Five
The Ancient Near East

Scope:

We continue our presentation of the basic introductory material by surveying the broader context of ancient Israel. Scholars call this world the ancient Near East, which in turn, is divided into three major geographical regions: Egypt, Canaan, and Mesopotamia. All three are important for understanding the Bible in general and Genesis in particular. Abraham is born in Mesopotamia, migrates to Canaan, and visits Egypt. Jacob is born in Canaan, lives for 20 years in Mesopotamia, returns to Canaan, and dies in Egypt. Joseph is born in Mesopotamia, moves to Canaan with his family at a young age, and spends his entire adult life in Egypt. In short, the book of Genesis provides a veritable tour of the entire ancient Near East. Knowledge of these regions greatly enhances our understanding of the biblical stories.

Outline

I. The Ancient Near East is divided into three major geographical regions: Egypt, Canaan, and Mesopotamia. [See appendix map: **The Ancient Near East c. 1400 B.C.E.**] All of these are important for understanding the Bible in general and the book of Genesis in particular.

 A. Abraham is born in Mesopotamia, migrates to the land of Canaan, and visits Egypt during his lifetime.

 B. His grandson, Jacob, is born in Canaan, lives for 20 years in Mesopotamia, returns to Canaan, and then spends the end of his life in Egypt, where he eventually dies.

 C. Joseph, in turn, is born in Mesopotamia, moves to Canaan with his family at a young age, and then spends his entire adult life in Egypt.

II. "Near East" is the term scholars use to refer to the area where Asia, Africa, and to some extent Europe all come together.

 A. *Ancient* refers to the period from c. 3000 B.C.E., when our written records first begin, though 333 B.C.E., at which point we move to the Greco-Roman period, also called late antiquity.

B. From the archaeological perspective, we divide the period into large epochs, Bronze Age and Iron Age, with the former further subdivided into three periods:

    1. Bronze Age (3000–1200 B.C.E.)

        a. Early Bronze Age (3000–2200 B.C.E.)

        b. Middle Bronze Age (2200–1550 B.C.E.)

        c. Late Bronze Age (1550–1200 B.C.E.)

    2. Iron Age (1200 B.C.E. onward)

II. The three main geographical regions of the ancient Near East are as follows:

A. Egypt, that is, the Nile valley, home of the Egyptians, contained mainly a homogeneous population.

B. Mesopotamia, that is, the Tigris and Euphrates valley, contained, in contrast to Egypt, a very heterogeneous population: it was the home of the Sumerians, Babylonians, Assyrians, Hurrians, and others.

C. Canaan, the land in between the two great powers listed above, in which lived the Canaanites and the Israelites, might be called "the third world" of ancient times.

    1. Canaan has rather amorphous boundaries; basically, we define it as the area bounded by the shore of the Mediterranean to the west and the Syrian Desert to the east.

    2. There was no unified political entity in Canaan (in contrast to Egypt especially, but Mesopotamia as well); instead, dozens of independent city-states dotted the landscape.

    3. In contrast to Egypt and Mesopotamia, there is no major river in Canaan. Instead, the people of Canaan were totally dependent on rainfall for growing crops.

D. There are three regions beyond the main Near East that have a role to play in biblical history: Persia (modern Iran), Greece, and Arabia.

III. It is important to note that all of these cultures were literate societies during the biblical period (with the possible exception of Arabia). Moreover, their literary remains often share striking similarities with the Bible, as we have seen already and as we will continue to demonstrate as the course unfolds. Examples include:

A. The Babylonian creation story, known as the *Enuma Elish*, discussed in Lecture Three.

B. The Gilgamesh Epic, which includes the Babylonian flood story, to be discussed in Lecture Seven.

C. The Canaanite epics of Aqhat and Kret, heroic figures in quest of a son, as is also the case with Abraham, as we will see in Lecture Nine.

D. The Egyptian Tale of Two Brothers and the *Iliad* of Homer both include a story that closely parallels an episode in Joseph's life; see Lecture Twenty-Two.

E. In addition, although literary texts are the most exciting discoveries in archaeological excavations, note that the most common written records found, by far, are economic and legal texts, detailing the everyday life of the ancient Near East. These, too, play a role in our study of the Bible, the best example of which are the Nuzi documents from northern Mesopotamia, which we will survey in Lecture Ten.

F. These numerous parallels lead us to the conclusion that Israel did not exist in a vacuum but, instead, participated to a large extent in the greater cultural world of the ancient Near East. At times, it is not just texts from the ancient world that illuminate the Bible but other matters as well. For example:

   1. The Tower of Babel story in Genesis 11:1–9 reflects the Mesopotamian ziggurat tradition, tall pyramid-like temple structures that were envisioned to connect heaven and earth.

   2. We get a second reference to this Mesopotamian tradition in the story of Jacob's dream in Genesis 28:10–22 Note that this dream occurs at the beginning of his journey to Aram, that is, northern Mesopotamia (modern-day northeastern Syria and southern Turkey). The Hebrew term there, *sullam*, is traditionally rendered "ladder," but we now know that it means "stairway" or even "ziggurat," if you will.

G. Our reading of ancient Near Eastern literature allows us to see important distinctions between the way the polytheistic world saw matters and the way ancient Israel understood the world. A discussion of Genesis 3 illustrates this. Note that the Tree of Knowledge is the central issue in this chapter, not the Tree of Life, though this second tree is also present in the garden.

1. Most ancient Near Eastern people saw eternal life as the ultimate quest for mankind

2. The Gilgamesh Epic has this as its main theme, and the story ends with Gilgamesh crying to himself in resignation of the fact that he will not achieve immortality and even the next best thing, rejuvenation, has slipped through his fingers.

3. Egyptians were the only people in antiquity who believed one could live forever after one's death in a pleasurable, positive afterlife.

4. Not so Israel, however, which places the Tree of Life in the Garden of Eden as a token nod in that direction, but there is no danger that Adam and Eve will eat from that tree because we all know that immortality is unattainable.

5. The main issue, instead, is the Tree of Knowledge, which demonstrates that for the ancient Israelites, the main quest was knowledge, and not eternal life.

Essential Reading:

Cyrus H. Gordon and Gary A. Rendsburg, *The Bible and the Ancient Near East*, pp. 32–108.

Michael Roaf, *The Cultural Atlas of Mesopotamia and the Ancient Near East*.

Supplementary Reading:

Bill T. Arnold and Bryan Beyer, *Readings from the Ancient Near East: Primary Sources for Old Testament Study*.

Victor H. Matthews and Don C. Benjamin, *Old Testament Parallels: Laws and Stories from the Ancient Near East*.

Questions to Consider:

1. One of the main points we made in this lecture is that no culture exists in a vacuum. Illustrate this point for ancient Israel.

2. Can you think of parallels to this issue in our contemporary culture, whether it be minority cultures in the American melting pot or America within the greater world today, or other cultures elsewhere in relationship to America?

Lecture Five—Transcript
The Ancient Near East

Welcome to our lecture on the ancient Near East, which is a natural continuation of our previous lecture. Did you notice how often in the last lecture I referred to other countries in the ancient world—Egypt, Babylonia, Assyria, Persia, and Greece? All of these countries make up part of what we call the ancient Near East. No country exists in a vacuum, and that is certainly true of Israel in the biblical period. Therefore, when we traced the history of ancient Israel in our last lecture we, by necessity, had to refer to all of these countries.

Let's talk about the ancient Near East, which in turn is divided into three major geographical regions: Egypt, Canaan, and Mesopotamia. All of these are important for understanding the Bible in general and the book of Genesis in particular. Abraham is born in Mesopotamia. He then migrates to the land of Canaan, and he visits Egypt during his lifetime. His grandson, Jacob, is born in Canaan. He lives for 20 years in Mesopotamia. He then returns to Canaan and he spends the rest of his life in Egypt where he eventually dies. His son, Joseph, in turn, is born in Mesopotamia. He moves to Canaan with his family at a young age and then spends his entire adult life in Egypt. In short, the book of Genesis provides a veritable tour of the entire ancient Near East. Knowledge of these regions, accordingly, greatly enhances our understanding of the biblical stories.

"The Near East" is the term that scholars use to refer to the area where Asia, Africa, and to some extent, Europe, all come together. "ancient" refers to the period from about 3000 B.C.E., when our first written records begin to appear, down to the year 333 B.C.E., at which point we move to the Greco-Roman period, also called Late Antiquity—which, according to what we said last time, is the end of the Biblical Period—and once again, the boundary marker is the conquest of Alexander the Great.

Now, if our historical records begin around 3000 B.C.E. and, as we saw in the previous lecture, Abraham is to be dated to about 1400 B.C.E., this means that there is a lot of Ancient Near Eastern history long before Israel comes on to the scene of history. From the archeological perspective, we divide this period into two large ages, the Bronze Age and the Iron Age. The Bronze Age commences around 3000 B.C.E and it takes us down to 1200 B.C.E. This, in turn, is subdivided into an Early Bronze Age, a Middle Bronze Age, and a Late Bronze Age. Of these three periods, the one that concerns us is the Late Bronze Age, which is about 1550 B.C.E. to 1200 B.C.E. That would be the time of the Patriarchs, the 14th century, or the 1300s, according to the last lecture, the time when we would date Abraham, Isaac, Jacob, and Joseph as well. Around 1200 B.C.E., the Bronze Age comes to an end and we move to the Iron Age. As these names imply, archeologists use these terms based on the commonest metal in use. Bronze, an alloy of copper and tin, was the main metal used for much of the Near Eastern history, until 1200 B.C.E. when iron implements begin to appear with much more frequency. To some extent, we are still in the Iron Age today because the number one metal that we use is steel, which of course is based on iron.

Now, the three main geographical regions of the Near East, which I referred to, are Egypt, Mesopotamia, and Canaan. Let's talk about them in some detail. Egypt, that is, the Nile valley, was the home of the ancient Egyptians. It was mainly a homogeneous population. Almost everybody who lived in Egypt would be called the Egyptians. Although from time to time, foreigners, of course, could reside there, as in the case of the Israelites at the end of the book of Genesis and in the book of Exodus. Mesopotamia we define as the Tigris and Euphrates Valley and it was, in contrast to Egypt, a very heterogeneous population. You had there Sumerians, Babylonians, Assyrians, Hurrians and others. We've already referred to Babylon and Assyria. The Hurrians are people in northern Mesopotamia that we will be talking about at other points in our course. The land between is the land of Canaan. The two great powers that existed on either side—Egypt toward the southwest and Mesopotamia toward the east and northeast—were the powers of antiquity and between, you have what might be called "the third world" of ancient times, the land of Canaan. No great power existed there, but it was there that one found the people known as the Canaanites and that was where the Israelites lived as well.

Canaan had rather amorphous borders. Basically, we defined it as the area bounded by the shore of the Mediterranean to the west and the Syrian Desert to the east. Remember, there were no real nation-states yet with the kind of national boundaries that one can see on a map today. In contrast to Egypt and Mesopotamia, there was no major river in Canaan. That is to say, Egypt had the Nile and Mesopotamia had the Tigris and Euphrates. That was not true of Canaan. The longest river is the Jordan River, but that's actually a very narrow river. There's not a lot of water to be found in it. It's a bit of a stream, even though it runs for more than a hundred miles. Instead of the dependency on rivers for their fresh water, the people of Canaan were totally dependent on rainfall for growing crops. That presents a difference between that land and the lands of Egypt and Mesopotamia. I also hasten to add that there is not a lot of rainfall in that region.

Another thing we can say about Canaan is the following. There was no unified political entity in Canaan, in contrast again to Egypt, where a single king known as the pharaoh ruled over the entire land, and that was also true in Mesopotamia. It might have been the king of Babylon or the king of Assyria, but for much of Mesopotamian history, a single political entity ruled over the Tigris and Euphrates Valley. Not so in Canaan; however, instead of a single king or a single empire of any sort, the land was carved into dozens of independent city-states, which dotted the landscape. We can actually talk about the geography of that region, which explains this phenomenon. The cultures of Mesopotamia and Egypt are what we call riverine societies. That is to say, they are based on those major rivers—the Nile and the Tigris and Euphrates. Because the water in those rivers needs to be coordinated—how much water can be used for irrigating fields, diverting water from those rivers—all of that requires some kind of national governmental administration. In the land of Canaan, however, where people did not use a river for their growing of crops, all water resources were local. The rainfall—which we already commented about for the irrigation or the watering of fields, and nearby springs and wells that could be dug deep into the ground for the procurement of drinking water—therefore, a single, independent city-state located in place "X" need not coordinate its water resource management with another city-state living maybe 10 or 15 kilometers away.

Each of these city-states, no matter how large or how small, would have had its own "king." "King" may be in quotation marks because these rulers ruled over an area maybe 10–15 kilometer radius away from their city where their fields would be located. The first people and the only people to actually ever unify the land of Canaan into a single, political entity would have been the people of Israel. First in the period of the Judges, the emergence of Israel where it was a loose confederation of 12 tribes; although even there, as we noted again in the last lecture, it wasn't a single political entity per se, but certainly it was under the early monarchy where David and Solomon ruled over the entire land. That's the only time Canaan actually appears in the political history of the ancient world as a single, unified entity.

In addition to these three main regions—Egypt, Canaan and Mesopotamia—we also have to mention three other regions that are beyond the main boundaries of the Near East that also have a role to play in biblical history. Two of these we've already referred to and they are Persia and Greece. The third is Arabia. Persia, which is modern Iran, is to the far east of Mesopotamia and, as you already know, they eventually would conquer Babylonia and rule over the land of Israel and the Jews of the entire ancient Near East. Greece is across the Mediterranean, the region of the Aegean Sea and, again, as we've already mentioned more than once, they eventually would conquer Persia and they, too, would rule over the land of Israel and Jews would fall under the rule of the Greeks. The third area is Arabia. It's the third area beyond the bounds of the main Near East and that is to the south and southeast of the land of Canaan. We don't have many mentions of Arabia in the biblical record, but we do find, from time to time, something of interest from our ancient sources that refer to Arabia, and in some cases, have an effect on the way we understand the Bible.

I want to mention here that the Bible typically refers to the land of Canaan with those words, "the land of Canaan." That is to say, "the land of Israel" is used in the Bible, but very rarely. The Israelites themselves understood that the country they lived in, or the region they lived in, was called "the land of Canaan." They themselves were the people of Israel, but their land was "the land of Canaan."

Now, it is important to note that all of the cultures that I have referred to were literate Gilgamesh Epic societies during the biblical period, with the possible exception of Arabia. Moreover, their literary remains, from Egypt, Babylonia, and these other places, often share striking similarities with the biblical material, as we already have seen and as we will continue to demonstrate as the course continues to unfold. Let's mention some examples here. We already have talked about the Babylonian creation story known as the *Enuma Elish*, which we discussed in Lecture Three when we talked about the holiness, which is established at the end of the biblical Creation story, the first account at the beginning of Genesis 2. The was the great literary classic of the ancient world from Babylonia and it includes a story of a flood, strikingly parallel to the biblical Flood story, and when we reach the biblical Flood story, we'll talk about the Gilgamesh epic and, in fact, we'll see some striking similarities between those two flood accounts. From Canaan, we have the epics called Aqhat and Kret. These are two separate epics. They are the epic of Aqhat and the epic of Kret, two heroic figures, both of whom share a motif with the story of Abraham and that motif is the quest for an heir, the quest for a son. We'll be talking about that as our course proceeds. These are written on clay tablets. This is true of the Babylonian material, the *Enuma Elish* and the Gilgamesh Epic. It's also true of these Canaanite epics.

From Egypt, we have a variety of stories that affect our understanding of the Bible and one stellar example from the book of Genesis is the Egyptian Tale of Two Brothers. Here we also can mention the *Iliad* of Homer because both the Egyptian Tale of Two Brothers and the *Iliad* of Homer include a story that very closely parallels an episode in Joseph's life. In Genesis 39, Joseph is enticed by the wife of his master, Potiphar. Joseph valiantly declines this seduction and, in turn, is then falsely accused of rape by Potiphar's wife. The same thing happens to the younger brother in the Egyptian Tale of Two Brothers; the same thing happens to Bellerophontes in the *Iliad* of Homer. All of this tells us that to some extent, the Israelites must have known about the literature of their neighbors, close neighbors in Canaan, neighbors further afield in Babylon, and even those across the Mediterranean in Greece.

I've used the word "epic" a couple of times here to refer to the Gilgamesh Epic and to refer to these Canaanite materials, and I should take a moment to talk about "epic" and "myth." We use the word "epic" to refer to those stories from the ancient world, which have human heroes. Gods may appear in them from time to time, but the stories are based on human heroes in particular, individuals like Gilgamesh or Kret. Myths, by contrast, are stories that deal with gods and humans do not appear in them. So, when we talk about the *Enuma Elish*, this would be a Babylonian myth, because it's talking about the various gods. We've already mentioned Marduk and Tiamat and other deities that appear in that story. So, keep this distinction between myths and epics because it is something that is convenient to remember as we work through our course.

Up until now, I've been talking about literary texts. The *Enuma Elish*, the Gilgamesh Epic, these Canaanite epics, the *Iliad* of Homer, the Egyptian Tale of Two Brothers—these are what are known as literary texts. That is, they create good reading. They were designed to be read as literature. But, most of the materials that we find in the ancient Near East when we do archeological excavations are not literary texts. By far, the commonest written records that one finds are economic texts and legal texts, which detail for us, in many ways, the everyday life of the ancient Near East. Now, these too play a role in our study of the Bible, but let's talk about the kind of texts that we are talking about here. Picture your file cabinet at home. Picture all the documents that you have in your file cabinet. That's what we find in the typical excavation of an ancient Near Eastern city—deeds, receipts, contracts, warranties even, business documents, and economic texts. This is not literature, but they tell us an awful lot about the ordinary life of an individual or a society in the ancient world.

It is this ordinary, quotidian material which frequently will shed some light on the Bible, as well. For example, in a future lecture, we're going to be talking about some of the customs that were in vogue during the time of Abraham and Sarah, and we will see that these customs are reflected in documents from a place called Nuzi in northern Mesopotamia. We don't have literary texts from Nuzi, but we have plenty of these economic and legal texts, which will inform the way we understand the biblical material. These economic texts truly are quite remarkable. It is not my primary interest, as you have already realized. My interest lies elsewhere, specifically in the world of ancient literature, *qua* literature, but there are experts in our field who can take this material from the ancient world and reconstruct an entire society, the economy of those countries. They can tell you how much wool was produced, how much wool was exported from Place A to Place B, or how much it costs to buy a bushel of barley. A bushel is, of course, a modern measurement, but the equivalent of a bushel of barley. They can tell you what the prices were for various commodities—for wine, for olive oil and all sorts of other items.

So, these are experts in this field and every once in a while that material will also help us understand the biblical material. Let me just give you two examples. In Genesis 23, Abraham buys a plot of land to bury his now-deceased wife, Sarah. He pays 400 shekels for that land. Is that a lot? Is that a little? Is that the standard? We have experts who can help us and we find out, we learn from this material, that it is basically a standard price for a plot of land, although we don't have the exact dimensions of that land in Genesis 23. Similarly, in Genesis 37, Joseph's brothers sell him for twenty shekels. These are weights, these are measures. A shekel is a particular weight. It's about ten grams and always referred to silver. That was the commodity you used for the purchasing, for the buying and selling. For twenty shekels, Joseph was sold as a slave. Again, is that a lot? Is that a little? Our sources inform us, and the experts, who worked on this, tell us that, in fact that, again is about a standard price.

The legal documents from the ancient world, as I mentioned, can help us understand other biblical stories still. Let's talk about Genesis 23 once more. I just referred to Abraham's purchasing the plot of land for four hundred shekels. In that story, we read something quite peculiar. It keeps on talking about Abraham not only buying the land, but buying the trees. What is the emphasis on the trees all about? When you buy land, don't you naturally buy the trees at the same time? Well, it turns out that in the ancient world that was not necessarily the case. There was a legal institution by which you could buy the land, but not the trees, which meant that somebody else had the use of the trees. Or, you could buy the trees, but not the land, which meant that you could have use of the trees, that is, the fruit that they would bear, and so on, but not necessarily own the land. In Genesis 23 when we have the statement that Abraham bought the land and the trees that were on the land, we now understand why the biblical text is telling us this. It's telling us this because these economic and legal texts from the ancient world inform us of the possibility of buying one without necessarily buying the other. In this case, Abraham bought it all, the trees and the land.

These numerous parallels that I'm referring to here—the literary ones and the economic and legal texts that I've just referred to—these collectively inform us that Israel did not exist in a vacuum. That's what I stated at the beginning of this lecture and hopefully we are illustrating that as we proceed here with all sorts of examples. Israel participated, to a great extent, in the greater cultural world of the ancient Near East. At times, it is not just written texts from the ancient world that illuminate the Bible; other matters help as well. For example, the Tower of Babel story in Genesis 11:1–9 reflects the

Mesopotamian ziggurat tradition. Let's define a few terms here. "Babel" is the Hebrew word for "Babylon," so the Tower of Babel is something that is situated in the city of Babylon in Genesis 11. A "ziggurat" is a tall, pyramid-like temple structure, which the people of Mesopotamia built. Archeologists have found these and there are still several of them standing, not in perfect condition anymore, but still standing in the ruined cities of ancient Iraq, ancient Mesopotamia. These structures, these ziggurats, were envisioned to connect heaven and earth. It was an ancient tradition in Mesopotamia to build these structures. If you look at chapter 11:2 of Genesis, it tells us that this structure that the people wished to build shall have its top, or its head, in heaven, and that matches perfectly what we know about the building of these ziggurats.

We have a second reference to this Mesopotamian tradition in the story of Jacob's dream, which occurs in Genesis 28:10–22. Note, by the way, that this dream occurs at the beginning of Jacob's journey, just as he's leaving the land of Israel. He's leaving because he has to flee the wrath of his brother, Esau, and he's going to leave to go live with his uncle Laban, the brother of his mother, Rebecca, in the land of Aram. Aram is northern Mesopotamia, more or less modern-day northeastern Syria and southern Turkey. The Hebrew word that is used there, *sullam*, is traditionally rendered as a "ladder," but we now know that, in fact, the word means, more specifically, "stairway" or even "ziggurat," if you will. So, it is no coincidence that as Jacob readies to leave the land of Israel, he dreams about something Mesopotamian. Again, in Genesis 28:12, we have the reference, just as we had in Genesis 11, that the top of this structure that he dreams about has its top in heaven. Then, the story goes on to refer further to the angels that were going up and down this "ladder," in quotation marks again; stairway, ramp, or ziggurat is more likely the meaning of our particular Hebrew word.

So, throughout all of the Near Eastern material, the book of Genesis comes alive. It is the wonder of biblical studies that from every corner of the ancient Near East, we are able to obtain material that illuminates the content of the Bible—literary texts, economic texts, legal texts and, occasionally, architectural material such as the ziggurat structure.

At this juncture, I want to return to our discussion about the second Creation story, which we treated several lectures ago. You will recall that we talked about the Tree of Knowledge, one of the two special trees that God planted in the Garden of Eden, the story of which is related in Genesis 2 and 3. In Genesis 2:9 God plants the Garden of Eden and in it he places the two trees, the Tree of Knowledge and the Tree of Life. Interestingly, in Genesis 2:17, when God issues the command to Adam, he prohibits him only from eating of the fruit of the Tree of Knowledge. There is no mention there of the Tree of Life, even though both trees were present in the Garden. Then, at some point, Adam clearly must have conveyed this information to Eve, even though that scene is not narrated for us, because when the snake tries to entice Eve to eat the fruit, she knows about the prohibition. I repeat, however, that we are dealing here, once more, only with the prohibition of the fruit of the Tree of Knowledge, or to use its full name, the Tree of Knowledge of Good and Evil. The Tree of Life is, once again, not mentioned at this point. The story continues with the eating of that fruit first by Eve and then by Adam, and that action, of course, leads to their banishment from the Garden of Eden, at the end of chapter 3. Notice how the focus throughout this story is on the Tree of Knowledge, with the Tree of Life receiving only an occasional mention.

Why, we may ask. Why the focus on the Tree of Knowledge, with little or no attention given to the Tree of Life. It is here that we may bring the larger picture of the ancient Near East to bear on our question. As we have illustrated in this lecture, looking at the material from the ancient Near East as a whole allows us to gain a greater understanding of what the biblical text is doing.

Most people in the ancient Near East saw eternal life as the ultimate quest for mankind. The best example of this is the Gilgamesh Epic from Babylonia. I already mentioned that this composition was the literary classic of the ancient world. We have early versions of this story, going back to the third millennium B.C.E. in the Sumerian language. The Gilgamesh Epic then developed over the course of centuries in Mesopotamia, indeed over the course of two millennia, until the standard Babylonian version was produced sometime in the 8th or 7th century B.C.E. In short, the Gilgamesh Epic has an exceedingly long tradition in ancient Mesopotamia, as its story was told and retold for generations.

The story, which is written over the course of twelve different cuneiform tablets in the standard version written in Babylonian, and based on these earlier precursors, relates for us the life of Gilgamesh, a legendary king from the city of Uruk in southern Mesopotamia. The dominant theme in this great epic poem is the hero's quest for eternal life. Once Gilgamesh witnesses the death of his dear friend, Enkidu, he comes to the realization that he himself will one day die. Gilgamesh does not want to die, however, and thus he sets his course on determining how he can live forever. That is what I mean by the quest for eternal life. That, again, is the main theme of this classic composition.

Gilgamesh goes on an episodic journey from place to place, trying to find out how he can achieve eternal life. It is in the course of this journey, in the course of this quest, that Gilgamesh learns about Utnapishtim, a man who indeed achieved immortality. Gilgamesh decides, therefore, to visit Utnapishtim and to learn his secret as, he figures, "If I can learn how Utnapishtim achieved immortality, then I, too, can live forever."

In the next scene of the epic, Gilgamesh visits Utnapishtim, at which point the immortal man tells our hero the story of the Flood. Two lectures hence we will come back and talk about the Babylonian flood story in greater detail and we will compare it to the biblical Flood story, For our present purposes, however, let me just note the following. When Utnapishtim tells Gilgamesh the story of the Flood, he ends it by saying, "But, my dear Gilgamesh, this event happened only once, and because of my heroism in surviving the Flood, the gods conferred upon me immortality, and upon my wife as well, but that will never happen again."

Utnapishtim then gives to Gilgamesh the next best thing. With immortality beyond his grasp, Utnapishtim tells Gilgamesh about a plant beneath the sea that will grant him a second life, rejuvenate him in some fashion. So, Gilgamesh goes down to the bottom of the sea, finds the plant, plucks it, and at least he has the ability to be rejuvenated. Before he eats the plant, however, a snake comes by, steals the plant and eats it, which, of course, represents the ancients' way of explaining why snakes rejuvenate, by molting and gaining new skin every year. We call this, an etiological story, a story that seeks to explain the origin of peculiarity in nature, such as why snakes molt. The Bible also has etiological stories, such as in the account we are talking about, Genesis 3, in which there is an attempt to explain why snakes move on their bellies, since they alone among animals have no legs, or later on, in Genesis 9, where the rainbow is explained as the symbol of the covenant. Back to the Gilgamesh Epic, though, the story ends with our hero crying, consoling himself, resigned to the fact that he will not achieve immortality and even the next best thing, rejuvenation, has slipped through his fingers.

Let's go to the other end of the Near East, to Egypt. The Egyptians actually believed that you could achieve immortality, in a sense. They were the only people in antiquity who believed that human existence continued beyond one's death in a very pleasurable, positive afterlife. Therefore, the Egyptians built such wonderful tombs, which would serve as houses of eternity during the afterlife. For the Egyptians, then, the afterlife, a type of immortality, was their main quest, and if you could afford it, while you were still alive, then you prepared your tomb. You spent all your resources to build that tomb. If you were the pharaoh, you could construct the largest tombs such as the great pyramids, which are still standing at Giza. Both of these peoples, the Egyptians and the Babylonians, had the idea that somehow, immortality is what we, as human beings, should seek to achieve.

Not so in Israel, however. Israel rebelled against this notion. Inside Genesis 2 and 3, or beneath Genesis 2 and 3, perhaps we should say, lies everything that I have just described about the ancient understanding of the quest of life, eternal life. Israel rejects it. The Tree of Life is in the Garden of Eden as a token nod in that direction, but on the surface, there really is no danger that Adam and Eve will eat from that tree. True, God expresses the concern that the human couple might eat from the Tree of Life and become immortal, in Genesis 3:22, but to my mind, once more, this is but a token nod toward the great quest of humanity in the ancient Near East. If this were really an issue, then one would expect God to prohibit the fruit of the Tree of Life from the outset. But such is not necessary, says the author of our story, because immortality is unattainable. Such was the belief in ancient Israel; it would be a pursuit after the wind and nothing more.

The main issue instead, I repeat, is the Tree of Knowledge, which demonstrates that for the ancient Israelites, the pursuit of knowledge was the true human quest. The Israelites understood that the human drive to discover, through our God-given intellectual capacity, is what propels our lives forward, and that through such discovery, one can discern not only the secrets of life in general, but the knowledge of God as well. This, for the ancient Israelites, defines us as human beings and is at the very core of their culture, society, religion and way of life.

Lecture Six
The JEDP Theory and Alternative Approaches

Scope:

In Lecture Three, we presented a unified approach to the two creation accounts, understanding the two stories as an integrated whole. Most scholars, however, would disagree, opting instead to assign the two narratives to two distinct authors, with no connection to each other. A survey of Genesis and the other books of the Torah, in fact, reveals a host of contradictions, for example, the names of Esau's wives and who transported Joseph to Egypt. The result of scholarly investigations is a theory about the authorship of the Pentateuch called the *JEDP theory*, which posits four separate sources, all independent of each other, brought together in more or less haphazard fashion by a later redactor. We will present this hypothesis and discuss both its good points and its problems.

Outline

I. Scholars have noted a number of contradictions in the book of Genesis, including the following:

   A. As noted earlier, we saw major differences between the two creation stories in Genesis 1–2.

   B. The number of animals that Noah took on board the ark differs: 6:19–20 states that one pair of each species shall be brought on the ark, while 7:2 makes a distinction between pure species (seven pairs) and impure species (one pair).

   C. There is divergent material concerning the identification of Esau's three wives; compare 26:34, 28:9 with 36:2–3.

Wives of Esau

Gen 26:34 and Gen 28:9	Judith, daughter of Beeri the Hittite
	Basemath, daughter of Elon the Hittite
	Mahalath, daughter of Ishmael
Gen 36:2–3	Adah, daughter of Elon the Hittite
	Oholibamah, daughter of Anah (daughter of Zibeon the Hivite)
	Basemath, daughter of Ishmael

D. Then there is the question of who took Joseph down to Egypt: Was it the Ishmaelites (Genesis 37:28, 39:1) or the Medanites (Genesis 37:36)? And note also the Midianites mentioned in Genesis 37:28.

II. Scholars developed the *documentary hypothesis*, or the *JEDP theory*, as a reasonable explanation for the composition of the Torah or Pentateuch.

  A. The Enlightenment led scholars to begin looking at the Bible with fresh eyes, as they turned away from the traditional view that the five books of the Torah or Pentateuch are divine in origin.

  B. Jean Astruc (1684–1766) took the first steps in this direction, while Julius Wellhausen (1844–1918) is the person credited with developing the JEDP theory in its classical formulation.

  C. Four separate sources are posited, written at different times in ancient Israel:

  1. J = Yahwist, 10th century B.C.E. ("Jahweh" is German for Yahweh)
  2. E = Elohist, 9th century B.C.E.
  3. D = Deuteronomist, 7th century B.C.E.
  4. P = Priestly, 5th century B.C.E.

  D. The four sources were then brought together by the redactor, called R, to create the Torah or Pentateuch in its final form in the 5th century B.C.E.

III. The social and cultural background of 19th-century Germany influenced Wellhausen's reconstruction of the development of the sources of the Torah or Pentateuch. He was a Protestant (Lutheran, specifically), and his anti-Jewish and anti-Catholic biases led him to date D and P after the time of the classical Prophets.

  A. Wellhausen dated J and E early, because they are essentially the basic narratives of ancient Israel, devoid of any overriding theology.

  B. Wellhausen saw the Prophets, dated to the 8th century B.C.E. (the time of Amos, Hosea, Isaiah, and Micah), as the earliest expression of ancient Israel's religious thought. The Prophets emphasized ethics and morality, the aspects of religion most heavily emphasized by Protestants.

C. Because D is mostly legal in nature and Jews continue to uphold the laws of the Torah, Wellhausen dated D to after the Prophets and viewed the legal tradition as a downward turn away from the religious ideals of the Prophets.

D. Similarly, because P is mostly cultic material and Catholics continue to re-create this worship system, with priests offering incense on an altar, Wellhausen also dated P to the late period, regarding cultic concerns as a downward turn away from the Prophetic ideal.

E. Nevertheless, even with the anti-Jewish and anti-Catholic bias at the heart of the documentary hypothesis, the theory took hold and continues to dominate biblical studies into the 21ˢᵗ century.

IV. As with all theories, the JEDP theory has pros and cons.

    A. The theory neatly explains the contradictions noted above, as well as others; for example, according to Leviticus (P), there is a hierarchy between priests and Levites, while according to Deuteronomy (D), there is no hierarchy; that is, all Levites are priests.

    B. However, what we may perceive as contradictions in an ancient text, as a result of our notions of rational logic, may not have been perceived as such by the ancient authors and readers. That is to say, the literary style in antiquity had its own narrative logic, which does not necessarily mesh with ours.

        1. For example, in Genesis 15, first God tells Abraham to look at the sky and count the stars, for as innumerable as they are, so will be his offspring (in verse 5)—then the sun sets in verse 12! By our standards, this is totally illogical, but based on the norms of ancient narrative logic, no problem is present.

        2. As another illustration, twice in Genesis 42, Joseph's brothers discover the silver in their bags and react with equal fear and trembling, first in verses 27–28 at an encampment on the way back from Egypt to Canaan, then again in verse 35 when they are telling Jacob all that transpired on their mission. Clearly, the brothers could not have been surprised by this discovery the second time! Yet once more, we must assume that such storytelling is in line with the norms and expectations of ancient narrative logic.

C. In the same vein, the literary study of biblical prose has demonstrated much greater unity to the narratives than the JEDP theory perceives.

D. The dates of the JEDP theory are all wrong, especially for the last two sources, D and P. Linguistic analysis demonstrates that the entirety of the Torah, and certainly Genesis, is composed in classical Biblical Hebrew, not Late Biblical Hebrew—the dividing point for these two strata is c. 550 B.C.E., in the middle of the Babylonian exile.

    1. All languages undergo change during their history, often gradual, but typically, there is radical change during and after times of political and social upheaval. (Note, for example, that Old English becomes Middle English upon the Norman conquest of Britain in 1066.) And thus it is with Hebrew, but the linguistic developments that one finds in the texts dated to the Exile and beyond are *not* to be found in Genesis.

    2. The easiest demonstration of this is the following: During the Persian period, loanwords from Persian enter the Hebrew language by the dozens, as can be seen by looking at the relatively short books of Esther, Ezra, Nehemiah, and others from that period. By contrast, not a single Persian loanword occurs in the very extensive five books of the Torah.

V. My approach is as follows:

A. I accept the obvious differences between P and D and recognize that the laws and cultic material in the Torah emanate from these two distinct sources. I am unwilling, however, to posit one source as earlier than the other.

B. Instead, I prefer to see P (essentially the book of Leviticus, along with portions of Exodus and Numbers) and D (essentially the book of Deuteronomy) as contemporary and competing systems of law and worship in ancient Israel.

C. Most importantly for our study of Genesis, I see the narratives as literary wholes, not to be subdivided into J, E, and P material.

1. A crucial example that illustrates this point—and resounds through the book of Genesis—is the deceiver deceived.

2. We will see the importance of literary wholes more fully in Lecture Fifteen.

Essential Reading:

Richard E. Friedman, *Who Wrote the Bible?*

Robert Alter, *The Art of Biblical Narrative*, pp. 131–154.

Supplementary Reading:

Richard E. Friedman, *The Bible with Sources Revealed*, esp. pp. 1–31.

William M. Schniedewind, *How the Bible Became a Book.*

Questions to Consider:

1. What other contradictions can you identify in the book of Genesis that could serve as additional fodder for the JEDP theory?

2. We noted the social, political, and religious agenda that underlay the development of the documentary hypothesis. Can you think of other theories in the humanities or the social sciences that developed in the 19th and 20th centuries with similar agendas at their heart?

Lecture Six—Transcript
The JEDP Theory and Alternative Approaches

In this lecture, I want to integrate the history of ancient Israel and the history of the ancient Near East, which we surveyed in the two previous lectures, with the question of the scholarly debate concerning the composition of the book of Genesis and the Torah as a whole. The question arises in large part due to the contradictions that appear in the book of Genesis and in the other books of the Torah. We have already talked about the differences between Genesis 1 and 2, the two stories of Creation, whether man was created at the end of Creation, as in story number one, or whether he was the first animate object created, as in story number two. Recall that there were different names of God that were used in those two stories; we will come back and talk about that in just a few moments.

There are lots of biblical stories in Genesis that have contradictions built into them. Let's look at some of those. The number of animals that Noah took on board the Ark—in Genesis 6:19–20 it states that he is to bring, God commands him to bring one pair of each species of animals onto the Ark. While in Genesis 7:2, just a few verses later, a distinction is made between the "pure" species and the "impure" species. Here, God commands Noah to bring on board seven pairs of the "pure" animals and one pair of the "impure" animals. So, we have a difference built into the story of Noah and the Ark. By the way, as an aside, let me point out that "pure" and "impure" here refers to those animals that may be eaten and, accordingly, may be sacrificed, and those animals that may not be eaten and may not be sacrificed. All of that is laid out for us in Leviticus 11 where the dietary laws of ancient Israel are presented. Another example of divergent material in the book of Genesis is the identification of Esau's three wives. Now, if you look at the passages in Genesis 26:34 and in Genesis 28:9, you put those together and you have a list of Esau's three wives and the names of his three fathers-in-law. If you then look at Genesis 36:2–3, you have another list of his three wives, where you have some of the same names. Both of his wives and his fathers-in-law, but in scrambled fashion, and you have other names that don't appear earlier. So, there is contradictory information. The two texts agree that Esau had three wives; they disagree on the names and how they are aligned with their particular fathers.

Another example is the question of who took Joseph down to Egypt in Genesis 37 and in Genesis 39:1, we have at least two, if not three, groups of people who are mentioned. We have the Midianites and the Ishmaelites and, in fact, a third group, the Medanites, who were mentioned at the end in the very last verse of Genesis 37. Most translations, however, render that word there as "Midianites" to bring it in line with one of the other two groups. But, in fact, it's a distinct group called the Medanites. Then, as we move beyond the book of Genesis into the other books of the Torah or the Pentateuch, other examples of such divergent information may be found. Moses's father-in-law is sometimes called Jethro; he is sometimes called Reuel. The mountain on which God gives Moses the Ten Commandments is sometimes called Sinai and it's sometimes called Horeb.

Now, these examples, and others could be presented as well, have been known for centuries. The ancient Jewish and Christian interpreters from antiquity through the Middle Ages recognize these examples of divergent information and they try to explain them as best they can, usually by dovetailing them in some fashion. For example, a particular scholar would argue that when God commands Noah to take on board one pair of each animal species at the end of Genesis 6, that is a general command, a general statement, which is then made more specific at the beginning of Genesis 7, where a distinction is made between the pure animals and the impure animals, so these explanations were used throughout the Middle Ages, for example.

By the 17th and 18th century, however, and into the 19th century, humanity had reached a new epoch and we call that the Age of Reason, the Enlightenment, the Age of Humanism, and biblical scholars, in particular, started rethinking these problems. Now, let's state the obvious, which we have not mentioned yet, that traditionally, in Judaism and in Christianity, the five books of the Torah or the Pentateuch, including Genesis, were believed to be the revealed Word of God. Now, nowhere in these books is authorship actually mentioned, certainly nowhere in Genesis. One could say that in Exodus, Leviticus, Numbers, and Deuteronomy, the laws that God gives to Moses are in his mouth. They are divine word, but the narratives, as a whole, disclose nothing about who wrote them, but the tradition arose through the process of canonization that these five books were, in fact, the Word of God. Again, in the Age of the

Enlightenment, with increased humanism in Europe, scholars began to question this doctrine of Judaism and Christianity. In particular, it was Christian scholars who led the way in doing so. What developed was something called the Documentary Hypothesis, or the JEDP Theory. First, questioning whether it was divine at all and once that was stripped from the debate, scholars were now able and open and willing to talk about human authorship and not a single unified text from the hand of Moses, but rather a text that was comprised of a variety of different sources.

The man who started the ball rolling was a man named Jean Astruc. He was a French physician who, in 1753, wrote a book in which he laid out the numerous differences that I have just described. He was a true renaissance man, a man who made major contributions to the field of medicine and, as you can see, to biblical studies as well. He was unwilling to remove Moses from the equation and so he basically believed that Moses had used preexisting documents to compile the books of the Pentateuch. That was Jean Astruc in 1753. A bit more than a century later in Germany, a great scholar named Julius Wellhausen created what is called the standard version or the classical version of the Documentary hypothesis, the JEDP theory, as a reasonable explanation for the compilation of the five books of the Torah or Pentateuch. As the theory's name indicates, he believed that there were four separate sources—J, E, D, and P—which are abbreviations for the presumed authors who lived at different times in ancient Israel.

Now, let me set the theory up in this way. According to Wellhausen, this is the classical expression of this theory. An individual whom we abbreviate as J, whom we call the "Yahwist," wrote a history of Israel in the 10th century B.C.E., beginning with the creation of the world and taking us through the life and death of Moses. He's called the Yahwist because when he refers to God, he uses the name "Yahweh," which we already have encountered. Now in German, Yahweh is spelled with a "J" and so we use the "J" abbreviation because that's how Wellhausen wrote. Although when we say the word "Yahwist," we typically spell it out with a "Y" and the word "Yahweh," the name of God, we render into English as a "Y" as well.

Wellhausen continued as follows. About a century later, someone who we call the "Elohist" wrote another history of Israel, a parallel account. He began with the life of Abraham and he went forward into the life and death of Moses as well. He used the name "Elohim" when he wrote this history of his and, therefore, we call him the "Elohist." The "E" source dated to the 9th century. The third source is called "D," the "Deuteronomist" and it dated to the 7th century. As the name implies, he is the author of the book of Deuteronomy. Unlike the other books of the Torah, Deuteronomy has no contradictions internal to itself. It reads fine as a single unified work; all agree on that. It does, however, contradict some previous statements that one finds in Exodus, Leviticus, and Numbers. But, "D" is its own source and it focuses solely on Moses.

So, we have three biblical authors—the Yahwist, the Elohist, and the Deuteronomist from the 10th, 9th, and 7th centuries. Note that the first of these, the Yahwist, is believed to have lived during the period of the united monarchy, during the time of David and Solomon, the 10th century. The second of these, the Elohist, lived during the time, according to this theory, of the divided monarchy, in the 9th century. The Deuteronomist, the third of them, is in the 7th century; this would place him after the fall of the kingdom of Israel when only the kingdom of Judah was still in existence in the south.

Then, there is a fourth author and that author is called "P," or the "priestly" source. It is, according to Wellhausen and those who subscribe to this theory, the latest of the four sources and it is dated to the 5th century B.C.E. That is, after the Exile, the post-Exilic period during the time of Persian rule. This author, the Priestly source, also takes his history of Israel back to Creation and moves forward to the time of Moses. He also uses the name "Elohim" when he's writing to refer to God.

The four sources—J, E, D, and P—so the theory goes, were then brought together by an individual whom we call the Redactor, or R; that's our word that we encountered before meaning "compiler" or "editor" who created the Torah or the Pentateuch in its final form, in the 5th century B.C.E. J, E, D, and P—10th, 9th, 7th, and 5th centuries, respectively—are brought together by this editor, R, the Redactor in the 5th century B.C.E. That is how the text of the Torah, in its final form, came to be. However, this editor, our compiler, our author, our creator of the Torah, did not iron out all of the difficulties. He left in the contradictions. So if one story has so many animals and the other story has another number of animals, or if one story has this number of wives or these names for the wives and another one has these names for the wives, he left them all in. He did not do what a modern editor might do which would be to dovetail all the information. All the traditions, in his mind, were held to be sacred and, therefore, he kept them all in and that is how, according to this theory, the text of the Torah achieved the form in which we now have it with all of that divergent material built into it.

Now, let me take a moment to go back to the 19th century and say a word about Wellhausen and his work. Every person, every scholar, is a product of his or her own times and Wellhausen was no different. It's important to point out the following. Wellhausen, as were many of the early proponents of this Documentary hypothesis, this JEDP Theory, was a German Protestant, specifically, a Lutheran scholar. The spirit of the times in Germany in the 19th century—and this was certainly true of Wellhausen—was very much anti-Catholic and anti-Jewish. Now, you may ask, how does that affect the scholarship that we are talking about? It does so in the following way. The two sources, J and E, which Wellhausen held to be the earliest of the two sources of the Torah, are basically the narratives—the very nice stories we have about Abraham and Jacob and Joseph and so on and they are, according to Wellhausen, largely devoid of major theological teachings. They are simply stories that describe these family traditions and the life of Moses.

Then, within the JEDP schema, if you take out J and E, the first two, and leave off the D and P for a moment, the last two, in the middle there, you have the 8th century B.C.E. That is the time of classical prophecy, the great biblical prophets of the 8th century—Amos, Hosea, Isaiah, and Micah, the first four prophets chronologically. The prophets of the Jewish Bible or Christian Old Testament emphasized morals and ethics as the number one thing that God demands of us as human beings. For Protestants, that is where the emphasis of their teachings is to be found. So, Wellhausen, as a Lutheran, held to that belief and he saw the biblical prophets as the number one expression of Israelite theology; the original genius of biblical Israel was to be found in that prophetic material. It was important for him to date the latter two sources, D and P, after the time of the biblical prophets. So D goes to the 7th century and P goes to the 5th century. Why? They do because D, the Deuteronomist, the book of Deuteronomy, is essentially all legal material. It is a collection of laws that Moses presents to the people of Israel. The Priestly material, the P source, is mainly cultic material about how to worship God, how to perform the sacrifices. Notice it is a priestly source because the priests were the officiators of the cult, the sacrifices.

Now, the D source for Wellhausen was associated with his contemporary Jews. They are the people who still uphold the laws of the Torah. Therefore, D is associated with contemporary, 19th century Jews and P was associated with the Catholics because Catholics still have priests offering incense on the altar in churches. Wellhausen, in his anti-Jewish and anti-Catholic way, felt the need to date this material late. He saw this as Israel's latter-day religion, not part of the original spirit of ancient Israel, part of the religion that became very much overly so involved with the observance of law and the sacrificial worship of God. The true spirit of Israel was in its prophets and the legal and cultic material took Israel away from that original genius. So, when Wellhausen set up his theory as he did, underneath it, very much part of the theory, is this bias that one can find in Wellhausen's scholarship.

Now, his theory remains very much in vogue today. More than 125 years later, scholars are still very much beholding to Wellhausen's system of J, E, D, and P. People have largely lost sight of the issues that I have just raised and so I bracket them off here as a tangential discussion because in the 21st century, nobody holds to these issues anymore, and yet the JEDP Theory took hold in such a way that it continues to dominate the scene of biblical scholarship.

As with all theories, there are pros and cons with the JEDP Theory. The theory neatly explains various contradictions and in some of these, I myself am willing to accept. For example, according to "P," who is the author of the book of Leviticus—all of the material in the Leviticus is seen as the P source—there is a hierarchy between the priests and the Levites. They are all within the priestly group, but there is a hierarchy between the priests who rank on top and the Levites who serve as their assistants. According to the book of Deuteronomy, however, the D source, there is no hierarchy. All Levites, everybody from the tribe of Levi can serve as a priest. So, that is a clear distinction between P and D in the legal, cultic arena, and I agree with this finding and this conclusion of the Documentary hypothesis. However, what we may perceive as contradictions in an ancient text, due to our notions of rational logic, may not have been perceived as such by the ancient authors, the ancient readers of the text. That is to say, the literary style in antiquity had its own narrative logic, which does not necessarily mesh with ours as modern-day readers. Ancient literature should be understood unto itself and modern literature can go in a different direction altogether.

Let me give you an example. In Genesis 15 God tells Abraham to look at the sky and count the stars, for as innumerable as the stars are, so will his offspring be. That's in Genesis 15:5. As we read on, seven verses later in verse 12, the sun sets. Now, by our standards, this is totally illogical. How can one go and look at the stars and then only later have the sunset? But based on the norms of ancient narrative logic, which is not necessarily Aristotelian and rational in our sense of the word, no problem is present. To put this in other terms, I would argue that nobody in ancient Israel would have stopped to ask the question, "How is it possible that God asked Abraham and took him outside to look at the stars in verse 5 and only later did the sun set in verse 12?" The problem would not even have been perceived because they had a different understanding of the way a narrative can operate. And so, I would not take this narrative, this chapter 15, and divide it up into different sources. I would like to see it as one unified story and accept that it has a narrative logic different from our own.

As another illustration, let us look at Genesis 42. Joseph's brothers discover the silver in their bags and they react with equal fear and trembling twice. On their way back to Canaan, Joseph, who is the viceroy of Egypt whom they don't recognize, before they left Egypt, he replaced the silver with which they had purchased grain into their bags. So, on their way home in Genesis 42:27–28, as they're traversing the Sinai on their way back from Egypt to Canaan, and again in verse 35 when they are telling Jacob all that transpired on their mission; both times they are surprised to find the silver in their bags. Now, obviously, they were very much surprised to find that silver the first time in verses 27 and 28. Clearly, the brothers could not have been surprised by this discovery the second go around when they were home with Jacob. But, the demands of the story are such that we need to read of their surprise the second go round as well when they are now in front of Jacob telling them all that transpired and emptying out their bags. So, the assumption here is that ancient storytelling has its own norms and expectations based on an ancient narrative logic and we do not have to impose our modern, rational ideas of the way a story is to be told on this ancient text.

In line with this statement, the literary study of biblical prose has demonstrated much greater unity to the narratives than the JEDP Theory perceives. So, while I'm willing to see examples of P and D being separated from each other because they clearly do understand the way God is to be worshipped and who can serve as a priest and so on in different ways, the stories I hold, and this is my alternative approach, should be read as units, even when you have contradictory information. We go back to what I said about the two Creation accounts. Yes, they differ from one another. Yes, they have contradictions. Yes, they use different names of God. But only by reading the two stories together, only by putting them together—the cosmocentric approach in the first story and the anthropocentric approach in the second story—do we have essence of that Israelite theology coming through, shining through very, very brightly.

Now, let me just say a word here about how you can identify a text according to the JEDP Theory. For example, if you're reading Genesis 1, you'll recall that we said that the name of God in that story is "Elohim." So, we have a choice. It's either an E story, the Elohist who uses that term for God, or it could be a P story, the Priestly source, which also uses the word "Elohim." How do we decide? Well, earlier, I said that the Priestly source goes back to the creation of the world, whereas the Elohist source only goes back to the time of Abraham. So you might say, "Well, therefore, it has to be the P source," and of course that's correct, but that would be circular reasoning. How do we know that the Elohist source only goes back to Abraham and the P source goes back to Creation? That's because, once you have the word "Elohim" there, you have to go down to a set of sub-criteria. That is to say, there are other elements in that story that point to the author of Genesis 1 according to the JEDP Theory as being P. Those elements are certain phrases that occur later on in P sources, P material—clearly, Priestly material in Exodus and Leviticus and Numbers—and so you hear echoes and that is why we associate Genesis 1 with the P source.

If you look at Genesis 2, you see the name Yahweh. It's true that it's a compound name, Yahweh/Elohim, and that's quite rare, as we noted. But, the presence of the name "Yahweh" there suggests that this is the J source and that's the way the adherence to the JEDP Theory proceeds, by taking the biblical text in the Torah or the Pentateuch and assigning it to one of the four. If it's in Deuteronomy, it's clearly D. If it's in Genesis through Numbers, one has to make the decision, J, E, or P. If the name Yahweh is present, it's J. If the name Elohim is present, it's either E or P, and you can go down to a set of sub-criteria, which define for us whether it's the P source or the E source.

I also have a problem with the JEDP Theory's dating of these sources. To my mind, they are all wrong, especially the last two sources, the D and the P source. Linguistic analysis demonstrates that the entirety of the Torah, and certainly Genesis, is composed in Classical Biblical Hebrew and not Late Biblical Hebrew. The dividing point for these two strata of the language is approximately 550 B.C.E. That would place us smack in the middle of the Exile and that's an important point here. Incidentally, much of my own research is based on this subject, the history of the Hebrew language. I do a lot of my own work, trying to figure out the kinds of changes that the Hebrew language underwent and when these changes occurred.

Now, all languages undergo change during their history. It's often a very gradual change. Typically, there is radical change during and after times of political and social upheaval. Note, for example, that Old English—let's just take our own language—Old English becomes Middle English. When? It changes upon the Norman conquest of Britain in 1066. All of a sudden, after that year, we see hundreds, if not thousands, of words from French entering the English language and they remain part of the English language down to the present day. It was the sociopolitical changes of the Norman Conquest in 1066 that vaulted English very radically from its Old English phase into its Middle English phase. Thus, it is with Hebrew as well. For it is the Exile that creates a great upheaval for the people of Israel as we've described—the loss of independence, the loss of Jerusalem, the loss of the Temple, and deportation and Exile in the land of Babylonia, Mesopotamia. So, all of this will change the manner of the Hebrew language and, therefore, we can see very clearly the differences between Standard Biblical Hebrew up to the time of the Exile and Late Biblical Hebrew from the Exile onward.

Now, the easiest demonstration of this is the following. During the Persian period, the late 6th, 5th, and 4th centuries, that is when the P source would be dated according to the JEPD Theory from Wellhausen down to the present day to those that adhere to this theory. During the Persian period, loan words from the Persian language entered Hebrew by the dozens. It's exactly parallel to what we mentioned, the use of French loan words in English during the Middle English Period. We can see these Persian loan words in books written in the 5th century, books such as Ecclesiastes or Qohelet, Song of Songs, Esther, Ezra, Nehemiah, and Chronicles. These are books from the Persian period. They are replete with Persian loanwords, especially works such as Esther, which is, in fact, of course, set in the land of Persia.

By contrast, when we look at the five books of the Torah—and that is quite a lengthy section of biblical material, the books of Genesis through Deuteronomy—not a single Persian loan word occurs in the very extensive corpus of material. To me, this says that these books must have been written before the Persian period before the 5th century, indeed, before the 6th century before the Exile. None of the markers, none of the features of Late Biblical Hebrew, which can be found in grammar, syntax, and lexicon, none of these are to be found in the Pentateuch. All of the sources must be pre-Exilic. To my mind, they are indeed mainly early Monarchic. So, I want to put P and D certainly before 586 B.C.E. in the Monarchic period and I would also like to place them into the earlier Monarchic period.

To sum this up, let me give you my view of matters. I accept the obvious differences between P and D, as I mentioned, and I recognize that the laws and the cultic material in the Torah emanate from different sources, two distinct sources. I am unwilling, however, to posit one source as earlier than the other. I simply prefer to see P, which is essentially Leviticus and portions of Exodus and Numbers, and D, the book of Deuteronomy, as contemporary and competing systems of law and worship in ancient Israel. Most important for our study of Genesis, I see the narratives as literary wholes—and I think I've said it before and I need to say it again, that's with a "w," W-H-O-L-E, literary wholes, literary units—not to be subdivided into J, E, and P material.

Let me conclude this presentation with one example, a crucial example that illustrates the point. One of the themes that resound through the book of Genesis is the deceiver deceived. The first deception occurs when Jacob fools his father, Isaac, in Genesis 27, and thereby obtains the blessing that should have been due to Esau. Jacob himself is deceived in Genesis 37 when his sons fool him into believing that his beloved son, Joseph, has been killed by a wild beast. The ringleader of those brothers was Judah. Judah, in the very next chapter, 38, is in turn, deceived by his daughter-in-law, Tamar. We'll be looking at that story later in our course. Now, the props, the physical way in which these deceptions occurred was the same in each of these three cases, a goat and clothing. Jacob used goatskins to cover up his smooth arms and neck so that he would appear hairy like his brother, Esau. His mother, Rebekah, cooked the goat to serve as a meal to Isaac and he wore his brother's clothing. Jacob's sons, in turn, Judah and the rest, took Joseph's garment, his famous coat of many colors, dipped it in goat's blood and presented it to their father, Jacob, in order to deceive him. In the very next chapter, Judah, in turn, is deceived by Tamar using clothing and a goat. She disguises herself with clothing and he pledges to pay her a goat as the fee for having intercourse with her as she is dressed as a harlot and he does not recognize her. So, the goat and clothing goes from one story to the next and unites all of these stories in one literary entity not to be subdivided into component parts.

Lecture Seven
Genesis 6–8, The Flood Story

Scope:

We return to our reading of the book of Genesis by looking in detail at chapters 6–8, the story of Noah and the flood. This story provides us with an excellent opportunity to apply information learned in the previous lectures. First, we will compare the biblical account to the flood story incorporated into the Gilgamesh Epic, the great literary classic of ancient Mesopotamia. We will note the many points of similarity, and we will emphasize several crucial differences. Second, we will read chapters 6–8 in two different fashions: in the light of the JEDP theory, which sees two sources intertwined in the text, and as a unified whole, in opposition to the above approach, thereby illustrating the contrasting methods.

Outline

I. The Gilgamesh Epic was the literary classic of the ancient Near East, read far and wide, either in the original Akkadian (Babylonian) by people educated in that language (even if it was not their native tongue) or in translations into other languages (Hittite, Hurrian, and so on).

    A. This lengthy (by ancient Near Eastern standards) composition is an epic poem about the search for immortality of the legendary king Gilgamesh (from the southern Mesopotamian city of Uruk).

    B. Among the scenes narrated toward the end of the epic is Gilgamesh's visit to Utnapishtim, the flood hero, who relates to Gilgamesh the story of the flood (occurring in Tablet XI of the 12-tablet composition).

II. The Babylonian flood story shares numerous similarities with the biblical flood story in Genesis 6–8, including the building materials for the ark, the dimensions, and the number of decks; the population of the ark and the detailed description of the flood; the mountaintop landing and the sending forth of a series of birds to determine that the land was dry; and finally, the fact that the hero sets everyone free and offers sacrifices to the deity. **(See Table 7a.)**

A. Note that all translations agree on two of the building materials for the ark: wood and pitch. The third item is the subject of some discussion, however. The consonants in the biblical text, namely, QNYM, can be read as either *qinnim*, "rooms, compartments" (thus the traditional rendering), or *qanim*, "reeds" (thus some recent translations). We favor the latter understanding, especially because reeds constitute the third building material in the Gilgamesh Epic flood narrative.

B. Not only do all the aforementioned elements appear in both the biblical account and the Babylonian version, but these elements parallel each other in the same order as well. Even where there is room for some variation, the order in the two stories remains constant.

   1. At the beginning of both stories, the first three elements appear in the order: materials, dimensions, number of decks.

   2. In both stories, the mountaintop landing appears before the sending forth of the birds, even though the alternative order is possible.

   3. At the end of both accounts, all are set free and the flood hero offers sacrifices, even though, once again, the alternative order is easily conceivable.

III. There are also two crucial differences between the two stories.

A. In the Gilgamesh Epic, it is not clear exactly why the gods decided to destroy the world, and it is also not clear why Utnapishtim was chosen to survive the flood. The biblical account includes a morality factor—the world was destroyed because of its immoral state; and Noah was chosen to survive the flood because he was righteous.

B. The biblical account introduces the covenant factor—God makes a covenant with Noah.

IV. The most likely explanation for the striking similarities between the two versions is this: The biblical account is borrowed from the Mesopotamian flood tradition, for the following reasons:

A. In general, greater societies influence lesser ones, and Babylonia was a major power in the ancient world, whereas Israel was a relatively minor player.

B. Flooding is typical of Mesopotamia but not of Canaan. The former gets more plentiful rainfall, and it has two major rivers running through the region, the Tigris and the Euphrates, both of which flood the Mesopotamian plain with relative frequency. The flood tradition obviously grew to legendary proportions, but presumably, one such real flooding formed the basis for the flood story. By contrast, flooding is impossible in the land of Canaan, with its lesser amount of rainfall and no major rivers.

C. The only geographical location mentioned in the biblical account is the mountains of Ararat, which are located in far northern Mesopotamia (around Lake Van, in modern-day eastern Turkey), near the headwaters of both the Tigris and Euphrates rivers.

D. As noted above, the Gilgamesh Epic was the literary classic of the ancient world; thus, people in other cultures would have been familiar with it. Indeed, a fragment of the epic dated to c. 1400 B.C.E. (relating a scene known from Tablet VII of the 12-tablet version) was found in Megiddo, a city in northern Israel, not far from modern-day Haifa.

   1. We have to assume that the local Canaanites at Megiddo were able to read this text in the original.

   2. From the city of Ugarit, located in far northern Canaan, on the Mediterranean coast in northern Syria, we have another cuneiform tablet, describing another episode from the life of Gilgamesh (though not one known from the 12-tablet version).

   3. How did somebody in, let's say, the 10th or 9th or 8th century in Israel know about the Gilgamesh Epic? It might have been translated orally, perhaps, into Hebrew or Canaanite (recall that Hebrew and Canaanite are dialects of the same language).

E. In addition, the biblical tradition has Abraham originating from Mesopotamia, before he moves to the land of Canaan. Thus, it is possible that the earliest Hebrews would have brought the flood story with them.

F. The additions in the biblical account suggest that the Hebrew version is an expansion of the Babylonian version. This is far more likely than assuming that the Babylonians excised material from an Israelite version.

G. The end of Genesis 8 also contains a particular item that is very non-Israelite.

    1. When Noah sacrifices to God, Genesis 8 tells us that God smelled the sweet savor of the sacrifices.

    2. Of all the many times in the Bible where we have reference to the Israelites offering sacrifices, this is the only place in the Bible where we have a reference to God smelling the sacrifices.

    3. God appears here almost in human fashion, which is something we would expect to find in the polytheistic world. Indeed, in Gilgamesh Epic, Tablet XI, line 161, we read, "the gods smelled the sweet savor" emanating from Utnapisthim's sacrifice.

V. Most scholars, especially those who adhere to the JEDP theory, believe that the biblical flood story is redacted from two separate sources. But was it?

A. Certain apparent inconsistencies in the biblical account, such as the number of animals that Noah brought onto the ark, have led scholars to propose that the biblical story has two layers, the Yahwist and the Priestly, which then were redacted into a single narrative.

B. There is an alternative approach, though, which we prefer, and that is to read the biblical account as a unified whole. By doing so, and only in this manner, does the biblical account match with the Gilgamesh version of the flood.

C. Just as Julius Wellhausen was presenting the JEDP Theory in its classical formulation in 1878, these Babylonian texts written in the Akkadian language, discovered during the British excavations of Nineveh in the 1840s and 1850s, were being read and analyzed by scholars in the 1870s and 1880s.

D. Most famously, a remarkable man named George Smith, working at the British Museum in London, discovered Gilgamesh Tablet XI containing a flood story closely paralleling the biblical account.

E. Only later, so great was Wellhausen's influence, did it occur to anybody that we should not think of the Flood story as a compilation of two texts. It cannot be the case, so goes the argument, that a redactor took this material from two hypothesized, smaller component parts and put them together in the very order that we actually find in the Gilgamesh Epic.

Essential Reading:

Nahum Sarna, *Understanding Genesis*, pp. 37–59.

Alexander Heidel, *The Gilgamesh Epic and Old Testament Parallels*.

Supplementary Reading:

Benjamin R. Foster, *The Epic of Gilgamesh*.

Andrew George, *The Epic of Gilgamesh*.

Questions to Consider:

1. How does the fact that the Gilgamesh Epic influenced the biblical flood story affect our understanding of the Bible as "sacred scripture"?

2. Imagine yourself as George Smith reading cuneiform texts in the British Museum during the 1870s. What kind of intellectual tools and abilities would you require to do this kind of work?

Table 7a: Flood Stories Compared:

The Biblical Story (Genesis 6–8) and the Gilgamesh Epic (Tablet XI)

			Story Elements According to JEDP Source Theory	
Order in story	*Genesis story element*	*Present in Gilgamesh Epic?*	*Yahwist (J) "Yahweh" (Lord)*	*Priestly (P) "Elohim" (God)*
1.	morality/immorality factor	no	6:5–8	6:9–13
2.	materials (wood, pitch, reeds)	yes		6:14
3.	dimensions	yes		6:15
4.	decks	yes		6:16
5.	covenant, population	no		6:17–22
6.	population	yes	7:1–5	
7.	flood	yes	7:7–10, 12, 16b, 17b, 22–23	7:6, 11, 13–16a, 17a, 18–21
8.	mountaintop landing	yes		7:24–8:5
9.	birds sent forth	yes	8:6–12	
10.	dry land	yes, but much less than in Genesis		8:13–14
11.	all set free	yes		8:15–19
12.	sacrifices	yes	8:20–22	

Lecture Seven—Transcript
Genesis 6–8, The Flood Story

In this lecture, we return to our reading of the Book of Genesis by looking in detail at chapters 6–8, the story of Noah and the Flood. This story provides us with an excellent opportunity to apply the information that we have learned in the previous lectures concerning the history of ancient Israel, the Near East, and the composition of the book of Genesis. First, we will compare the biblical account to the flood story incorporated into the Gilgamesh Epic, the great literary classic of ancient Mesopotamia. We will note the many points of similarity and we will also emphasize the several crucial differences. Second, we will read Genesis 6–8 in two different fashions: in the light of the JEDP Theory, which sees two different sources—the Yahwist and the Priestly—intertwined in the text, and as a unified whole, in opposition to the JEDP approach, thereby illustrating the two methods in contrast to each other.

First, a prelude to the Flood story occurs at the beginning of Genesis 6:1–8. We'll talk about this much more in our next lecture. For the moment, let's just point out that in that story, we are given a vignette, a scene that describes for us the depravity, the corruption, and the lawlessness to which the world has sunk. We previously have read of two murders in the biblical text. In Genesis 4, Cain kills Abel and Lamech kills an unknown man as well. What we're seeing here in Genesis 4, in Genesis 6, as we lead up to the Flood, is an increase in man's transgressions, and once we've also taken into account the fact that Adam and Eve were unable to abide by God's command, we can see that the world is not turning out as God had intended. Therefore, we move to the story of the Flood in which God decides to destroy the world that he has created and to begin anew.

Let's talk about the Gilgamesh Epic again. It was the literary classic of the ancient world. It was read far and wide, either in the original Akkadian language—Akkadian is the technical term we use for the Babylonian language. It was read by people educated in that language not only in Babylon where it was the native language, but also in surrounding lands—or it was read in translations into other languages such as Hittite and Hurrian, both of which were spoken and used in Anatolia, modern-day Turkey to the north of Mesopotamia. The Gilgamesh Epic, as we've already noted, is a very lengthy composition by ancient Near Eastern standards. It is written over the course of twelve cuneiform tablets written on clay and it is an epic poem about the legendary king, Gilgamesh, who came from the southern Mesopotamian city of Uruk. We've already talked about his search for immortality. Now, among the scenes narrated towards the end of the epic is Gilgamesh's visit to Utnapishtim, the flood hero, who relates to Gilgamesh the story of the flood. This occurs in Tablet XI out of those twelve tablets.

The Babylonian flood story shares numerous similarities with the biblical Flood story in Genesis 6–8. Let's go down the list and detail them. The chart in the course booklet will help you as a guide here. The first thing we notice is that God commands Noah to build an ark. Similarly, the god Ea in the Babylonian story commands Utnapishtim to build a vessel and three elements are noted there—the materials to be used, the dimensions of the ship, and the fact that the ship shall be divided into a series of decks. Now, the materials, which are provided in both stories, are the same three building materials, wood, pitch and reeds. If you read your biblical text, you'll see that the words "wood" and "pitch" are very clearly there. There is a debate among biblical scholars about the third item in that list, the reeds. The older biblical translations translate this Hebrew word as "compartments," sometimes as rooms or cells, but other translations take the word to mean "reeds." This has to do with the transmission of the biblical text in antiquity, the nature of the way the vowels are indicated, and there is a slight difference between *qinnim,* which means "compartments" or "rooms," and *qanim,* which means "reeds." We take it as the latter and the translation of Everett Fox, which is one of the books that I have already recommended, in fact, translates it that way. So, the same three elements that occur in the Gilgamesh story's list of building materials—wood, pitch, and reeds—occur in our biblical text as well—if your translation reflects something else, that's fine, but I prefer the reeds there, as I've indicated—and then the dimensions and the decks.

Next, the god in the Gilgamesh Epic story commands Utnapishtim to go on board the ark with himself and his family and representative members of the animal kingdom. That, of course, is exactly what God instructs Noah at this point, and then, the Flood occurs. The lengthiest part of the Gilgamesh story, Tablet XI, is the description of the flood—the waters, the rain, all of that great thunder and lightning, all that big show is described there in great detail.

Similarly with the biblical account, all of Genesis 7 describes for us in great detail the surging of the deeps and the rain coming from above, and the Great Flood emerging the highest mountains on earth.

The next element we have in the Gilgamesh Epic is how the vessel in which Utnapishtim and his family and the animals who were resident came to a landing on a mountaintop. That is exactly what happens next in the biblical story. Next, Utnapishtim sends forth a series of birds to determine that the land was dry. That, too, occurs in the biblical story in a famous episode with which we are all familiar as Noah sends forth a series of birds. Eventually, the dove does not return and he determines that the land was dry. Both Utnapishtim, the flood hero in the Babylonian story, and Noah in the biblical story next set everybody free. All the residents of the ark, or the vessel, are set free, and the final scene is narrated with sacrifices made to the deity. Utnapishtim does this in the Gilgamesh Epic and Noah does this at the end of Genesis 8:20–22 in the biblical account.

Now, note that not only are all these elements present, one by one, as we work through the two stories that we are comparing here, but that they are also in the same order. Now, in certain cases, of course, there is no opportunity for a variation in the order. That is to say, you have to build the ark before the flood comes, and the flood has to come before it lands on a mountaintop and so on. But even where there is room for variation, the two stories proceed, element by element, in the same order. Let me give you an example of that. In the Gilgamesh story, the materials, the dimensions and the decks, are given in that order; in the biblical story, the materials, the dimensions and the decks, are given in that order. Of course, you may say, "Well, that is perfectly logical. How else would you instruct somebody to build a vessel?" Nevertheless, it is still noteworthy. Perhaps at the end is where we can see the room for some variation. That is to say, it might have been possible to send out the birds first and then have the ark land on a mountaintop. But no, in both stories, the mountaintop landing occurs first and then the birds were sent forth. Most important, I think, the place for the best possibility for a variation is at the very, very end of the story, where it's very possible that the flood hero, Noah or Utnapishtim, could have done the sacrifices before letting everybody go free. But no, in both stories, all are set free and then the sacrifices occur. So, I repeat the statement here. Element by element, the two stories, the Gilgamesh Epic, Tablet XI, the Babylonian flood tradition, and the biblical story with

Noah as its hero in Genesis 6–8, tell the tale, one by one, element by element, in the same order.

Now, there are also two crucial differences between the two stories and this is extremely important to note. The biblical account includes a morality factor built into the story, which is lacking in the Gilgamesh Epic. If we read the Gilgamesh Epic, it is not clear exactly why the gods have decided to destroy the world, and it is also not clear why Utnapishtim himself has been chosen to survive the flood. He seems to be a favorite of one of the gods, but otherwise, we are given no information as to why that individual among all the others in the society was chosen to survive. Contrast the biblical account, we've already mentioned that the reason for the Flood is given—the world has to be destroyed because it is now in an immoral state; it has too much crime, too much this, too much that, and that is why God decides to destroy the world, Genesis 6:1–8. Moreover, we are told why Noah himself was selected. He was chosen because he was a righteous man, Genesis 6:9. So, the biblical account introduces very strongly the morality factor into this narrative.

The second difference that we find is the covenant factor. Now, in the biblical story, right before the population of the ark is described, the story is interrupted for a moment because God tells Noah that he is establishing a covenant with him. He makes a covenant with Noah. This will be described in detail in Genesis 9, but it's already mentioned here in Genesis 6:17–19, where the word "covenant" comes into play. There's a bond, there's a linkage, and there is this closeness between God and Noah that is part of the covenant concept.

Now, we need to address the question, how is it that these two stories are related? There are three options, I would say. Option number one is that the biblical story was borrowed from the Babylonian story. Option number two is that the Babylonian story was borrowed from the biblical story, and one could hypothesize a third option, as well, and that is that it's possible that both the biblical and the Babylonian stories were borrowed from an unknown source, which we'll call "Source X." Of those three options, the one that is the most likely explanation, by far, is that the biblical account is borrowed from the Mesopotamian flood tradition, the first of the three options that I laid out, and let's give a variety of reasons why we arrive at that conclusion.

First, in general, greater societies influence lesser societies. As we have noted, within the world of the ancient Near East, Babylonia was a major power, a major player in the entire ancient world throughout the duration of the ancient Near East, whereas Israel was a relatively minor player on the geopolitical scene of the ancient world. It's true that during the time of David and Solomon, they achieved a time of greatness and glory, an empire, but otherwise Israel was basically a backwater, politically and culturally. Greater societies influence lesser ones, and that is the first of the reasons why we would assume that the biblical story is borrowed from the Babylonian one.

Secondly, flooding—the nature of the destruction of the world is via a flood—flooding is typical of Mesopotamia, but not of Canaan. The former, Mesopotamia has more plentiful rainfall than Canaan and, you'll remember, it has two major rivers running through the region, the Tigris and Euphrates, both of which flood the Mesopotamian plain with relative frequency. A flood could not be possible if the story began, originated in the land of Canaan. If God were to destroy the world in a story that originated in the world of Canaan, it might come through other means, such as drought—the exact opposite, lack of rain. But, one could not imagine somebody in the land of Canaan, in the land of Israel, creating a story where a flood wiped out the world. This would be another reason, our second reason why we believe that the story originates in the land of Mesopotamia.

I should take a timeout here to note that archeologists indeed have found evidence for the flooding of individual cities in Mesopotamia. That is to say, one can see an entire silt layer covering up the archeological remains of a city in Mesopotamia along the banks of the Euphrates or the Tigris after which the city was rebuilt. It is very likely that one of these floods—some of which go back to pre-historic times—the archeological record can show things from the 4th and 5th millennia B.C.E., before our written records begin in the year 3000, and we can see such floods of such Mesopotamia cities in the plain of modern-day southern Iraq. Most likely, it was one such flooding, or a series of such floods, which served as the basis for the Mesopotamian flood tradition. That started the whole ball rolling, which eventuates in Tablet XI of the Gilgamesh Epic, the story that Utnapishtim narrates to Gilgamesh.

A third reason for concluding that the biblical story was borrowed from a Mesopotamian prototype is the only geographical location mentioned in the biblical account. I refer to the mountains of Ararat, which are mentioned at the beginning of Genesis 8. Ararat is to be found in far northern Mesopotamia—the region around Lake Van, in modern-day eastern Turkey, near the headwaters of both the Tigris and Euphrates rivers.

Fourth, perhaps most crucially, as noted above, the Gilgamesh Epic was the literary classic of the ancient world, so people in other cultures would have been familiar with it. I mentioned the fact that we have copies of it from outside of Mesopotamia and that it was translated into Hittite and Hurrian, for example. One of those copies that we have from outside Mesopotamia, very strikingly, was excavated at a place in northern Israel called Megiddo, not far from modern-day Haifa in the modern country of Israel. It dates to around 1400 B.C.E. It's a relatively small fragment and it is not even a scene from the flood story, but in fact, it tells us that the Gilgamesh Epic, as a whole, was known and could be read in the Babylonian original to people in the land of Israel around 1400 B.C.E. This is exactly the time of Abraham as we have dated him.

There's not quite yet an Israelite people that we can speak of and so we have to assume that it was Canaanites in the land of Israel living in the city of Megiddo that were able to read this text in the original. Far north in Canaan, there's another city called Ugarit, which we'll be talking about later in our course. From the city of Ugarit, which is on the Mediterranean coast in northern Assyria, we have another cuneiform table, which describes another scene from the life of Gilgamesh. So, the Gilgamesh hero and the Gilgamesh Epic, and all of these traditions, were known to people in the west, the Canaanites, who could read this material, apparently in the Babylonian original. Now, we may ask, how could somebody from ancient Israel have learned about this? What were the routes of transmission? It's one thing to have a Babylonian text excavated in Megiddo concerning Gilgamesh, but how did somebody in, let's say, the 10th or 9th or 8th century in Israel, know about this? Well, the culture was so great that it's hard to imagine anybody would not ever have heard of the Gilgamesh story. It might have been translated orally, perhaps, into Hebrew or Canaanite—Hebrew and Canaanite being dialects of the same language—and through such means, people in ancient Israel would have learned of the flood story.

There's another reason we can point to it in support of our conclusion. Remember that the biblical tradition has Abraham originating in Mesopotamia, before he moved to the land of Canaan. Thus, it is possible that the earliest Hebrews would have brought the flood story with them, Abraham and his entourage when they moved from Mesopotamia, into the land of Canaan and it remained a story that was told and eventually was incorporated into the biblical account concerning Noah.

Finally, let's look at the additions that are in the biblical story. Let's go back and recall that the biblical story includes two items that are not to be found in the Babylonian story. They are, A, the morality factor—or perhaps we should call it the "immorality factor," which leads to the whole flood story—and, B, the use and presence of a covenant. These are exactly the kinds of additions one would expect the people of ancient Israel to add to an ancient Near Eastern story. That is to say, remember that Israel does not live in a vacuum. Israel knows the literature and the culture of its neighbors throughout the ancient Near East. But when it takes ancient Near Eastern literary material, it doesn't just take it and import it and incorporate it for no reason; it uses that material and places upon it the distinctively Israelite, theological imprint. In this case, gods do not destroy worlds for any cause and, in particular, human beings are not selected for any reason. There is closeness between God and man and, therefore, the "immorality issue" is raised at the beginning of the Flood story and the covenant concept is incorporated as well.

Now, it is far more likely that the Israelites took the Babylonian story and incorporated these distinctively Israelite theological issues into that story than to assume the opposite, that the Babylonians borrowed this story from the Israelites and somehow excised the material in that version. These are the reasons that collectively direct our attention to the conclusion that, indeed, it was the biblical Israelites who knew of this material from ancient Babylonia and incorporated it into their tradition. Let's review them. First, the greater societies influence the lesser. Second, the flooding is something associated with Mesopotamia, not Canaan. Third, there's the mention of Ararat in far northern Mesopotamia. Fourth, there's the fact that the Gilgamesh Epic was the literary classic and we have a fragment from Megiddo in the land of Israel. Fifth, there's the idea that Abraham may have brought this story with him from Mesopotamia. The earliest Hebrews may have known of it and brought it with them as they moved from Mesopotamia to Canaan. And, sixth, the additions in the biblical account suggest that the Hebrew version is an expansion of the Babylonian story. Taken collectively, these issues—these points that I have raised—point to the conclusion that the biblical story is borrowed, in this case, directly from the Babylonian flood tradition, as incorporated into the Gilgamesh Epic.

I also can mention here, by the way, a particular item that is in the story, which is something very, very non Israelite. That is at the very end of the story, in the end of Genesis 8, when you have the sacrifices that Noah offers to God, it tells us that God smelled the sweet savor of the sacrifices. This is the only place in the Bible where we have a reference to God smelling the sacrifices. We have dozens, if not hundreds of times in the Bible where we have reference to the Israelites offering sacrifices in the form of sheep and goats and cattle, and wine libations and olive oil, and grains, cereals and so on to their God, but never does God smell the sacrifices. This is a very anthropomorphic statement. God appears here almost in human fashion. That is something we would expect to find in the polytheistic world when they write about their gods and, indeed, that is exactly what we find toward the end of the flood account in the Gilgamesh Epic where we are told that when Utnapishtim sacrifices to the gods, the gods smell the sweet savor. It's almost as if the biblical words in Hebrew were a direct translation of the Babylonian story. This was left in the biblical account. It doesn't sound perfectly Israelite; it sounds very much non Israelite, but it is still there. It doesn't violate in any real way any theological dogma or dictum of ancient Israel, but it is interesting to note that only here at the end of the Flood story, Genesis 8:20–22, where the sacrifices occur, that God appears in this anthropomorphic fashion, smelling the sweet savor of Noah's sacrifices.

Now, let's talk about this story, the Flood story, in conjunction with the JEDP Theory which we talked about in the last lecture. Most scholars believe that the biblical flood story—certainly those scholars that are the majority who would adhere to the JEDP Theory—they believe that the biblical Flood story is redacted from two separate stories. If you look through Genesis 6–8, you will notice that the name of God is sometimes "God Elohim" and sometimes "Lord Yahweh," and, therefore, according to this theory, there must be two sources present. One of them is clearly the J source because the name "Yahweh" is only used by the Yahwist, and the other is the P source that uses the word "Elohim." Most of the material is ascribed to the P source, the Priestly source, and some of the material is ascribed to the J source, the Yahwist source. Again, the chart in the course booklet illustrates this for you.

This explains the apparent inconsistencies in the biblical account, as we've already noted, most importantly, the number of animals that Noah brought onto the ark. So, for example, at the end of Genesis 6 where he is commanded to bring one pair of each species of animals onto the ark, the word "God" is used there at the end of Genesis 6; this must be the Priestly source, because the word is "Elohim." At the beginning of Genesis 7, where now "the Lord" or "Yahweh" commands Noah to bring on seven pair of the pure animals and one pair of the impure animals, as I've just indicated, the word "Lord" is used there and therefore this has to be "Yahweh," the Yahwist source. There, the theory goes and builds up the idea that we have two sources, the Yahwist and the Priestly, one dated to the 10th century, you'll recall, and one dated to the 5th century, and these two were brought together by our redactor in the 5th century.

But, there is an alternative approach—and that is the one that I would like to suggest here—that is to read the biblical account as a single unified literary whole. By doing so, and only in this matter, does the biblical account match with the Gilgamesh version of the flood. Let me explain what I mean by that. As you work through the Gilgamesh story, you will remember that, element by element, we proceed from the beginning to the end, paralleling exactly the same order in the biblical story, or looking at it the other way, the biblical story parallels, element by element, unit by unit, the Gilgamesh Epic. Again, these elements are the materials, the dimensions, the decks, the population, the flood, the mountaintop landing, the sending forth of the birds, the dry land, everybody being set free and the sacrifices at the end.

If you were to divide the biblical accounts into two separate sources, some of those elements wind up in the P document and some of those elements wind up in the J document. We would be led to believe by the adherence of the Documentary Hypothesis that the redactor took the P material and the J material and put it together and, *voilà*, the story wound up looking exactly like the Gilgamesh Epic account. Now, part of the problem here has to do with the history of discovery. That is to say, the division of the biblical material into its separate sources is a part of scholarship that goes back to the 18th and 19th centuries, as we noted in the last lecture, culminating with Julius Wellhausen in 1878 presenting the JEDP Theory in its classical formulation.

Exactly in those years, in the 1870s and 1880s, these Babylonian texts written in the Akkadian language on cuneiform were being excavated in Iraq by early British archeologists and they were brought to the British Museum in London. It was there in the British Museum that a remarkable man named George Smith, who was actually an amateur—he was an engraver who was fascinated with this material, who learned to read cuneiform and learned the Babylonian, the Akkadian language—volunteered his time in the British Museum to read these tablets that were being unearthed in Iraq and sent to London. It was there in the 1870s and 1880s, when he was working, presumably after hours, after he left his day job, when he, this amateur scholar, discovered Gilgamesh Tablet XI, which he read and saw the flood story paralleling the biblical account. He describes how the scene of Utnapishtim sending forth the birds jumped off the page—as it were, not quite a page, but a cuneiform tablet—into his eyes and he realized how closely the two stories were related.

But by this point, the JEDP Theory was already, if I can use the word, dogmatic among biblical scholars, so great was Wellhausen's influence. It didn't occur to anybody until sometime later—and I'm not the originator of this idea—that we should not think of the Flood story as a compilation of two texts. In fact, we should look at that Gilgamesh text and think that, indeed, the biblical account is taken, piece by piece, item by item, and must be a unified whole. Let me illustrate the problem with just looking at the end of the biblical Flood story. In Genesis 8:1, we have the mountaintop landing and in Genesis 8:6, we have the birds being sent forth. The mountaintop landing is ascribed to P and the birds being sent forth is ascribed to J. Then, the next section tells us that Noah set everybody free; that's ascribed to P. Then, there's the last section of the sacrifices that he offers to God and that's ascribed to J. So, it goes back and forth—P, J, P, J. Some verses ascribe to P, then to J, then to P, then to J.

But, we would have it that the redactor took this material and put it together in the very order that we actually find in the Gilgamesh Epic, and I would hold that that can not be the case. There is just too much coherence in this text to assume that what we are dealing with are two separate compositions, which were compiled by a redactor. This coherence points to a single biblical story of the Flood, borrowed from the Babylonian flood tradition. A larger, unitary view of the biblical material, as I am proposing here, explains the text, to my mind, far better than any view that divides the biblical text into its hypothesized—and I emphasize that word—hypothesized, smaller component parts.

Lecture Eight
Genesis 9, Covenant

Scope:

The covenant mentioned briefly in Genesis 6:18 is treated in greater detail in Genesis 9. This lecture focuses on this crucial concept in biblical studies and on how the notion of covenant distinguished ancient Israel from other cultures and religions of the ancient Near East. We also will look ahead to chapters 15 and 17, in which God establishes a covenant with Abraham. In 9:3–4, God permits man to eat meat (though not blood); this passage leads us back to the creation accounts, where we note that man was allowed to eat only vegetation. We will use this passage as a springboard to discuss the vegetarian ideal that permeates the Bible.

Outline

I. There are two major distinctions between the gods of the polytheistic religions and the single God worshipped in Israel, the quantitative and the qualitative.

    A. The quantitative is well known. The religions of other cultures in the ancient world were polytheisms, characterized by the belief in many gods. By contrast, in Israel, only one God was worshipped. But the picture is more complicated, for there is no radical step from polytheism to monotheism. Instead, the process occurred in stages.

        1. The religion of ancient Israel throughout most of the biblical period was a monolatry, that is, the worship of one God.

        2. Only later, during the Babylonian Exile, did the religion of ancient Israel develop into a monotheism, that is, the belief in one God.

    B. The background for the distinction between Israel and the other religions of the ancient world may be found in the societal difference.

        1. Egypt, Babylonia, and the other great powers were complex societies, governed by kings and vast bureaucracies, while Israel was a simple society, based on a tribal structure with one individual leader at the head.

2. Given that the gods are a projection of human society onto the divine realm, one can understand how Egypt, Babylonia, and the other great powers developed the notion of a pantheon of deities, while Israel, by contrast, fostered the worship of one god (which, as noted above, eventually developed into pure monotheism).

3. Unfortunately, we do not have written remains for other semi-nomadic, tribal, pastoral peoples who lived in the desert and in the desert-fringe, and so we do not know what their religious outlook would have been like.

C. We also note that the worship of the deity in antiquity was a local affair. Gods could be worshipped only in their own locale or realm.

1. Such was true in ancient Egypt, for example, where Khnum was the god of Elephantine (near modern-day Aswan) but could not be worshipped in the region of the Nile Delta in the far north.

2. Several biblical passages indicate that Israel had the same understanding about the worship of Yahweh.

   a. Moses asks Pharaoh for permission for the Israelites to leave Egypt to worship God in the Sinai for three days (Exodus 7:16, 8:23).

   b. David states that moving to Philistia would require him to worship other gods (1 Samuel 27:19).

3. During the Babylonian Exile, however, the theology of Israel underwent a change. Israel now believed that it could worship Yahweh outside the land of Israel. The background for this transformation is the fact that Assyria and Babylonia were international empires, which had an effect on religious ideas, not just geopolitics.

4. Moreover, Jews living in exile and worshipping their God in Babylon, concluded that He must be the God of the entire world and that the Babylonian gods are not gods at all, only figments in the imagination of the people who worship them.

D. This quantitative distinction, however, is only half the equation. The other part of the equation is the qualitative distinction.

  1. Gods in the polytheistic world were, by and large, seen as nature deities, associated with the earth, sky, sun, moon, desert, sea, and so on.

  2. Yahweh, by contrast, was perceived by the Israelites as a god of history, exalted above all of nature, manifesting himself in human history.

  3. One can point to the Aten cult developed by Akhenaten, an Egyptian pharaoh c. 1350 B.C.E., as an example of another monolatry.

   a. However, the god Aten was still a nature deity, the god of light.

   b. Akhenaten ruled for about a decade and when he died, the old priesthoods came back and reestablished the worship of the other Egyptian gods in their temples.

  4. A key passage to understand the distinction is 1 Kings 19:11–12, in which Elijah makes a trip to Mount Sinai to visit God.

   a. There was a great wind, an earthquake, and a fire—all elements of nature—but nowhere was God to be found in those powerful displays of the natural world.

   b. God spoke to Elijah in a still, small voice—communicating directly with human beings through the divine word.

II. The concept of covenant (*berit*)—a bond between God and man—was possible because of Israel's unique view of the deity.

  A. The first covenant in the Bible is between God and Noah, representative of all mankind (see Genesis 9).

  B. The second covenant in the Bible is between God and Abraham, representative of the people of Israel (see Genesis 15 and Genesis 17).

III. The concept of covenant speaks to the closeness between God and man in Israel's understanding of the world. By contrast, the other peoples of the ancient world saw a distance between man and the gods.

    A. Notwithstanding the chasm between man and the gods in the polytheistic world, ancient peoples believed that that gap could be bridged in certain instances.

        1. The first method was by the gods coming down to earth and having sexual intercourse with females. We find this in a variety of ancient mythologies, including that of ancient Greece. Note, moreover, that this is what occurs in Genesis 6:1–4 to epitomize the depravity of mankind.

        2. At other times, certain humans could achieve divine status. Such, for example, was the belief among the Egyptians, who considered every pharaoh to be divine. In addition, Imhotep, the builder of the first pyramid, was deified after his death.

    B. By contrast, notwithstanding the closeness between God and man, as concretized through the covenant, for ancient Israel, the gap could never be bridged. Again, if a bridging of the gap appears in Genesis 6:1–4, it is simply an ancient Near Eastern mythological fragment that is used for the specific purpose of a prelude to the flood story.

IV. Another interesting topic pertaining to how ancient Israel understood the divine is the gender of God. On the one hand, one could argue that the God of Israel was devoid of gender (unlike the polytheistic deities) or gender-neutral, if you will, but these ideas are rather modern and fall outside the worldview of ancient Israel. More likely, the average ancient Israelite would have understood the God of Israel as a male deity.

    A. The Hebrew language has grammatical gender, and God is always referred to with masculine nouns, verbs, and pronouns.

    B. The metaphors usually attached to God suggest that he was seen as a male deity. For example, the prophets of Israel saw the covenant between God and Israel in terms of a marriage, with God as the male partner and Israel as the female partner.

C. At the same time, one must readily admit that the ancient Hebrew writers sometimes used female imagery, such as presenting God as a mother caring for her children.

V. God apparently had some ideals in store for humanity the first go-round, which mankind could not live up to. Accordingly, God permits greater flexibility in Genesis 9, by allowing humankind to eat meat now; but this does not detract from the vegetarian ideal that permeates the Bible.

   A. In Genesis 1, God commands a vegetarian diet for both humankind and the animal kingdom.

   B. Genesis 9 adds something new: Because man cannot live up to this ideal, humankind is given permission to eat meat, with the proviso that no blood can be consumed.

   C. Leviticus 11 presents the dietary laws specific to Israel, with a general prohibition against eating carnivores.

   D. Isaiah 11 presents the prophet's eschatological view of world history, in which vegetarianism will define the end of days.

Essential Reading:

Gary A. Rendsburg, "An Essay on Israelite Religion," in Jacob Neusner, ed., *Approaches to Ancient Judaism*, pp. 1–17.

Supplementary Reading:

Gary A. Rendsburg, "The Vegetarian Ideal in the Bible," in L. J. Greenspoon, R. A. Simkins, and G. Shapiro, eds., *Food and Judaism*, pp. 319–334.

Questions to Consider:

1. Do you think that other cultures in the ancient Near East might also have developed a monolatry or a monotheism? Explain your answer.

2. What other commands from God are present in Genesis 9:1–7 that relate to our discussion in this lecture?

Lecture Eight—Transcript
Genesis 9, Covenant

Welcome back. In our previous lecture concerning the Flood story in Genesis 6–8, we mentioned the covenant concept, which is one of those elements that is found in the biblical Flood story, but which is lacking in the Babylonian flood narrative. That issue, the covenant, is explored in more detail in the following chapter in the Bible, Genesis 9, and I want to devote this lecture to that concept. I also want to talk about God, Israel's conception of God, and how it differed from the conception of the deities among the other peoples in the ancient Near East. Then, we'll bring these two issues together, Israel's understanding of the divine and the covenant concept.

There are two major distinctions concerning the issue of the deity—Israel's understanding of God, in contrast with the other peoples of the ancient Near East. The polytheistic religions, which everybody else followed, as that term implies, mean that they worshipped many gods. In Israel, only a single God was worshipped. That is the quantitative distinction. There's also a qualitative distinction, and we'll come back and talk about that in just a few minutes. Let's focus, however, on the quantitative. It is, of course, a well known distinction. Most people realize that ancient Israel worshipped the one God, while everybody else in the ancient Near East worshiped and believed in multiple deities. The picture, however, is a bit more complicated than I have just suggested, for there is no radical step from the polytheism of the other peoples of the ancient Near East to the monotheism of ancient Israel. Instead, that process occurred in stages.

Now, the religion of ancient Israel throughout most of the biblical period was a monolatry, that is, the worship of one God. We've actually talked about this concept in our previous lectures, but we haven't given it a label. So let me talk about that term, "monolatry." What it means is, etymologically, the worship of one. That is to say, "mono" is a prefix that most people will recognize meaning "one," and the suffix on that word—L-A-T-R-Y—appears in the English word "idolatry," for example, the worship of idols. Therefore, monolatry means the worship of one and that stands in slight contrast to "monotheism," which is the belief in one God. Now, let's expand the definitions of those two.

Monolatry is the worship of one God without necessarily denying the existence of other gods. Monotheism is the belief in one God and that means, yes, denying the existence of all other gods. The best way to understand this distinction is with the following. If you were to ask an ancient Israelite, while that society was still in its monolatrous stage, "What about those gods from the other countries? What about the gods that the Egyptians believed in, Ra, and Horus and Isis, or those Babylonian gods, Marduk and Ishtar, and some of the other deities? Or, how about over in Greece where they worship Zeus and Apollo and Aphrodite?" The answer of an average Israelite would have been, and this is still in their monolatrous stage, "Yes, those are deities." The existence of those deities would not have been denied, but this Israelite would have said to us, "But they are for other peoples in the world to worship; they are not for us to worship. We worship the one God, the God of Israel, Yahweh." This is in contrast to Israel in its later stage, after it develops into a monotheism, by which point this average individual would have responded to that same question in the following way, "No, those are not gods at all; they are merely figments in the imagination of the people who worship them." Hopefully, that will help you understand the distinction between monolatry and monotheism.

Now, let's put this in some sort of chronological scheme. If we assume that Abraham is the originator of the monolatrous, which eventually develops into monotheistic tradition, then the shift from polytheism to monolatry among the people of Israel would occur around 1400 B.C.E., which, of course, is the date we have already affixed for Abraham. Now, the shift to monotheism will occur in the Babylonian Exile during the Exile, around 550 B.C.E. That means for most of the biblical period, as I've indicated, Israel's religion was a monolatry.

Now, let's talk about why these things occurred, the shift from polytheism of the ancient world to the monolatry of Abraham and his descendents and his followers, the people of Israel. Very frequently, when we study the ancient world, we can answer such questions as the who, and the what, and the when, and the where and the how. The why is always a more difficult question to answer, but let's give it a stab because this is, indeed, such a crucial question. Scholars—particularly those who are involved with the social sciences such as anthropology and sociology—have divided up, or occasionally divide up, the societies of the world into complex societies and simple societies, and if you take that approach, we may have our answer here. That is to say, the other cultures of the ancient world, certainly Egypt and certainly Babylonia, and the other great powers about whom we know so much from their written remains, were complex societies. There was not just a single king or a pharaoh ruling over these realms, but there was a royal family and a government bureaucracy, all of whom took part in the administration of the country. Israel, by contrast, was a simple society. Israel was pastoral, it was tribal, it was semi-nomadic, and presumably, a single tribal leader took care of everything. Anthropologists have noticed, for example, that this is how people, to this day, who live in desert or desert-fringe regions, run their societies, with a single leader. If we think about the Arabian Peninsula, for example, we may consider the term "sheikh" who is in charge of basically everything in the tribe and, therefore, the whole concept of administration and linkage on people to their leader is, in fact, much more direct and much simpler.

Now, in the psychology of religion, scholars very often talk about how the gods are a projection of human society into another realm, into the divine realm. So, if you have a complex society as existed in Egypt or in Babylonia, you project that into the world of the gods and, therefore, you have multiple deities in the pantheon, and that's what happened in Egypt and Babylonia. Israel, by contrast, because of its simple desert or desert-fringe society, could understand and could come up with the concept of a single god to worship, a single connection between that one god and that one people. This is highly theoretical I hasten to add because the comeback should be, "Well, what about the other desert peoples in the ancient world? If this is true of Israel, shouldn't this be true of the other people who live in the desert and in the desert fringe who also had a semi-nomadic, tribal, pastoral society?" Unfortunately, we can't answer that question because the only such people from antiquity for whom we have written remains is the people of Israel who transmitted the biblical material through the centuries and the millennia down to the present day, in the Hebrew original as still read by Jews down into the 21st century. What about the other desert peoples? We know their names because the Bible refers to them by name. We have people such as the Ishmaelites and the Midianites and all sorts of people mentioned in the Bible, but unfortunately, we don't have their remains and so we don't know what their religious outlook would have been on this question. So, I raise this issue and I present this information to you as food for thought, although I hasten to emphasize, once more, that this is theoretical, hypothetical, with some validity to it, but cannot be proved to the extent that of course we would like.

The shift from monolatry to monotheism during the Babylonian Exile—there we're standing on firmer ground. This we can actually talk about because we can actually see what occurred. Before we move to that, I have to add here one other item that's important for understanding the religion of ancient Israel in its earliest stages, and that is to say the worship of God was a local affair. This wasn't only true of Israel. This was true of everybody in the ancient world. Gods were worshipped in a single place in a single country, sometimes in a single city, and that is to say that the gods of Egypt would be worshipped in Egypt and the gods of Canaan in Canaan and the gods of Babylon in Babylonia and so on. In Egypt, for example, sometimes it meant that a particular god could be worshipped in only his or her particular city. Let me take, for example, the god Khnum who was worshipped in Elephantine in the far south, more or less, modern-day Aswan. That was his territory. That was his region. That was where his temple stood and that's where his worshippers worshipped him. If you found yourself further north in Egypt, let's say, in the Delta, hundreds of miles away from Aswan, Khnum could not be worshipped because you were then in the realm of other deities. That's also true of Israel during its earliest stages.

Let me give you the examples from the Bible that speak to this. You'll remember in the book of Exodus that Moses and the Israelites that were in the land of Egypt, Moses is before Pharaoh and he's asking for permission for the Israelites to worship God. He says to Pharaoh that, "We would like to go into the desert for three days to worship our God." Pharaoh never responds with a statement such as, "Why don't you just worship him right here in Egypt?" There is an understanding between them that this cannot be done, so this is an example of how deity worship had to be localized. Yahweh could be worshipped only in his land, which eventually would be the land of Israel, but at this earlier stage was the Sinai tract, which is a bit of a no man's land in between Egypt and the land of Canaan, the homeland of the Israelites.

Similarly, later on in the Bible in the Book of 1 Samuel, David and Saul have a relationship, which isn't quite the loving relationship that we would expect between father-in-law and son-in-law. Saul is becoming less and less popular among the people. David is becoming more and more popular among the people and, of course, eventually, would succeed Saul as the king of Israel. At one point, Saul actually tries to kill David in a rage and David has to flee the country. When he flees the country and goes to live with the Philistines—which is just a few miles away, probably no more than ten, fifteen, twenty miles west of his homeland in the mountainous region of Canaan—he went down to the coastal plain where the Philistines lived, and David is quoted in the book of 1 Samuel as saying that "Saul's men have driven me from the inheritance of God"—and that means the land of Israel—"and I have to go worship other gods." So, he moves twenty or thirty miles away, let's say, to live with the Philistines, and he must worship other gods. So, that's the local worship of a deity. That was true of Israel and it is true of everybody in antiquity.

What happens during the Babylonian Exile, however? The large population of Judah goes into exile and now is living in Babylonia, Mesopotamia. Who do the people of Judah worship when they arrive to that country, to that region, in the 6th century B.C.E.? They do not worship the Babylonian gods. No, they continue to worship their God, the God of Israel, Yahweh. How did this happen? Why was it possible in the 6th century when it, in fact, did not occur earlier on as we've illustrated with examples of Moses and David? The answer is that the world had changed in the intervening centuries. There had been two large world empires, the Assyrian Empire and the Babylonian Empire, both of which we've talked about, both of which were truly international, ruling over large swaths of land, most of the Near East united under a single monarchy, united under a single political entity. This has an effect on the theology of the people of Israel and perhaps the theologies of others, as well, although for the present, our concern is Israel and it is, of course, from them that we have the most information.

So, when the Israelites go off into Babylonia in exile, they are now in a new world, which is totally international and, therefore, the religion, the worship of their God, has become international as well. Yahweh does not have to be worshipped only in the land of Israel, he now can be worshipped in other places as well, including in

Babylonia. He could not be worshipped by offering sacrifices in the temple, which could be done only in Jerusalem, and of course, that Temple was now destroyed. Nevertheless, the people could still have their devotion to Yahweh and develop other forms of worship, presumably, in the manner of public prayer, which probably developed for the first time during the Babylonian Exile. So, if you're worshipping Yahweh in Babylon, the next logical question to ask is, "Well, what about these Babylonian gods? What about Marduk and Ishtar and Nabu and Sin and the other members of the pantheon of Babylon?" So the conclusion of the Jews now living in exile was that these gods, presumably, are not gods at all because here we are in Babylon worshipping our God, whom we have brought with us from Jerusalem, from Judah, as it were. He must be the God of the entire world and, therefore, the Babylonian gods are not gods at all, but indeed are figments in the imagination of the people who worship them, and that is how you have the shift from monolatry to monotheism. Now, all of this takes us well beyond the book of Genesis, but it is a remarkably interesting account of how the development of the worship of God and the belief in God changed over time in the history of ancient Israel.

Now, all of that is the quantitative distinction with which I began. Now, we have to talk about the qualitative distinction. The quantitative is only half the equation; the qualitative is the other half. The gods in the polytheistic world were, by and large, seen as nature deities. They were associated with the elements of nature—the earth, the sky, the sun, the moon, the desert, and the sea. These are all parts of nature. Yahweh, by contrast, was perceived by the Israelites as a god of history. He was exalted above all nature and he manifested himself in human history. That is the crucial distinction here between these two groups. That's the qualitative one. The polytheistic deities associated with nature and we've already talked about a sun deity, a moon deity, and a sea deity when we were talking about Genesis 1 in the earlier part of our course. Now, let's talk about the contrast on the qualitative side with the following illustration.

There actually was one other attempt in antiquity to worship only one god and that occurred in Egypt in the 14th century, about 1350 B.C.E. It was an experiment by the Pharaoh Akhenaten, who decided to close down the temples to all the other gods in Egypt, and so, the worship of Horus and the worship of Ra and the worship of Khnum, and all of these deities that I have referred to, would no longer occur and those priests were put out of business, basically. The temples were closed and only a single god, the god Aten, was to be worshipped. You can hear the name of the god Aten in the name of this pharaoh, Akhenaten, at the end of his name, but Aten was still a nature deity, he was the god of light. So, here is a monolatry. Here is another example in the records from the Ancient Near East of a people, or at least of a single experiment for a brief amount of time with the worship of one god, just like the Israelites. But, notice that the distinction is still to be held on the qualitative side because for the Egyptians, the worship of this one god was a nature deity associated with light. For the Israelites, of course, as we mentioned, God was always simply a God of history who could not be pinned down to a single aspect of nature. The end of this Egyptian story, by the way, is that Akhenaten ruled for almost two decades and when he died, the old priesthoods came back and reestablished the worship of those other Egyptian gods in their temples. So, this is a blip, as it were, on the radar screen of thousands of years of ancient Egyptian history, but it does indicate for us that there was at least one other time when another people went to the worship of one god, again, on the quantitative side, qualitatively very different from what was going on in ancient Israel.

Let me illustrate this idea of the God of history in ancient Israel with a passage in First Kings 19. It is as a key passage to witness the distinction I'm talking about. It's a story about Elijah who decides to make a trip to Mount Sinai to visit God. There he is in the desert. He actually has to flee from Ahab and Jezebel, the king and queen of Israel, and he flees into the desert for personal safety. There he is at Sinai and then we are told that there was a great wind, but God was not to be found in the wind. Then, an earthquake, but God was not to be found in the earthquake. Then, a fire, but God was not to be found in the fire. What are those? Wind, earthquake, and fire—those are all elements of nature, but nowhere was God to be found in those powerful displays of the natural world. Then, the story comes to its conclusion that God spoke to Elijah in a still, small voice. That is the idea of God in ancient Israel. He communicates directly with human beings through the divine word and all the thunder and light shows, sound and light shows, thunder and lightning shows that one can imagine, as First Kings 19 presents, that is not where God is to be seen. That is a crucial passage and that illustrates for us how Israel understood its deity.

Now, let's talk about the concept of the covenant. Because Israel understood its God as a God of history, that deity, therefore, held a close relationship with mankind. Mankind in general, as illustrated by the covenant with Noah and the people of Israel, in particular, which will be formulated with the covenant between God and Abraham that is described twice in the book of Genesis—Genesis 15 and Genesis 17. The covenant is a bond between God and man. The Hebrew word is *berit* and this word covers a wide array of terms in English—covenant, contract, treaty or bond. If country A and country B entered into a treaty, then that would also be called a *berit*, so basically, the covenant between God and man or God and the Israelites, in particular, is a treaty relationship, as it were. There are stipulations. God says, "I'm your God" and the people are to worship only that God. Or, in the case of the covenant between God and Noah in Genesis 9, God has stipulations that he presents to mankind. You'll remember that we talked about the book of Genesis as a book of origins, two origins—the origins of mankind, in general, and the origins of the people of Israel, in particular. Therefore, we have these two covenants—the one in Genesis 9 between God and Noah built into the first eleven chapters of Genesis, which give us the universal view of mankind and then, the covenant with Abraham occurring after Genesis 12, when the story of Genesis moves to a discussion of the relationship between God and the people of Israel, in particular.

Now, the concept of the covenant speaks to the closeness between God and man in Israel's understanding of the world. By contrast, as I've suggested here, the other peoples of the ancient world saw a distance between man and the gods. Here, there is a paradox, for notwithstanding the chasm between man and the gods in the polytheistic world, these peoples of the ancient world believed that the gap could be bridged in certain instances. That is to say, man operates in his realm and the gods operate in their realm, the realm of nature, and there is a distance between them and yet, that distance, great as it is, can be bridged in two ways. The first method was by the gods coming down to earth and having sexual intercourse with females. We find this in a variety of ancient mythologies, including that of ancient Greece. Note, moreover, that this is what occurs in Genesis 6:1–4 to epitomize the depravity of mankind. Now, you'll recall that that passage in Genesis 6 is the passage that leads up to the Flood. When the biblical author needs to talk about the depravity, the low state of the world, which is what demands God to destroy it and to start afresh, the text utilizes this mythological idea in Genesis 6 of gods mating with females. Now, various biblical translations treat this differently, but it actually says in the Hebrew original that, "the gods were mating with females." Later, biblical interpretation would remove some of that language because it was seen as too pagan, too polytheistic and too mythological. But, it is quite possible that the Bible, which is typically devoid of mythology because with only one God, you cannot have these kinds of mythological ideas, especially a God who is not tied to nature but is, in fact, a God of history. Nevertheless, in this one place, and specifically in this one place, we have this mythological fragment. That is to say, Israel would not have understood, would not have accepted the idea, of deities mating with human women, but the text allows it to be introduced at this one point as the prelude to the Flood.

At other times, the gap between mankind and the deities in the polytheistic world could be bridged by certain humans achieving divine status. Such, for example, was the belief among the Egyptians, who considered the Pharaoh to be divine. The Pharaoh was considered the son of Ra, the sun god. That is to say, the son, the S-O-N of the S-U-N, sun god, Ra, and every pharaoh had a divine status. There were other individuals in the Near East who achieved divine status and here I can mention Imhotep; he was the builder of the first pyramid and later, Egyptians deified him, presented him in divine statues. We've talked about Gilgamesh a number of times in this course. If we move to Mesopotamia, we see the same thing happening. He was a legendary king, but later on in Mesopotamian tradition, Gilgamesh is also deified. We can also refer to Prometheus in the Greek realm where the distinction between his human status and his divine status is blurred. So, yes, certain individuals could achieve divine status. So that gap, a great chasm between the world of the gods and the world of man in the polytheistic world, can be bridged in certain instances—by gods coming down to earth, as we've suggested, and by certain humans becoming divine.

By contrast, in ancient Israel, there is closeness between man and God, as concretized through the covenant, and yet that gap could never be bridged. So, there's that paradox. In the polytheistic world, there's a great distance between the gods and mankind and yet it could be bridged. In Israel, there's closeness between God and mankind and yet it could not be bridged. If it appears in Genesis 6, I repeat, it's simply an ancient, Near Eastern, mythological fragment that is used for the specific purpose of a prelude to the Flood story. Otherwise, God is God and man is man.

I want to say a few words here about the gender of God. It's an interesting topic, as long as we're on the topic of how Israel understood the divine. Let's consider that question, as well. While, on the one hand, one could argue that the God of Israel was devoid of gender—and this would be unlike the polytheistic deities who, clearly, were either masculine or feminine and who frequently mated with each other and had children and had all kind of humanlike relations between and among them—the God of Israel could be seen as gender neutral, if you will. Now, these ideas are rather modern and they fall outside, I think, the worldview of ancient Israel. More likely, the average ancient Israelite would have understood the god of Israel as a male deity. The Hebrew language has grammatical gender and God is always referred to with masculine nouns, verbs and pronouns, and, therefore, the Israelites would have understood God in that fashion. Furthermore, the metaphors usually attached to God suggest that he was seen as a male deity. For example, the prophets of Israel saw the covenant between God and Israel in terms of a marriage. I've mentioned that this Hebrew word, *berit*, means a bond, a partnership, an alliance, a treaty, a covenant, and, indeed, it can be used metaphorically for marriage. When the prophets use this terminology, God is seen as the male partner and Israel is seen as the female partner. Accordingly, I repeat most Israelites would have understood God in masculine terms. At the same time, one readily must admit that the ancient Hebrew writers sometimes used female imagery when talking about God. Yes, they occasionally present God as a mother caring for one's children. So, I don't want to say that it was beyond the realm of possibility that they saw God in female terms, but by and large, the deity was understood as a masculine entity.

Now when we look at chapter 9 in the book of Genesis and look at some of the details there where the covenant concept is laid out for us, we note a few very important points. Some of the language there in Genesis 9 repeats the language that we saw earlier in the Bible in Genesis 1. So, for example, in Genesis 9:1, it says, "God blessed

Noah and his sons and said to them, 'Be fertile and increase and fill the earth.' " Well, that's a passage that we've seen before in Genesis 1. This is the traditional "be fruitful and multiply"; the translation I'm using says, "Be fertile and increase." This is intentionally repeating that language because Genesis 9, in the aftermath of the Flood, is to be seen as a new world, as a new creation. God is beginning again. The line from Adam goes down to the Flood, goes down to Noah; that whole mankind is wiped out and now we begin again, a fresh start, with Noah, so the language is going to repeat.

However, God apparently had some ideals in store for humanity the first go round that mankind could not live up to. Therefore, there are going to be some commands here that allow for some greater flexibility. One of them is in the realm of diet. You'll remember that in Genesis 1, man and the animal kingdom were to eat only vegetation. Here we have, in Genesis 9, the permission to eat meat. All creatures can be eaten. There will actually be some limitation to that in Leviticus 11 for the people of Israel, where the dietary laws are laid out with only certain animals permitted to be eaten. But, in general, mankind and the animal kingdom are now given the permission to eat meat. However, the proviso is that they cannot eat blood. Let me quote from verses 3–4, "Every creature that lives shall be yours to eat. As with the green grasses, I give you all these. You must not, however, eat flesh with its lifeblood in it." That is to say, blood was the symbol of life and so while man is now given permission to eat meat, he cannot eat blood. Blood has to be removed as much as possible from the animals that are to be eaten. There were various ways to do this that were practiced not only in Israel, but actually as we know, elsewhere in the ancient world. For example, the method of slaughtering the animal with one, quick knife-cut through the neck, which drains out most of the blood through the arteries and veins, which flow through the neck.

There is a vegetarian ideal built into the Bible as we see in Genesis 1. It will be repeated and referred to again in Isaiah 11, where the prophet Isaiah presents an eschatological view of the world. It is in that vision of Isaiah where he states that at the end of days, at the end of time, vegetarianism will once more be part of mankind and the animal kingdom, where the lion shall learn to eat straw like the ox. This is the wonder of the Bible, how all of these passages are interfacing and interrelating to one another. You have to read

Genesis 1, Genesis 9, and Isaiah 11 all in tandem, keep all that in mind, as you work your way through the biblical text.

Lecture Nine
Genesis 12–22, The Abraham Story

Scope:

Abraham is introduced at the end of chapter 11, and there is additional material about his life in chapters 23–25, but the main core of the Abraham story is chapters 12–22, bounded by the first and last times that God speaks to Abraham (12:1–3 and 22:16–18). This lecture presents an overview of the narrative, focusing on the interrelated themes of God's granting the land of Canaan to Abraham and Abraham's quest for an heir. We will see how Lot, Eliezer, Ishmael, and Isaac are all candidates for this role, but how the story eliminates the first three, one after another, thereby leaving only Isaac as the true heir.

Outline

I. Israel's understanding of God as a deity who reveals himself in history has far-reaching implications for ancient Israel.

A. Statements in Deuteronomy 32:7 and Psalms 78:5–6 command the people to recall their history. It is no surprise, then, that the biblical books developed as they did, especially the great narrative that commences with Genesis and continues through Kings, presenting the entire history of Israel from Abraham through the destruction of Jerusalem in 586 B.C.E.

B. As indicated, that history begins with the personality of Abraham, and it is to his story, which commences at the end of Genesis 11 and the beginning of Genesis 12, to which we now turn.

II. We note several literary devices in the story.

A. The story begins with a conflict between the statement that Sarah was barren (11:30) and the promise by God that Abraham would be a great nation (12:2). All literature is driven by conflict, which creates the drama. In this case, the reader wishes to read on to see how the conflict between the promise from on high (12:2) and the facts on the ground (11:30) will be resolved.

B. Note the verbs predicated of Abraham in verses 4–5, "went forth" and "took." We would expect these two verses to appear in reverse order. But the storywriter narrates the tale in dischronological fashion in order to emphasize the point that Abraham immediately followed God's command. God told Abraham to "go forth" in verse 1, and Abraham immediately obeyed in verse 4, as indicated by the verb "went forth."

III. The Abraham story brings a host of potential heirs into the picture.

    A. First, we are directed to focus our attention on Lot, but he is a nephew. Thus, we ask ourselves: Can he count as offspring? Perhaps, but then Lot departs in Genesis 13.

    B. We next are introduced to Eliezer, an adopted son (to be discussed further in the next lecture). Is he the one? The answer is no, because as soon as Eliezer is introduced in Genesis 15, we are informed that he will not be Abraham's heir.

    C. At last, finally, after much travail, Abraham gains a natural-born son, Ishmael, son of Hagar, a servant woman presented to Abraham by Sarah (again, more on this in the next lecture).

    D. But wait, in Genesis 21, another son is born to Abraham, Isaac, son of Sarah, confirming the more specific promise made to Abraham in Genesis 17 that Sarah would bear him a son—especially noteworthy in light of the introductory statement in Genesis 11:30 that Sarah was barren.

IV. God makes two interconnected promises to Abraham.

    A. God promises to Abraham the land of Canaan.

    B. God also promises that Abraham shall have offspring.

V. The stage is too crowded, with Abraham, Sarah, Hagar, Ishmael, and Isaac all present; thus, there is a literary need to remove several characters from the stage.

    A. Hagar and Ishmael depart in Genesis 21.

    B. Abraham, Sarah, and Isaac remain toward the story's end, though this scene will be challenged with God's command to sacrifice Isaac in Genesis 22, for which see Lecture Eleven in detail.

VI. Note the manner in which all comes full circle, with the language in 22:16–18 echoing that of 12:1–3; we will note this again in Lecture Eleven and return to this issue in greater detail in Lecture Fifteen.

Essential Reading:

Robert Alter, *Genesis*, pp. 50–107 = Robert Alter, *The Five Books of Moses*, pp. 62–112.

Supplementary Reading:

Everett Fox, *The Five Books of Moses*, pp. 53–95.

Questions to Consider:

1. How did Israel's unique understanding of God affect the production of literature in ancient Israel?

2. In what way is the conflict in the story increased before it is resolved? Why would the author have constructed the narrative in this fashion?

3. The most unique episode in the Abraham story, which we did not discuss in this lecture, is the account in Genesis 14. What makes this story so different from the other stories in Genesis 12–22?

4. Another story that we did not discuss is the Sodom and Gomorrah episode in Genesis 18–19. What do you think is the main point of this narrative?

Lecture Nine—Transcript
Genesis 12–22, The Abraham Story

In this lecture, we arrive at the story of Abraham, which provides for us our segue from the universalistic message that is presented in Genesis 1–11, to the particular story of the people of Israel and its origins. This will carry us from Genesis 12 through the end of the book, Genesis 50 and, indeed, for the rest of the biblical books through the end of the canon, as well. This also provides the segue from what we will call the "a-historical" or non-historical material to the historical material, as we see in the person of Abraham. That is to say, as we talked about in a previous lecture, the material before Genesis 12 cannot be placed into an historical timeline or a historical context, so individuals such as Noah cannot be placed in history per se.

That is not the case with Abraham, however; as we've spoken about, we can talk about when Abraham lived, and indeed, we'll come back and talk about that topic in greater detail in our next lecture. In this lecture, I want to talk about the story of Abraham, not only the content of that story, but also the literary devices that are to be found in the narrative. We've talked about the sophisticated nature of ancient Israelite writers, we've seen examples of it when we studied chapter 1 and chapter 2 of Genesis, and we'll see much more of that in this lecture, as well.

Let's talk about what's going to be happening here; we are going to be talking about history. Now, the understanding of God, who reveals himself in history, which we emphasized in the previous lecture, has far-reaching implications for ancient Israel. We have statements elsewhere in the Bible, in the book of Deuteronomy 32:7 and in Psalms 78:5–6, which command the people of Israel to recall their history, to talk about what has happened in the past, and to learn the message and the morals of that history. It is no surprise, then, that the biblical books developed as they did with the great narrative that commences with the book of Genesis and continues through the book of Kings. It presents the entire history of Israel from its origins, which are traced back to Abraham here in Genesis 12 through to the destruction of Jerusalem in 586 B.C.E., which is how the book of Second Kings comes to a conclusion. So, with that as a reminder as to the importance of history and the telling of history for the people of Israel, let's go to the beginning of that history as described in Genesis 12.

Abraham is actually introduced at the end of Genesis 11. Genesis 11 includes a genealogical chain, which links Noah and his son, Shem, down to Terah, the father of Abraham and Abraham at the very end of Chapter 11. Based on what I said a moment ago, individuals such as Noah and Shem are in the world of legend, yet Abraham and, presumably, his father, Terah, are in the world of history. So, somewhere in this lineage that we have at the end of chapter 11 in the book of Genesis, somewhere in that list, we have to see a segue—the movement from this "a-historical" or non-historical, legendary context to the time of Abraham. Exactly where, we don't know, but we can assume not only Abraham as historical, but presumably his father Terah, as well.

We're introduced to the family at the end of Genesis 11. At this point in the narrative, Abraham is called "Abram," a shorter form of his name and his wife Sarah is called "Sarai," a variant form of her name. Their names will be changed in chapter 17 of Genesis and we will refer to them with those more familiar names, Abraham and Sarah. Just note, however, when I read biblical passages, I will be reading their names as "Abram" and "Sarai," until we come to Genesis 17, but I'll refer to them with those more familiar names, "Abraham" and "Sarah." So there we have the family tree of Abraham at the end of Genesis 11. We find that he has two brothers, one of whom has died, but that deceased brother has a son named Lot, who is Abraham's nephew. Of course, we have Abraham, as I mentioned, his father Terah, and his wife Sarah. They're living in northern Mesopotamia. The birthplace of Abraham is a place called Ur—Ur of the Chaldees, more particularly—and that is also a topic that we'll talk about in our next lecture.

The story of Abraham propels forward in Genesis 12:1. Let me read that

> The Lord said to Abram, "Go forth from your native land and from your father's house to the land that I will show you.
>
> And I will make of you a great nation and I will bless you; I will make your name great, and you shall be a blessing. I will bless those who bless you, and curse him that curses

you; and all the families of the earth shall bless themselves by you.

That's Genesis 12:1–3. It's a command from God to Abraham to go forth, to leave his homeland, northern Mesopotamia, and to go to the land that God will show him. It's not defined yet, but it's clear as we move on through the rest of Genesis 12, that it is the land of Canaan. We probably should take a moment here to note that the speech from God to Abraham is seen as perfectly normal. God has already spoken to other characters already—to Adam and Eve, to Noah, for example—and here he speaks to Abraham. This is simply part of the mindset of ancient Israelites—that God could speak directly to human beings. We talked about this in the previous lecture as well, the close connection between God and Israel means that he speaks, as we saw in the story of Elijah, in a still, small voice. God's communication to Abraham is seen as direct and perfectly natural, requiring no explanation here. The text simply begins, "And the Lord said to Abram." He tells him that he will become "a great nation."

Our story begins, accordingly, with conflict. Conflict is what creates literature. Where's the conflict? In Genesis 11:30, within the context of the genealogical material with which we were provided at the end of Genesis 11, we are told that Sarai was barren, she had no child. That's Genesis 11:30. Now, here, in Genesis 12:2, we have the promise by God that Abraham would be "a great nation." There's our conflict. How is he going to be a great nation if this couple doesn't even have a single child? I repeat—all literature is driven by conflict, which creates the drama. In this case, the reader wishes to read on, as we do with all literature, to see how the conflict between the promise from on high and the facts on the ground will be resolved.

Now, in Genesis 12:4–5, we read on, "Abram went forth, as the Lord had commanded him; and Lot went with him. And Abraham was 75 years old when he left Haran." Haran is that place in northern Mesopotamia; they began their journey and stopped in Haran, en route to Canaan. Genesis 12:5, "Abram took his wife, Sarai, and his brother's son, Lot, and all the wealth that they had amassed, and the persons that they had acquired in Haran, and they set out for the land of Canaan."

Now, I want you to pay particular attention to the two verbs that are predicated of Abraham here in Genesis 12:4–5. Genesis 12:4 begins, "Abraham went forth," and we're actually told that Lot went with him. Then Genesis 12:5 begins that, "Abraham took his wife, Sarai," and Lot, and the entire entourage, and his wealth, and so on. Now, in the course of moving from Place A to Place B, which almost everyone has done at some time in his or her lifetime, typically, these verbs would appear in the opposite order—in the reverse order. We take everything first and then we go forth. But in this wording, Abraham "went forth" and then he took. We have to stop and ask why that is. The answer is quite clear—because God's initial words to Abraham in Genesis 12:1 were, "Go forth from your land," so on and so forth. "Go forth" was God's initial command to Abraham, close quote, at the end of Genesis 12:3, where God finishes speaking to Abraham and then, in Genesis 12:4, Abraham went forth.

The author of this text wants you to know that Abraham immediately obeyed God's command. In reality, he must have taken everything with him first and then gone forth, but that's not the way the text is worded. The text is worded first with Abraham going forth and then with him taking everything. Literature is not reality. Reality is our real life. Literature is a reflection of a reality, of a real life, and the story can be cast in the way that it so desires, the author handling the words. The message you are supposed to have is immediate obedience, even if it creates an impossibility of Abraham having gone forth before he took everything. Note that there is no statement to that effect, but that the reader needs to gain this message on his or her own. These texts demand reader involvement, reader input. One must be an active reader, an active participant in the reading process as you work through the biblical text to gain the message. God commands and Abraham does what God told him to do immediately.

Lot is mentioned, actually, in Genesis 12:4, as having gone forth with Abraham and then he's mentioned in Genesis 12:5, obviously, as among all the people and items that Abraham took with him. There appears to be, then, some sort of focus on Lot, who is Abraham's nephew. The camera, as it were, is focusing our attention on Lot. The spotlight is not only on Abraham, the spotlight is here on his nephew, Lot. Why? The reason is because God has promised Abraham "a great nation," and they have no children. Abraham and Sarah are childless and, therefore, it appears that the author wants us to start thinking about Lot as the potential heir for Abraham, the potential resolution to the conflict that has been introduced here into this story. As we read on in Genesis 12—as Abraham and the entourage makes their way into the land of Canaan—in verse 7, God speaks to Abraham a second time and he says, "I will assign this land to your offspring." Again, we, as readers, start thinking about this. Can Lot, a nephew, can he count as offspring? Perhaps he can. That Hebrew word, which is "seed" or "offspring," is as amorphous or as ambiguous or as pliant as are the English words. Usually that means, a child—a son, perhaps, in particular—but in this case we begin to think, as readers of this text, "Hmm, maybe a nephew can actually fulfill God's promise here in some fashion."

When we move ahead to Genesis 13, however, we realize that Lot is indeed a loose trail. He is not going to be the one who is the resolution of this conflict. He's not going to be the fulfillment of God's promise. Why? What happens in Genesis 13? There is a conflict between Abraham's shepherds and Lot's shepherds—a quarrel of some sort over watering rights, presumably, which is very common in the Near East. So, Abraham and Lot reach an agreement that they should separate themselves from one another, which is what they do in Genesis 13:11–12, with Lot moving on in one direction and Abraham remaining where he was, in the land of Canaan. We then read in Genesis 13:14, God now speaks to Abraham a third time and he says, "Raise your eyes and look out from where you are to the north and south, to the east and west," verse 15 now, "for I give you all the land that you see to you and your offspring forever." He is repeating the promise from before and now, Genesis 13:16, "I will make your offspring as the dust of the earth so that if one can count the dust of the earth, then your offspring, too, can be counted."

The conflict that was resolved, that was introduced at the beginning of our story, has actually been increased at this point. That is typical of the way literature operates. When a conflict is introduced—typically at the beginning of a text—the conflict increases. The drama has to increase before it reaches its resolution. How has it increased in our particular case? It increased in two ways. Abraham and Sarah and Lot were on our stage, if we understand this for a moment as a stage presentation, as a stage production. We saw these three characters, we walked with them, as it were, from northern Mesopotamia to the land of Canaan, and we thought of Lot as the potential resolution of this conflict. He, however, has now exited the stage, leaving only Abraham and Sarah onstage, and therefore, the conflict has been increased. Furthermore, the promise from God has been increased. Previously, it was, "offspring." Now, it's going to be innumerable offspring, "as the dust of the earth," and if you can number the dust of the earth, so shall your offspring be. Yet, we have no children here whatsoever forthcoming from Abraham and Sarah. There's increase in the conflict and, therefore, we, the readers, want to read on and see how this story will resolve itself.

We move ahead now to Genesis 15 and God speaks to Abraham yet a fourth time. He says, "Fear not, Abram. I am a shield to you. Your reward shall be very great." That's Genesis 15:1. The fourth time God speaks to Abraham with a similar promise; this time, it's "reward." Let's review what these four statements were, then—great nation, offspring, innumerable offspring and now, great reward. Abraham, until this point, has not spoken back to God and finally, he does. He has the gumption, as it were, to speak back in Genesis 15:2 and he says, "Oh, Lord God, what can you give me, seeing that I shall die childless, and the one in charge of my household is Damascus Eliezer? Since you have granted me no offspring, my steward will be my heir." Here, we are introduced to a new character, Eliezer. We now know Eliezer's relationship with Abraham was not only that of servant to master, but also as adopted son to adoptive father. We'll talk about this in the next lecture. We'll talk about some of the legal and social background of this story, as we now know from other sources in the ancient Near East.

So, here he's presented as another potential heir to Abraham. Abraham says to God, "What good is it if I die childless because Eliezer is going to be my heir, my trusted steward?" As soon as he's introduced to us, however, he's taken away from us because God continues in his response to Abraham here in Genesis 15:4: "The word of the Lord came to him, meaning to Abraham in reply, 'That one shall not be your heir. None but your very own issue shall be your heir,'" and when God says, "That one shall not be your heir," it's almost as if we can see the finger of God pointing in the direction of Eliezer, saying, "No, this individual will not be your heir, your very own issue will be your heir." That phrase, "Your very own issue," is an unambiguous statement that Abraham will have his own son. It's a Hebrew idiom, "your very own issue." It means, a son, a child—in particular, a son of your own. Here is the statement being made clearer for us as the readers, in case we thought that somehow offspring could mean something else—a nephew, an adopted son, whatever—here will be a natural-born son.

We now move to chapter 16 in Genesis, the next chapter. Okay, God has promised Abraham a son, but how is it going to happen? Sarah—still unable to become pregnant, to bear child—gives as a gift to Abraham, her handmaiden, Hagar, who becomes a second wife to Abraham. Again, we know the legal backgrounds of this. It turns out that this was Sarah's legal responsibility based on the marriage contractual arrangements that existed in the ancient world. In case a woman was unable to have children, it was her duty to present to her husband a handmaiden with whom he could have intercourse and, therefore, have a son. Again, we'll survey this material in the next lecture, as well. It is through Hagar, then, that Abraham finally has his own natural-born son. That individual is Ishmael, who is born at the very end of Genesis 16.

Now, this brings us to the midpoint of our story. This is the resting place of the story, as it were. We, the readers, now learn that, indeed, God promises and God fulfills that promise. This birth of Ishmael answers the story on a theological level. That is to say, God makes promises and God keeps promises. He promised Abraham a son, even if the language began in some ambiguous fashion, in Genesis 15, it became unambiguous and in Genesis 16 that natural-born son was born to Abraham—Ishmael, through Hagar. I repeat, that answers our problem theologically. It does not, however, resolve our conflict on a literary level and, in this case, the literary must override the theological.

Why do I say that? If we go back to Genesis 11:30, the verse we looked at previously, notice the emphasis there is on Sarah. It says, "Sarai was barren"; she had no child. Think of how the text could have been worded. We like to call that a "countertext." A countertext is a passage that is not present in the Bible. It is another wording that the author could have chosen. The author could have said, "Abram had no child," or perhaps, "Abram and Sarai were childless as a couple." But no, Abram's name is not mentioned in Genesis 11:30. It is "Sarai had no child"; she was barren. Therefore, on a literary level, not until Sarah gives birth will the story reach its ultimate resolution. The conflict, accordingly, still remains not on a theological level, I repeat, but on a literary level, and the literary overrides the theological. Therefore, we have a second half of the story, which commences in Genesis 17.

It is no surprise that at this point in Genesis 17, as we enter the second half of our story, that this is where we have the names of our two characters changed. Abram becomes Abraham and Sarai becomes Sarah. I also note that the name of God changes at this point. Up until this point, only the words "Yahweh" or "Lord" have been used. Here, in Genesis 17, the word "God" or "Elohim" comes into use as well. So to mark the change of names of Abraham and Sarah, we also have, indeed, a second divine name for God at this point. Furthermore, the covenant concept is introduced here in Genesis 17. It was mentioned previously in Genesis 15 in passing and much more specifically here in Genesis 17, with much more verbiage devoted to the covenant that God establishes with Abraham at this point. The symbol of that covenant will be the circumcision ritual, which is also described here in Genesis 17.

More important for the drama that we are presenting here in the Abraham story, it is here where God promises to Abraham and Sarah that Sarah also will have a child. In Genesis 17:16, God says, "I will bless her. Indeed, I will give you a son by her. I will bless her so that she will give rise to nations, rulers of peoples shall issue from her." Abraham's immediate reaction is to state to God, "You've given me my son. You've given me Ishmael. You fulfilled your promise to me." God says, "Nevertheless, you will have a son through Sarah and his name will be Isaac. Not to worry about Ishmael. Ishmael will also be a great nation," and, it states here in Genesis 17 that twelve chieftains will derive from the line of Ishmael, but that the covenant will continue on through Isaac who is to be born to Sarah.

There are a couple of intervening chapters here. In Genesis 18, we have the visit by the angels and, again, they are manifestations of God—to repeat a comment that we made earlier—that, again, talk about the promise to Sarah that she will have a child named Isaac. We then have a story in Genesis 19 about Sodom and Gomorrah and their destruction. Then, we have a story in Genesis 20 about the visit of Abraham and Sarah to the palace of a foreign king, King Abimelech, the king of Gerar, the city in the land of Canaan. Not until Genesis 21 is it indeed stated that Sarah gives birth to Isaac, at the beginning of Genesis 21.

Now, why do I mention all of this? I want to contrast with you the conception of Hagar and the promise that she will have a child in Genesis 16, and the birth of Ishmael, which occurs in Genesis 16. That is to say, in one single chapter, the story of Hagar giving birth to Ishmael is narrated in contrast to the story of Sarah here in Genesis 17–21. We learn in Genesis 17 that Sarah will give birth, but it doesn't occur immediately. The drama is stretched out. We have intervening stories and not until the very, very last moment, not until Genesis 21 after all this material has been narrated, we the readers still can't wait for Sarah to give birth, finally, her conception and pregnancy result in the birth of Isaac in Genesis 21. The point is this—all pregnancies last the same nine months. The issue here is the way the narrator tells the passage of time. That is to say, nine months can pass in one chapter, as it does in the case of Hagar in Genesis 16 or, it can be drawn out. It can be extended with intervening narratives, as happens in the case of Sarah with other stories intervening before she finally gives birth to Isaac in Genesis 21.

Now, I want to talk about the promise that God made to Abraham back in Genesis 12 and 13, and the interrelationship of them. He promised him a child—a son, in particular. Of course, first, we had Ishmael and then we had Isaac. He also promised him the land of Canaan. These two are intertwined. Isaac and the land of Canaan are going to be intertwined in our narrative throughout the book of Genesis. That is to say, you'll recall that Abraham and Jacob both traverse the entire Near East. Abraham, born in Mesopotamia, moves to Canaan, goes to Egypt at one point in Genesis 12. This is the story that we skipped over, but we'll come back to it. In the case of Jacob, born in Canaan, he moves to Mesopotamia, but comes back to Canaan, goes to Egypt, and dies. Isaac, by contrast, will never leave the land of Canaan. He's born in Canaan, he lives his entire life in Canaan, and he dies in Canaan. That's because of the promise that interlinks the gift of the land of Canaan to Abraham and the birth of his son, Isaac. Again, there's no statement to this effect anywhere in the book of Genesis. The reader has to determine this for his or her own self. That is to say, you have to go through all of this material and realize on your own that Isaac never leaves because he is intertwined with the covenant and the gift of the land of Canaan.

Now, as we come to Genesis 21, our stage is too crowded. What do I mean by that? In Genesis 21, we're going to assume Abraham is front and center stage, and he has with him his wife, Sarah, and his newborn son, Isaac, and he also has with him his wife, Hagar, and his firstborn son, Ishmael. That presents five characters on our stage. Now, this is what's called a "crowded stage" because in theater or perhaps, more particularly, we can mention opera here, it's a very difficult thing to have five individuals. There are too many principals here. Let's talk about opera where you can have solos and duets and trios and, occasionally, quartets. Almost never does one encounter a quintet in opera. A couple of geniuses attempted it and did it successfully, most importantly Mozart in Act IV of *The Marriage of Figaro* and Bizet in Act II of *Carmen,* although that latter one is not always produced on the stage because of the difficulty of having a quintet, so that's what you have here. You have five principal characters on the stage when we reach Genesis 21. The stage is too crowded. There is a literary need to remove several characters from the stage and that's what occurs in Genesis 21 when Hagar and Ishmael are removed from the scene. They depart from Abraham at this juncture.

That leaves, on our stage, Abraham, Sarah, and Isaac. Could we have a better ending? Could we have a better ending to the great story of Abraham with his wife, Sarah, and his son, Isaac? Just when you would think that the story should be, "And they lived happily ever after," what occurs? Genesis 22:1–2, a new command from God that Abraham should go and sacrifice his son, Isaac. We'll come back and talk about that story in greater detail in a future lecture, but what I want to point out at this juncture is the following—this is the way literature operates. That is to say, you've all had the experience of reading a novel and you come to a particular juncture where you're saying to yourself, "There're 50, 75, 100 pages left in this story and it looks as if all of the drama, all of the conflict is being resolved. What's going to happen?" Perhaps you thumb through those pages and look to the end to try to figure out what more could the story be telling. What happens? The narrator—let's say it's a 350-page novel and the author's somewhere around page 275 or 300—introduces a new conflict. There's a new drama, a new issue here that requires your attention and that needs to be resolved before the story can come to its ending. That's exactly what happens here in Genesis 22:1–2, when God tells Abraham to go sacrifice Isaac.

As almost everybody must know, that does not occur. He comes very close to sacrificing Isaac, but a voice from God prevents him from doing so at the very last moment. Only then, when that story comes to its conclusion, do we have the idea of Abraham and Sarah and Isaac continuing onward as our trio onstage. But, before we come to that point, we have to have this additional conflict at the end of our story, before we can reach the ultimate conclusion of the Abraham narrative.

The story comes full circle at this point. We'll come back and talk about Genesis 22, as I indicated, in a future lecture, but for the present I want to draw your attention to Genesis 22:16 and 18 where we have very similar language to what we had in Genesis 12:1–3. God is promising Abraham once more that he will be blessed and that the nations of the earth will be blessed through him. Those two passages are the first and last times that God speaks to Abraham in the book of Genesis. There is a little bit of material in Genesis 11 before we come to God speaking to Abraham in Genesis 12. There will be more material about Abraham, including the death of Sarah and Abraham's own death in Genesis 23–25. But, the beginning of Genesis 12 and the end of Genesis 22 are the beginning and the end of Abraham's relationship with God, serving as bookends as the story comes full circle and reaches its conclusion.

Lecture Ten
When and Where Did Abraham Live?

Scope:

This lecture addresses the two questions announced in the title. There is considerable scholarly debate concerning both issues. The dates proposed for Abraham range from c. 2000 B.C.E. to c. 1400 B.C.E. As indicated in Lecture Four, I adhere to the latest possible date. Scholars also debate the location of Ur, the birthplace of Abraham: Is it to be identified with the great Sumerian city in southern Mesopotamia, or is to be located in another city with the same name in northern Mesopotamia? In this case, I adhere to the latter opinion. This lecture surveys the different arguments for the various opinions and presents the reasons in favor of a late date (1400 B.C.E.) and a northern Ur (to be identified with Urfa in modern-day southern Turkey). The lecture also discusses the ancient city of Nuzi (in modern-day northern Iraq), whose archives have provided social and economic parallels to the book of Genesis, as well as the site of Ugarit (in modern-day northwestern Syria), whose epic compositions provide an important thematic parallel to the patriarchal narratives.

Outline

I. One question that continues to vex scholars is: When did Abraham live? By asking this question at all, one clearly is approaching the subject from the maximalist standpoint (see Lecture Four). The minimalists, of course, would not even bother to ask the question.

   A. A standard view places Abraham as early as 2000 B.C.E. This dating typically is based on a literal acceptance of the number of years presented in the Bible, such as the statement in Exodus 12:40 that the Israelites lived in Egypt for 430 years. There are problems with this approach, however.

      1. The numbers that appear in the earlier biblical books, including Genesis, are part of the epic style; they should not be taken literally. Note especially the repeated use of the number 40.

      2. Only from the time of Solomon onward do we get an accurate chronology reflected in the text. This is

attributable to the establishment of the monarchy, with royal scribes now keeping accurate records in the palace.

B. A second option dates Abraham to c. 1400 B.C.E., which is the year that I presented in Lecture Four. This dating is based on the judicious use of the genealogies presented in the Bible, in accordance with the Near Eastern custom of preserving family lineages accurately.

    1. Note that the individuals who appear in the Exodus account (most famously Moses but also such individuals as Nahshon and Zelophehad) are three to five generations removed from the sons of Jacob. This suggests a period of about 100 years for the Israelites in Egypt.

    2. To this day, people in the Near East frequently are unable to tell you how old they are (witness the story related to me by my teacher Cyrus Gordon), but they are able to recite their genealogies with great accuracy.

II. A second question scholars ask is: Where is Abraham's Ur? To which city does Ur of the Chaldeans refer?

A. One view proposes the great Sumerian city of Ur in southern Mesopotamia. [See appendix map: **The Ancient Near East c. 1400 B.C.E.**]

    1. This great urban center was not known to scholars until excavations in the early part of the 20th century by the British archeologist Sir Leonard Woolley, who around 1920 announced to the world that he had found the birthplace of Abraham.

    2. However, in truth, there is little evidence to support this position.

B. A second view locates the Ur from which Abraham came in northern Mesopotamia, specifically, at the venerable city of Urfa in southern Turkey. A number of reasons for this view are presented.

    1. Joshua 24 states that Abraham came from beyond the Euphrates, which works for the location of Urfa, which is in the north, beyond the Euphrates, but not for Ur in southern Mesopotamia, which is on the western shore of the Euphrates River.

2. If one were to journey from southern Ur to Canaan, as per the details provided in Genesis 11, the route would not take one via Harran. This would be the case, however, if Urfa is the birthplace of Abraham.

3. As Genesis 24 and 29 show, when people from Abraham's inner circle (his servant and his grandson Jacob, respectively) return to the family homeland, they journey to the region of Aram Nahariam, that is, northern Mesopotamia.

4. The local tradition among the Jews, Muslims, and Christians of Urfa, in southern Turkey, is that their city is the birthplace of Abraham.

5. The designation in Genesis 11:28 and 11:31, "Ur of the Chaldeans" (*Ur Kasdim*) suggests that the Ur from which Abraham came is the less famous Ur. The great metropolitan center of Ur in southern Mesopotamia would not require an additional descriptive phrase, such as "of the Chaldeans."

6. In line with the above comment, note that the Greek historian Xenophon places the Chaldeans as neighbors of the Armenians, that is, once again in northern Mesopotamia.

III. Once we realize that Abraham came from northern Mesopotamia, we can explain why several customs attested among the Hurrians are reflected in Genesis.

A. The peoples of Mesopotamia, working from south to north were the Sumerians, Babylonians, Assyrians, and Hurrians. Hurrians were in the far north in the northern parts of the Tigris and Euphrates River Valley.

B. The main source of this evidence is the city of Nuzi, in northern Mesopotamia (near the modern city of Kirkuk in northern Iraq; see appendix map: **The Ancient Near East c. 1400 B.C.E.**), which yielded several thousand important cuneiform tablets, dated to c. 1350 B.C.E., providing details about the legal and socioeconomic practices in the town.

1. Childless men would adopt their servants to be their heirs, which explains the relationship between Abraham and Eliezer (see Genesis 15).

2. These adoption contracts furthermore state that if a natural-born son is born, the natural-born son will supersede the adopted son.

3. Marriage contracts from Nuzi state that if a woman is unable to conceive, it is her legal duty to present to her husband a slavewoman as a second wife. This parallels Sarah's presentation of Hagar to Abraham in Genesis 16—and note that Sarah takes the initiative here, because it is her legal responsibility to act.

IV. There are literary parallels from ancient Ugarit (a city in northern Canaan on the Mediterranean coast; see appendix map: **The Ancient Near East c. 1400 B.C.E.**), concerning the childless hero, that are relevant to our story.

A. The Epic of Aqhat concerns the hero Dan'el, a legendary king of Canaan, and his quest for a son, which culminates in the birth of the heroic lad Aqhat.

B. The Epic of Kret, a legendary king devoid of family, has a similar theme.

C. Note that Ugarit also flourished during the 14th century B.C.E.

D. The combined evidence of Ugarit and Nuzi suggests that the 14th century, during which both cities flourished, is the most likely time period when Abraham lived

Essential Reading:

Cyrus H. Gordon and Gary A. Rendsburg, *The Bible and the Ancient Near East*, pp. 109–130.

Cyrus H. Gordon, "The Patriarchal Narratives," *Journal of Near Eastern Studies*, vol. 13 (1954), pp. 56–59.

Supplementary Reading:

P. Kyle McCarter (with Ronald S. Hendel), "The Patriarchal Age," in H. Shanks, ed., *Ancient Israel*, 2nd ed., pp. 1–31.

Questions to Consider:

1. In the long run, does it really matter when and where Abraham lived? Or is this just a case of scholarly curiosity?

2. If the stories in Genesis 15–16 reflect actual ancient social and legal customs (adoption, marriage), why does the biblical text not make this point more clearly?

Lecture Ten—Transcript
When and Where Did Abraham Live?

This lecture addresses the two questions announced in the title. When did Abraham live and where is Ur, the birthplace of Abraham. There is considerable scholarly debate concerning both issues. The dates proposed for Abraham range from circa 2000 B.C.E. to circa 1400 B.C.E. As I indicated earlier, I adhere to the latest possible date, 1400, stretching back to 2000, as well. Scholars also debate the location of Ur, the birthplace of Abraham. Is it to be identified with the great Sumerian city in southern Mesopotamia or is to be located in another city with the same name in northern Mesopotamia? In this case, I adhere to the latter opinion. The different arguments for the various opinions will be surveyed in this lecture and the reasons for our conclusions in favor of the later date—1400 B.C.E.—and a northern Ur—to be identified with Urfa in modern-day southern Turkey—will be presented. This lecture also will discuss two cities from the ancient world, the city of Nuzi—in modern-day northern Iraq—whose archives have provided social and economic parallels to the book of Genesis, and the city of Ugarit in northwestern Syria, on the Mediterranean coast, whose literature provides an important thematic parallel to the story of Abraham.

Let's turn now to the first of the questions we seek to answer: When did Abraham live? By asking this question at all, one clearly is approaching the subject from the maximalist standpoint. You'll recall the division that we referred to earlier among scholars between maximalists and minimalists. The minimalists, who don't see Abraham as a historical figure, would not even bother to ask this question. The maximalists, however, deal with this issue. When did Abraham live? A standard view places Abraham as early as 2000 B.C.E. How did scholars arrive at this dating? This dating is based mainly on a literal acceptance of the number of years presented in the biblical text. Let me explain. We begin, as our starting point, with the date of the exodus. Now, there is a general, scholarly consensus that the exodus from Egypt occurred in approximately 1200 B.C.E.—perhaps 25 years before that, maybe 50 years before that, maybe twenty-five years after that date—but more or less, 1200 B.C.E. That's not something that all scholars agree upon. In the book of Exodus 12 we are told that the Israelites lived in Egypt for 430 years. That would take us back 1630 B.C.E., or perhaps 1650 B.C.E., for the time of the entry of the Israelites into the land of Egypt—that is to say, the story of Joseph and his brothers at the end of the book of Genesis.

Incidentally, there is a statement in Genesis 15 where God tells Abraham that his descendents would be living in a land not their own, for slaves, for 400 years. How do we dovetail the 400-year statement in Genesis 15 with the 430-year statement in Exodus 12? The answer seems to be that the statement in Exodus 12 refers to the entire period of the Israelites' residence in Egypt, 430 years, whereas the statement in Genesis 15 talks about only the 400 years of slavery. The implication being that for 30 years the Israelites lived as free and prosperous individuals in Egypt and that, again, would be consistent with the story of Joseph and his brothers. The pharaoh, under whom Joseph served, looked kindly upon the Israelites. So we have 30 years and the 400 years of slavery for a total of 430 years of the Israelites living in Egypt. This gives us a date, again of 1630 or 1650 B.C.E., perhaps even earlier, 1700, for the time of Joseph. You then work back with Jacob, Isaac, and Abraham and you are close to the year 2000 B.C.E.

This, of course, takes somewhat of a literal approach to the number of years that these individuals lived. The years of the three patriarchs are far beyond the norms of any human lifespan. Abraham, we are told, lived to be 175, Isaac 180, and Jacob 147, and that totals more than 400 years. Clearly, they overlapped to some extent, and so the lifespan of these three individuals is somehow seen to be about 300 years or so and that takes us back to Joseph in the 17th century to Abraham in the 20th century, B.C.E., or perhaps as early as 2000 B.C.E. That will give you some indication as to how scholars figure out the date of Abraham and arrive at 2000 B.C.E. There's a problem with this approach, however, to my mind, and that is, it accepts these numbers all too literally. These numbers are not to be taken in the literal fashion. They are, instead, to be seen as idealized numbers.

Now, let's talk about the number of years that appear in the Bible. In the earlier parts of the Bible, the books of Genesis and Exodus that we're talking about, down through the time of David and Solomon, on the one hand. Then, the years that appear especially in the book of Kings and the latter books of the Bible such as the book of Chronicles and the book of Esther, which are from the time of Solomon onward, the monarchic period and the Exilic and post-

Exilic periods. Now, there is a difference between these two sets of figures that appear in the earlier material and the later material. The difference is as follows. In the earlier books, there was no strict counting of years. There is an epic tradition in the biblical narrative. I have not given you this equation yet. Let me give it to you now.

Biblical narrative is comprised of history plus epic. There is an historical tale that is being told, as we've discussed, and there's an epic overlay and the number of years that appear in these stories and some of the other grossly exaggerated numbers such as the 600,000 Israelites who left Egypt—adult males, that is. This is part of the epic storytelling tradition. This style of writing came to an end in Israel with the arrival of the monarchy. That's because with the arrival of the monarchy, you have a new type of writer who is writing texts, and that is the royal scribe keeping royal annals in the palace. These become much more accurate in their presentation of the years because the annalistic style of writing keeps track of years more accurately than the epic style of writing. So, the introduction of the monarchy under David and Solomon, in particular, brought with it royal scribes and, in fact, in the book of Samuel and in the book of Kings, we have the names and the titles of these individuals—scribes, recorders and so on—who clearly were keeping track of the years of the monarchs.

Therefore, from Solomon onward, we have exact dating. When we talk about the destruction of Judah in 586 B.C.E., or the destruction of Israel in 721 B.C.E., by the hands of the Babylonians and Assyrians, respectively, we are able to affix these events to specific years, or debate, perhaps, one-year differences, so that yes, some scholars may say 587 instead of 586 or 722 instead of 721. But, that's as far as the debate goes because we have such accurate records being kept by the royal scribes in Jerusalem in the south, Samaria, the capital of Israel, in the north, and of course, by the Assyrian and Babylonian royal scribes in Mesopotamia as well, but that's not true of the earlier biblical material, as I indicated. Therefore, one sees the same numbers repeating over and over again, especially the number 40. The Flood lasts 40 days and 40 nights; Moses is on top of Mount Sinai 40 days and forty nights; the Israelites wander in the desert for 40 years. When we reach the book of Judges, events or spans of time take place over the course of 40 years, or sometimes, twice that number, 80 years, and sometimes half that number 20 years. The reign of David is 40 years and the reign of Solomon is 40 years.

I indicated that under David and Solomon you had royal scribes coming into place in the palace and that's true, but the accurate kind of record keeping for the years of the king seems to have taken place only with the arrival of the divided kingdom. Under David and Solomon, you have the end of the epic tradition and so, we can see with those two things that we have a bit of the transition period where they are still talking about forty years this and forty years that. These things can't possibly always happen in multiples of 40, and notice that the period of time that the Israelites were enslaved in Egypt, according to Genesis 15, is also 400 years—that is, ten times forty.

These are, I repeat, idealized numbers and they should not be taken literally. Instead, we can use other information that the Bible provides for us to try to fix the date of Abraham and that is the genealogical material. The peoples of the ancient world and traditional people in the Near East to this day keep very accurate genealogies. They are able to tell you, at least on their father's, father's line, the lineage going back six, seven, eight, nine, or ten generations and they transmit this material accurately, again, especially on the main patrilineal line.

As we look in the Bible, we see something quite fascinating. We see an internal consistency with all the genealogical material that's presented. Furthermore, if we look at the books of the Torah from Exodus through Numbers, we see a number of characters mentioned who are, in their genealogies, three or four generations removed from the sons of Jacob who entered Egypt. Well, let's give the best example, the best and well known example, Moses and brother Aaron and his sister, Miriam. They are the children of Amram, who is the son of Kohath, and Kohath is the son of Levi. Levi is one of Joseph's brothers among the sons of Jacob. That is to say, Levi must have been, along with Joseph and the other brothers, among those Israelites who went to Egypt and lived there freely and prospered under the pharaoh under whom Joseph served. It was his son, Kohath, who must have been the first to experience the slavery and his son, Amram, who was clearly involved in this period as well. And, it was his children, Moses, Aaron, and Miriam, who were the leaders of the Israelites as they left Egypt. Even if we assume that

Moses and Aaron and Miriam as leaders were already advanced in age to some extent, then they would have had a younger generation who would have been leaving Egypt as well. That's why we say three or four generations of Israelites is all there was during the entire period of the going down to Egypt, the slavery in Egypt and the leaving of Egypt.

So, on the one hand, you have a biblical statement of four hundred years in slavery and, on the other hand, the genealogy suggests three or four generations. This is true not only of Moses and his siblings, but it's true of other characters. Nahshon, for example, who was the brother-in-law of Aaron, is descended from Judah, another one of Jacob's sons, five generations away. Zelophehad, a man mentioned in the book of Numbers, is again, five generations removed from Joseph, so the entire slavery must have occurred in about a 400-year period because three or four generations are about a century, assuming 25 or so, perhaps 30 years per generation.

Now, let me tell you a story that was related to me, which is very relevant here, by my teacher, Cyrus Gordon. Cyrus Gordon was involved in the field of biblical studies and archeology quite early on in the 20th century and in 1931, he made his first trip to Iraq to work in some excavations. The scholars—they were mainly Americans and some British—hired the local villagers in northern Iraq to work on the excavations. Gordon noticed within a week or so, that among the workers was a father-and-son team and the son was a very serious, judicious, earnest worker of great value to the excavation team. So one day at lunch—Gordon had already learned enough Arabic to speak the language—one day at lunch, he complimented the father on what a good son he has and what a good worker he was and, of course, the father thanked him. Making that kind of small talk as one does, the next question that came out of Gordon's mouth, as probably any American might ask, was, "How old is your son?," an innocent question. The father responded, "By Allah, I do not know." That's a very common way in Arabic speech. "By Allah, I do not know. He may be 20, he may be 30, he may be 40, but you are a smart man and you can figure out how old he is. He was born one year after the British occupied Iraq."

That happened in 1917 toward the end of World War I, as the Ottoman Empire was coming to an end, and that means the son was born in 1918. That means, in 1931, when this conversation took place, this young man was 13 years old, which Gordon said was exactly what he looked like, a young teenager. But, when asked to provide an age for his son, the father did not know and I repeat his words, "He may be 20, he may be 30, he may be 40; by Allah, I do not know," using round numbers, using inflated numbers, and, in fact, ending with the number 40. I still use this story in my classes today to teach my students. I was a student in Professor Gordon's class and when we came to the passages in Genesis concerning the ages of the patriarchs and how was it possible for Abraham to live to be 100 and Sarah to be 90 at the birth of Isaac, he related this story to us and it still sticks to me today.

We are talking here about people in the Near East who have been untouched by modernity and one can still find such individuals in villages of northern Iraq, isolated in the mountains of that country or of southern Egypt. This would not be true of Middle Easterners who have been exposed to the West in some fashion—people, educated individuals, in downtown Cairo or in Egypt or in downtown Beirut or Lebanon, many of whom can speak English and French and, therefore, have learned the ways of thought that dominates our world as well, and that probably can tell you how old they are or how old their children are. But in that world of these rural villages, you can still see how these individuals are unable to tell you how old they are or their children. At the same time, I have no doubt that this individual, to whom Professor Gordon was speaking, would have been able to recite his genealogy back, as I indicated, six, seven, eight, nine, or ten generations, and when I'm faced with the biblical material that sits before me and I say, "So what am I going to do? Am I going to take these years, which do not accord with the genealogies, or do I take the genealogies because three or four generations can only be a century, it can't be 400 years?" I take the latter route because that is consistent with the Near Eastern custom of preserving very accurate family lineages, but not taking account of how old a particular individual is or how many years have passed from Point A on a timeline to Point B.

Therefore, if Moses and the contemporaries of the Exodus lived around 1200 B.C.E. and the slavery was about a hundred years only, that puts Joseph around 1300 B.C.E. He, in turn, is the great-grandson of Abraham and again, using 25 to 30 years per generation, that brings Abraham back to about 1400 B.C.E. Even if we assume that yes, Abraham was older than the average dad when Isaac was born, still it doesn't put us nearly as far back as something like 1600, 1800, or 2000. That is how I—and those scholars who would take this route as well—date Abraham to about 1400 B.C.E., approximately.

A second question scholars ask is, "Where is Abraham's Ur? To which city does Ur of the Chaldees refer?" Now, one view proposes the great Sumerian city of Ur, in southern Mesopotamia. Let's talk about that city. It was a major metropolis in the ancient world. The Sumerians were the first literate people in Mesopotamia and probably the first literate people in the world. They created a great civilization with major, metropolitan centers, urban centers, of which Ur is probably the most famous. Now, the city was not known to scholars until the early part of the 20th century when a British archeologist named Sir Leonard Woolley went to excavate the place. There he uncovered the great grandeur, lots of gold, remarkable architecture, including the ziggurat in the city of Ur and, literally, thousands of cuneiform documents telling us about the history, culture, economics and so on of the city of Ur. Woolley had announced to the world that he had found the birthplace of Abraham. This was around 1920 and, in fact, he published a book called *Ur of Chaldees,* but there wasn't a single shred of evidence in all that documentation that we have at Ur, in southern Iraq, that this was indeed the birthplace of Abraham. But Woolley, because he was such a well known archeologist, and eventually was knighted Sir Leonard Woolley, convinced the world that he had found the birthplace of Abraham. The idea being that the founder of the monotheistic tradition held sacred to Jews, Christians and Muslims alike could only have come from a city such as Ur in southern Iraq.

What did scholars believe before Woolley did his excavations at Ur? A second view believes that the Ur from which Abraham came is to be found in northern Mesopotamia, specifically, the city of Urfa, still called that to this day, in southern Turkey. As you can see from the first syllable of that name, it retains the name Ur from ancient times. In the 19th century, before the rise of archeology, the local tradition among the peoples of Urfa—Jews, Muslims and Christians—was that this was the birthplace of Abraham. Indeed, as you drive into the city of Urfa to this day, there is a sign, "Welcome to Urfa, birthplace of Abraham." Now, the people have no recognition, no idea about the scholarly debate; they simply hold it as a tradition and we know that this tradition goes back into the Middle Ages and probably further back than that. Now, not every local tradition can be said to be accurate, but in this case, there is a lot of biblical evidence that points to the correctness of this identification.

A couple of points can be raised in that regard. First, Joshua 24 states that Abraham came from beyond the Euphrates. Now, this works for the location in northern Mesopotamia, southern Turkey, but it does not work for Ur in southern Mesopotamia, modern-day southern Iraq because that city of Ur is actually on the Euphrates and to be pedantic, it is on the western shore of the Euphrates River, so that when you went from Ur to Canaan, you wouldn't have to cross the Euphrates. Urfa in the north, however, is beyond the Euphrates and that is where Abraham came from, in my estimation. It's consistent with the statement in Joshua 24.

Secondly, we're told in Genesis 11 that when Terah and Abram and Sarai and Lot set off on their journey from Ur to Canaan, they stopped in the city of Haran, and that is where Terah died, and it was from there that Abraham continued onward chapter 12, from Haran to go on to the land of Canaan. Now, if you were to go from Ur in southern Iraq to Canaan, you would never go through Haran; it is simply not on the way. But, if you began in this northern Ur, you would indeed go through Haran on your way to Canaan. The geography makes sense once more, and I note all scholars agree on the location of Haran, there's no question about that. There is still a city by that name, a relatively large city in southern Turkey near the border with Syria. So, as you would go from this Urfa to Canaan, you would indeed pass through Haran. That would not work, however, for the southern location of Ur that's been proposed.

A third point, as two later chapters in Genesis show, chapters 24 and 29, when people from Abraham's inner circle—and I have in mind here, his servant in Genesis 24 and his grandson Jacob—return to the family homeland, where did they go to visit the relatives that did not journey onward? They go to the region of Aram in northern Mesopotamia. They do not go to southern Mesopotamia. So, when you bring all of this information together and you add to it the local tradition that I have referred to among the Jews, Muslims and Christians of Urfa in southern Turkey, this has to be the birthplace of Abraham. I should note that, most likely, this northern location of Ur is indeed related in some fashion to the southern location of Ur. That is to say, the great urban center of Ur of Sumer had colonies throughout the Near East and probably the northern Ur was established as such a colony of the great city of southern Ur—an outpost, a trading outpost, a commercial venture of some sort.

Let's use an analogy—London, the great city of London, England, and London, Ontario. We know, of course, that London, Ontario must have been founded by people who came from London, England, but let's make one further point on that. If I just said, "London," you would correctly think I was referring to London, England. If I have to refer to a second London, I have to add another term and I will indeed say, "London, Ontario." That's why the Bible, to my mind, says "Ur of the Chaldees" or "Ur of the Chaldeans" because if you just said "Ur," people would know that you're talking about the great Ur, the one in the south. By having to add that term, that expression "Ur of the Chaldees," "Ur of the Chaldeans"—the Hebrew expression is *Ur Kasdim*—that tells us we are talking about a lesser known Ur that has to be identified in some way. Finally, to point out that the ancient Greek historian and geographer, Xenophon, informs us in one of his works that the Chaldeans were neighbors of the Armenians. That is to say, in modern-day Turkey, and that works once more by placing the birthplace of Abraham, Ur of the Chaldees, using this information from Xenophon in Urfa in Southern Turkey.

Once we realize that Abraham came from northern Mesopotamia, we next can explain why several customs attested among the Hurrians are reflected in the book of Genesis. Now, I mentioned the Hurrians before in an earlier lecture. Let's talk about them. The peoples of Mesopotamia, working from south to north were the Sumerians, Babylonians, Assyrians, and Hurrians. They're in the far north in the northern parts of the Tigris and Euphrates River Valley. Now, the Hurrians are known to us from a number of different sites, but the most important Hurrian city is a city called Nuzi, in northern Mesopotamia. It is extremely close, within a kilometer or so, of the modern city of Kirkuk in northern Iraq in Kurdish territory. The city of Nuzi—the heyday of Nuzi was the 14th century B.C.E., the time of the patriarchs, according to our dating—and the city of Nuzi yielded several thousand very important cuneiform tablets written in the Babylonian language, although written with lots of Hurrian words in them, no surprise given the fact that it was a population of Hurrians. These tablets give us the legal and socioeconomic practices of that city at that time. We learn two things, two different practices that illuminate for us customs in the book of Genesis that we mentioned in the previous lecture in which we now can go into in greater detail.

There are, from Nuzi, a series of adoption tablets. These are cuneiform tablets and they tell us about how men would adopt sons. Why did men do this? These were childless men, apparently, and they needed an heir and so they would adopt their servants to be their heirs, which explains the relationship between Abraham and Eliezer in Genesis 15. You'll recall that Abraham says to God that, "My servant, Eliezer, will be my heir." Well, how is it possible for a servant to be one's heir? We've all heard of stories of wealthy individuals leaving their gold watch, perhaps, to their trusted butler, but that's about as far as we would go in our culture. But in ancient Nuzi, men indeed adopted their servants, if they were childless, to be their heirs.

Now, why would a man do this? They would do this because it was important to have a son. You needed somebody to take care of you in your old age. When you died, the funeral rituals had to be undertaken by your son. and then all sorts of other relationships between fathers and sons were necessary. Why would a man like Eliezer or any other such individual from Nuzi enter into such a contractual arrangement? Probably because this person came from a poorer family, a less well-off family—perhaps lower-middle class, perhaps even lower class— and this was a way of earning and gaining an inheritance somewhere down the road when the man you served would pass away. So, it worked for both parties for the adoptive father and the adopted son, and so we assume that underlying Genesis 15 is a relationship of this ilk. These adoption contracts furthermore state that if a natural-born son is born, the natural-born son will supersede the adopted son. That is indeed what happens in the story of Genesis when God says to Abraham, "No, that one—meaning Eliezer—will be your heir, but he who issues forth from you, your natural-born son, will be."

We also have marriage contracts from Nuzi, as we indicated in the previous lecture, and it states in these marriage contracts that if a woman is unable to conceive, it is her legal duty to present to her husband one of her slave women, handmaidens, as a second wife. This explains why Sarah presents Hagar to Abraham in Genesis 16, and note, if you look at that story, that it is Sarah who takes the initiative there. Abraham doesn't make the suggestion. Sarah does; it is her legal responsibility to act. Again, underneath the pages of the Bible—in this case, Genesis 16—is a legal tradition that tells us what the marriage relationship was between Abraham and Sarah, what their marriage contract would have looked like with such a clause built into it. Sarah gives Hagar and that's how Ishmael comes to be born.

I also mentioned Ugarit. Ugarit is a city in far northern Canaan, modern-day northwestern Syria on the Mediterranean coast. It flourished also in the 14th century and into the 13th century, the time we are talking about. We have literary texts from Ugarit, two epics. The epic of Aqhat, which concerns the hero Dan'el, a legendary king of Canaan, and his quest for a son. He is childless and it culminates in the birth of the heroic lad, Aqhat. We have a second story, called the epic of Kret, about a legendary king, as well devoid of family. This piece of literature, this composition, has a similar theme, too. These two Canaanite stories demonstrate that a childless hero's right for a son was a popular motif in antiquity. This is built into the story of Abraham as well.

The combined evidence of Ugarit and Nuzi, presented here in this lecture, suggests that the 14th century, during which both Nuzi and Ugarit flourished, is the most likely time period when Abraham lived.

Lecture Eleven
Genesis 21–22, Abraham Put to the Test

Scope:

Lecture Nine presented the "big picture" of the story of Abraham; in this lecture, we will look at the last two chapters of that narrative in great detail. Our approach will be a close reading of the text; that is, we will focus on the different literary techniques used by the author. One such device, for example, is the naming technique; we will note how Ishmael is never referred to by name in chapter 21, even though he is a major presence in the story. The attentive reader realizes that this is a sign that Ishmael is to be written out of the story at this point, which indeed, is the case. Another device is the accumulation of the words *father* and *son* in 22:7–8—in contrast to the usual economical style of writing encountered in biblical prose—as a harsh reminder to the reader of what is occurring here: A father is about to sacrifice his son.

Outline

I. The style of literature in ancient Israel (and in the ancient Near East as a whole) was an oral-aural one. A single reciter held the text and read it aloud, while the gathered group listened. This style of reading demands reader input and involvement.

II. We introduce here several additional literary devices not previously discussed in the course. Prime among them is alliteration, which occurs frequently in the Bible, in prose texts as much as in poetry.

   A. An excellent example occurs in Genesis 21, with the use of the rare verb *millel*, "utter," in verse 7 (used here instead of the common verb "say").

   B. This verb is selected by the author to create the alliterative effect with nearby verbs, namely, *mûl*, "circumcise," in verse 4 and *gamal*, "wean," in verse 8.

III. A second literary device that we may consider is the naming technique. Note that Ishmael is never referred to by name in Genesis 21; instead, a series of other terms is used, including *son*, *lad*, and *child*.

A. The author employs this literary technique as a sign to the reader that Ishmael is to be written out of the story at this point.

    1. Note, however, that there are no villains in the story, because Ishmael, too, is noble and he, too, will become a great nation (see verse 18 and, earlier, see already 17:20).

    2. Muslim tradition, in fact, which also traces its origins back to Abraham, does so through Ishmael, as opposed to the Jewish tradition, which reaches back to Abraham via Isaac.

B. This clears the way for Isaac to be the only son of Abraham, as stated in Genesis 22:2.

    1. In reality, Isaac is not the only son of Abraham, because Ishmael remains a son. This is a case of literary expressionism, exaggerating reality to stress the point.

    2. As proof of Ishmael remaining a son of Abraham, we take a quick glance ahead at Genesis 25:7–9, where both sons are present to bury their father upon his death.

IV. We use the term *aqedah* (Hebrew for "binding") to refer to the story of the binding of Isaac in Genesis 22.

A. How could God command Abraham to sacrifice his son? What is going on here?

    1. First, we note the larger literary pattern. Just when the story seems to be winding down, with the removal of Ishmael and Hagar from the stage, leaving only Isaac and Sarah at Abraham's side (see Lecture Nine)—at this very point—the author throws us a curveball. A new crisis arises: God commands Abraham to sacrifice Isaac. This pattern is well known from the modern novel.

    2. Next we note that this is only a test, as indicated in Genesis 22:1. This information is conveyed to the reader to ensure that we focus our attention on Abraham without having to worry about Isaac.

B. The statement in Genesis 22:1 leads to the identification of another literary technique in the story: The reader knows something that the character does not know.

    1. We know that God is only testing Abraham, that the sacrifice of Isaac will not really occur, but Abraham does not know this; thus, we focus our full attention on Abraham to see whether or not he will pass the test.

2. If we had not been told this information in verse 1, all of our emotions and sympathies would be on Isaac—what will happen to this boy?—but because we have been informed that this is "only a test" (compare the interruption of a television or radio show: "This is a test of the Emergency Broadcast System"), our eyes are solely on Abraham. We need not worry about Isaac, because we know that he will be fine.

3. The author wants our eyes solely on Abraham to such an extent that no mention whatsoever is made of Sarah. Where was she when all this took place? Did Abraham not consult with her? Did she wonder where her husband and son were for three days? Again, storytellers craft their stories to keep the focus where they want it. The introduction of Sarah into this episode would obfuscate the picture—we need to focus solely on Abraham. (Compare, in the movie *Monkey Business*, how we are asked to suspend disbelief when we see Harpo Marx go into a marionette box during a children's show, yet we do not see the puppeteer who is operating the marionettes.)

4. And the author never lets us forget what is happening here, with the repeated use of the words *father* and *son* in verses 7–8.

C. A simple comment: The story illustrates the move from child sacrifice (practiced by Canaanites and others in the ancient Near East) to animal sacrifice (practiced widely—and the only kind of sacrifice in ancient Israel, where child sacrifice was prohibited).

1. We have evidence of child sacrifice from the site of Carthage, a Canaanite or Phoenician outpost in the western Mediterranean (in modern-day Tunisia).

2. Archeologists there found hundreds of infant skeletons burnt, showing that they were indeed sacrificed to one of the gods.

D. A more complex analysis: The story is the culmination of Abraham's spiritual odyssey. [We noted this briefly in

Lecture Nine, and we will return to this issue in greater detail in Lecture Fifteen.] The words of God's first speech to Abraham in Genesis 12, about how he will be blessed, echo here in chapter 22, the last time that God speaks to Abraham.

Essential Reading:

Nahum Sarna, *Understanding Genesis*, pp. 154–163.

Robert Alter, *Genesis*, pp. 97–107 = Robert Alter, *The Five Books of Moses*, pp. 102–112.

Supplementary Reading:

Shimon Bar-Efrat, *Narrative Art in the Bible* (consult the pages listed for Genesis 21–22 in the index on p. 289).

Jacob Licht, *Storytelling in the Bible*, pp. 115–120.

Questions to Consider:

1. Readers (critics?) of the Bible often ask, "What kind of God would command Abraham to offer his son?" How do you react to this question?

2. At the end of the story, in Genesis 22:19, we read, "Abraham then returned to his servants." What do you find odd about this statement? How do you explain the wording?

Lecture Eleven—Transcript
Genesis 21–22, Abraham Put to the Test

Welcome back. This lecture is devoted to Genesis chapters 21–22, the last two chapters of the Abraham saga that we looked at in an earlier lecture in broad outline. We're going to read these two chapters in close detail and, in doing so, we will uncover a variety of literary techniques that are used by the biblical author. Before doing that, however, I want to speak about biblical literature in a much broader context. One thing that we've noted so far is the manner in which the reader has to be directly involved in these stories—reader input, reader participation. Why is that the case? Why is that so more about this literature than, let's say, modern English literature?

The answer is that in ancient times, and this is certainly true of ancient Israel, ancient literature had an oral, aural quality to it—O-R-A-L, A-U-R-A-L—oral, aural. That is to say, from the mouth and into the ear; one person held the written text. There may have been an oral tradition that indeed was passed down orally, but we know nothing about that material and about that tradition because all we have is the written material that is incorporated into the Bible. And so, somehow and some time in ancient Israel, these texts were written down and they were written either on papyrus, which was imported from Egypt, or of course, made from another kind of reed plant that grows from the Jordan River banks, or they were written at a later time on parchment—animal skins that could be obtained from any of the herds or flocks that were present in ancient Israel. But, there was a single, written text, let's say. Yes, there may have been other copies, but the physical work that was needed to actually make copies—importing papyrus, skinning and preparing the skins of an animal in the case of parchment, procuring ink, and writing them out by hand—all of that meant that there were very few copies of these ancient texts circulating in antiquity. And so, we have one person who would be the "reciter" who held the text in his or her hand, and an audience of people would listen.

How we understand this and in what settings this may have occurred—we don't know the answers to these questions necessarily. They may have occurred in urban settings, in town squares, at the city gates, or maybe in more pastoral settings with the shepherds at night with their flocks resting and the shepherds having worked a hard day, and maybe somebody related or narrated one of these stories. It is because of this "oral/aural" nature of the story that the reader has to always be present at the moment because, unlike silent reading, which did not exist in antiquity, you can't "go back," turn the page back or rewind, as it were, and read that material over again. The reciter, the narrator, the reader—by reader here, I mean the individual who is actually doing the reading aloud—is already on to the next paragraph or the next page, and so you are always present. You are demanded to be involved with the reading process.

Furthermore, the oral/aural nature will explain why there is so much alliteration built into the biblical text, into the Hebrew original. Not all English translations can capture this in the same way and, most frequently, they do not. But, I want to point out an excellent example of this and note it as the first of the literary techniques that we'll survey in this lecture as we look at Genesis 21 and 22. The example I bring to you occurs in Genesis 21:7 with Sarah, "Who would have uttered to Abraham that Sarah would suckle children?" Now, the word there that I have translated as "uttered" is not the normal word for "said." The text could have used the regular word to say, "Who would have said to Abraham," but instead, it is a very rare—an exceedingly rare—Hebrew verb and in Hebrew it is *millel*, and notice the "m" and "l" sounds in that word, *millel*: "Who would have uttered to Abraham?" I'll say the whole passage in Hebrew, in fact, "*Mi millel la'avrha ham.*" We hear the "m" and "l" sounds repeated in that passage.

Now, why did the author pick this very rare verb, which I have translated as "uttered," just to give a variety, a synonym to the word, "say"? In fact, it's a rarer verb in English, of course, because nearby, you have other words that have the "m" and "l" sounds in it alliterating. Those are, most important, three verses earlier, in verse 4, where you have the Hebrew word, *mûl*, meaning "to circumcise," where Abraham circumcised his son, Isaac. We have the verb *gamal*, with "g," "m," and "l" sounds in verse 8 meaning, "to wean," because in the very next verse, verse 8, we read that, "the child grew up and was weaned." And so, you hear those "m" and "l" sounds in relatively common verbs, "to circumcise" and "to wean," and accordingly, in verse 7, between those two, the author reached deep into the Hebrew lexicon to pluck a word, a verb, *millel*, meaning, "to utter," producing the alliteration. The audience who would be listening to this text would be able to appreciate the artistry of the author in utilizing that word and not the regular word, "to say," or any other synonym that might have been possible.

That's our first literary device that I want to discuss with you as we proceed to Genesis 21. The second literary device to note is what we call the naming technique. Now, when you read the biblical text, you should pay attention to the way characters are named, whether their actual proper names are used or whether other terms are used instead. In this chapter, Genesis 21, one of the noteworthy characters who appear throughout is Ishmael and yet, Ishmael is never referred to by name here. You'll remember from our previous lecture that this is the chapter when Ishmael and Hagar will depart from our stage, our crowded stage. They will leave and yet Ishmael's name is never used. Let's look at the chapter and let's look at the text and see how he is referred to.

In verse 9 we read, "Sarah saw the son whom Hagar, the Egyptian, had borne to Abraham playing." It doesn't say with whom he was playing and some texts translate that as "mocking" or "sporting," presumably the object there is Isaac, but it's not stated explicitly. "Sarah saw the son whom Hagar, the Egyptian, had borne to Abraham playing," or mocking or making sport. In verse 10, she said to Abraham, "Cast out that slave woman and her son for the son of that slave shall not share in the inheritance with my son, Isaac." She's using other terms, which make it very clear that, indeed, this is Ishmael, but she's not mentioning him by name. The term she uses, moreover, tells us the way she viewed Ishmael; we have Sarah's vantage point here by those terms. "Cast out that slave woman and her son." She is the slave woman and that is the son of a slave. That's Sarah's take on it. We then read in verse 11, "The matter distressed Abraham greatly, for it concerned a son of his." For Abraham, this is indeed his son, and now we have Abraham's take on this. He doesn't want to dismiss Ishmael from the household just because Sarah has suggested that he do so because this is his son. So yes, this is the same word that was used when Sarah referred to Ishmael, but of course there it was "the son of a slave woman," almost in derogatory fashion. Here, it is Abraham referring to this young man as his son.

In the very next verse, God says to Abraham, "Do not be distressed over the boy," or we might want to translate this as "lad." This is the neutral, the dispassionate view. God views Ishmael in the most neutral terms. He's a boy; he's a lad—not necessarily any emotional attachment to the individual. And then, as we read on in the story, when Hagar and Ishmael do depart, it says in verse 14, "He placed them"—that is, the items that Abraham was giving to Hagar, bread and water—"He placed them over her shoulder together with the child and sent her away." Then, when they run out of water, Hagar says in verse 16, "Let me not look on as the child dies." Now we have the word "child." Why? We have this word because this is a mother and a child. This is a vantage point of Hagar in the third-person narration together with the child, and then, in her own direct quoted speech, "Let me not look as the child dies;" that is to say, Ishmael will be referred to as either "son," the vantage point of Abraham, or as "boy" or "lad," the vantage point of God, or as "child," the vantage point of his mother. That's the naming technique. This is the brilliance of these literary creators in ancient Israel.

Now, back to the main point; the lack of a name for Ishmael, in this story, is an indication that he has one foot out the door or one foot off the stage already. He is being written out of the story and, therefore, his name has been removed from him. Yes, it is my opinion that the ancient readers in Israel, the listeners to this story, would have been so attuned to this story that they would have understood this message very clearly, this literary technique, and would have appreciated it.

As an aside, let's point out that when Ishmael leaves here, this doesn't mean that he is a, quote, "bad boy" or anything like that. There are no villains in our story; everybody is heroic. Indeed, in this chapter, in verse 18, God reminds Hagar that Ishmael will be a "great nation." We already saw that promise made to Abraham in Genesis 17:20 where God told Abraham that 12 chieftains would descend from Ishmael. I repeat—there are no villains; everybody in the biblical material is noble. Isaac may be the chief bearer of Abraham's tradition, but Ishmael himself is a son and is equally noble. Similarly, in the next generation with Isaac's two sons, Jacob and Esau, Jacob will be the main bearer of the tradition; he will be the chief heir, but this doesn't mean that Esau is to be seen in a negative light. He, too, is noble. In this sense, the Bible is similar to the Homeric material. When we read *the Iliad*, we see the battle between the Achaeans and the Trojans, but neither side is to be seen as the bad side or the good side. The Trojans—Hector, Priam, and Paris—are as equally heroic as the Achaeans—Achilles, Odysseus, and Agamemnon.

I also want to note that Muslim tradition traces its linkage, its origins, back to Abraham, whom they see as the first prophet through Ishmael. You'll note that Ishmael goes off in this chapter into the desert and the Muslims arise in Arabia, the desert regions of Arabia, and spread from there throughout the Near East in the 7th century C.E. They were familiar with the Jewish and Christian material in the Bible, and they saw Ishmael as their linkage back to Abraham, as opposed to the Jewish tradition, which as we've noticed, reaches back to Abraham via Isaac.

The removal of Ishmael from our stage, from our scene, clears the way for Isaac to be the only son of Abraham, as it is stated in Genesis 22:2. Now, this is not perfectly accurate information. Let me read that passage. God says in Genesis 22:2, "Take your son, your only one, Isaac, whom you love, and go to the land of Moriah and offer him there as a burnt offering on one of the heights that I will point out to you." Now, obviously, Isaac is not the only son of Abraham. Ishmael, even though he may have left our stage, is still clearly a son of Abraham and, indeed, when Abraham dies in Genesis 25:7–9, three chapters hence, both sons, Ishmael and Isaac, will be present to bury their father. So, he's not really an only son, but the text calls him, "Your son, your only one." This is a case of literary expressionism, exaggerating the reality to stress the point to bring out the emotional attachment, the author calls Isaac Abraham's only son at this point in Genesis 22:2.

With that, we are able to segue into our reading of this crucial chapter, the story of the Aqedah, as it is known in the Jewish tradition. The word *aqedah* means "binding" because that is the extent to which Abraham was able to carry out the actions that God commanded of him. He was able to bind Isaac on the altar and, indeed, was able to raise the knife to kill him before sacrificing him to God, as God commanded, but that's as far as he went when a voice from God commanded him to go no further and not harm the child. Therefore, it's called in the Jewish tradition, the binding of Isaac or Aqedah, and that verb, "to bind," is used in verse 9.

Christians typically refer to this story as "The Sacrifice of Isaac." Clearly, that's not absolutely accurate because Isaac is indeed not sacrificed in this chapter, but Christians will use that term because they see in this story a pre-figuration of Jesus as well. How could God command Abraham to sacrifice his son? What is going on here? First, let us note the larger literary pattern, which we talked about in our previous lecture, but it's worth reiterating that material here again. Just when the story seems to be winding down with the removal of Ishmael and Hagar from the stage, leaving only Isaac and Sarah at Abraham's side, at this very point the author throws us a curveball. The new crisis arises. The drama must continue. The drama must be propelled forward with a new conflict. God commands Abraham to sacrifice Isaac, and as I indicated in the previous lecture, this pattern is well known from the modern novel.

The next point to note here is the way Genesis 22:1 is worded. It reads, "Some time afterward, God put Abraham to the test." Now, what is the purpose of that verse, verse 1? What is the purpose of that information? Let us propose again a countertext. Again, a countertext is a wording that could have been used, which was not used. The author could have begun Genesis 22 with verses 1 and 2 together in some fashion, such as the following. Let me propose a different wording here. "Some time afterward, God said to Abraham, 'Take your son, your only one, Isaac, whom you love, and go to the land of Moriah—and so on—and sacrifice him.' " In that proposed wording, God simply says to Abraham to go sacrifice Isaac. No indication there that this is a test. Now, if we had been told the story in the way I have just suggested, I submit that our emotional attachment would be with Isaac. What is going to happen to this boy? We would have all of our sympathies and emotions linked up to this boy who is about to be sacrificed. But, by telling us that this is a test, that God put Abraham to the test, the author is deflecting our attention away from Isaac and making us focus our attention on Abraham. We the readers know this, but only the readers are aware of this—that God is only testing Abraham here, that the sacrifice of Isaac will not occur—but Abraham does not know this. He's unaware of this. We, the readers, are told this is a test. For Abraham, this is real in verse 2 when God tells him to go sacrifice Isaac, so we focus our full attention on Abraham to see whether or not he will pass this test.

This is a literary device by which the readers of the story know something, but that the character in the story does not know something. Now, typically, when a story is written, the author and his or her readership have a set of agreed-upon rules, as it were. That is that the characters in the story and the readers have the same information. At times, however, you can depart from that norm, as we have here, where the readers know something that the characters don't know or, in this case, the individual character of Abraham. Sometimes we can have the other departure, as we indeed will see in our next lecture, where the opposite can occur—where the characters know something, but the reader has not been informed of something until much later on in the story when the reader becomes aware of the same information that the character or characters have known all along.

When I say in verse 1 that God put Abraham to the test, I'm suggesting here that the word "test" is like our word "test," as we hear it when we're watching television or listening to the radio and there is an interruption and we are told that, "This is a test of the Emergency Broadcast System." When we hear that, we know that there is no real imminent threat or danger, that missiles have not been launched against America, right? That is what we mean when we say it's "a test of the Emergency Broadcast System." This is a test to Abraham. This is not really going to happen. The intention of that verse is to move our focus away from Isaac, as I suggested, and bring it to Abraham and solely on Abraham.

Now, the author wants our eyes solely on Abraham to such an extent, that the text makes no mention whatsoever of Sarah. Let's consider her here for a moment. Where was she when all this took place? Did Abraham not consult with her? God told Abraham to go sacrifice Isaac, the son, whom not only Abraham, but also Sarah had been waiting for, for so long. Both have such an attachment to this boy, wouldn't it have been possible or logical for Abraham to go to Sarah and say something like, "You're not going to believe what God told me to do now! I have to go sacrifice Isaac!" But no, we have no such statement. Did she not wonder where her husband and son were for three days? They went off for three days, according to this story. Again, storytellers craft their stories to keep the focus where they want it. Remember what I said in a previous lecture. Literature is not reality; it is a reflection of reality. In real life, perhaps Abraham did inform Sarah what he was about to do, but in this story, the author does not give us that information. He discloses no such text whatsoever because the introduction of Sarah into this episode would obfuscate the picture. It would introduce an unnecessary character.

This is a story solely about Abraham, and our focus must remain on Abraham. Yes, Isaac needs to be there in the story, naturally, but we're not focusing on Isaac. As we've indicated, we need to focus solely on Abraham. Sarah's presence in the story would totally cloud the issue and so we just remove her or don't include her in this story.

Let me give you a parallel, one of my favorites, out of a 20th-century motion picture, and I have in mind here a scene from the Marx Brothers movie called *Monkey Business*. In that movie, the Marx Brothers are stowaways on a ship and, needless to say, word goes out that they are indeed stowaways, and they have to spend most of their time hiding from the captain and the first mate who are searching for the stowaways. In one scene, the first mate is chasing Harpo—it's always Harpo, of course—through the ship and Harpo makes a quick turn into a room, which turns out to be the children's room where there is a puppet show, a marionette show of Punch and Judy type that the children are enjoying. What does Harpo do? He goes behind the puppet box and into the puppet box after he becomes part of the Punch and Judy show, which the children are now laughing at and roaring about in even louder laughter and voices. What happens? The first mate comes into the room and he sees Harpo there, and he also goes behind and into the box where the puppeteer is working the puppets. However, there is no puppeteer there. We do not see the individual who is operating the marionettes. We see only the first mate and Harpo struggling with each other.

Now, in real life, we know that puppets cannot work without a puppeteer. But when the camera goes behind the puppet box and into it, in fact, we don't see that individual there. We see only the first mate and Harpo. Why—because that third individual would cloud the issue. It would have our eyes focus on another individual who is unnecessary to this scene. Film, like literature, is a reflection of reality; it is not reality. And so, in our story, Sarah cannot be used as a character. We are asked to suspend disbelief when we look at that scene in *Monkey Business* and we're asked to suspend disbelief, I would suggest, here in our story as well, no Sarah present whatsoever.

Let's look at a couple of more literary devices that are used in the narration of the Aqedah, the binding of Isaac. The biblical story typically is economical in its writing style. Do you recognize the fact that the entire life story of Abraham is told ten or eleven or twelve chapters in the book of Genesis, which takes up, in an average English translation, maybe twenty or twenty-five pages? That is contrast to the very long-winded literary style that we have in modern American or modern English literature, where, as we've indicated, stories go on for hundreds of pages, and it is that economical style of writing in the Bible that dominates most of the time in the prose narratives. Every once in a while, however, the storywriter can include extra verbiage when he or she would like to do so. I say "he or she." Most likely, the author of these biblical texts were males, so, for most of the time, I'll probably be content to just refer to them as "males" and use the word "he."

Now, in this case, our author in verses 7 and 8 has included the words "father" and "son" repeatedly, more so than we ever would need in reading the story. Let me read those verses here, "Then Isaac said to his father, Abraham, 'Father?' and he answered, 'Yes, my son?' and he said, 'Here are the fire and the wood, but where is the sheep for the burnt offering?' And Abraham said, 'God will see to the sheep for his burnt offering, my son.' " Did you hear how many times the words "father" and "son" are used there? Especially, verse 7, "Then Isaac said to his father, Abraham, 'Father,' and he answered, 'Yes, my son.' " Shall we do a countertext? How about a simpler wording? "Then Isaac said to his father," or maybe, "And Isaac said, 'Father?' And he answered, 'Yes, my son?' " That would be much simpler and probably more natural, but here we have the piling up of these words, "father" and "son," to remind us, the reader, that this is not just a father and son going for a stroll in the woods, but this is indeed a father going out to sacrifice his son at the command of God.

Similarly, in the next verses, verses 9 and 10, we have a slowing down of the actions as well. That is to say, years pass very quickly in the biblical narrative. Take a look, for example, at the break between the end of Genesis 16 and the beginning of Genesis 17. At the end of chapter 16 Abraham is 86 years old. At the beginning of Genesis 17 he is 99 years old. Nothing at all is narrated about those 19 years that intervene. It is a quick fast forward from Abraham Point A to Abraham Point B, with no words whatsoever, yet at other times, the author can slow down the action, present something in slow motion, as it were. I think this is what's happening in verses 9 and 10. "Abraham built an altar there, he laid out the wood, he bound his son, Isaac, he laid him on the altar on top of the wood, and Abraham picked up the knife to slay his son." Do you hear all those verbs predicated of Abraham? He built the altar, he laid out the wood, he bound his son, Isaac, he laid him on the altar on top of the wood, and he picked up the knife. Step by step, instead of, again, countertext, the author could have said something like, "Abraham prepared to sacrifice Isaac," and we know what you have to do to prepare a sacrifice. You have to build an altar and you have to do this and you have to do that and you have to tie up the animal on the altar and so on and use the wood. But, instead, every single action, it's as if we are being led through these actions, slowly, deliberately, as we watch Abraham going through these actions slowly, deliberately.

The focus keeps growing narrower. If we were filming this, we would see Abraham building the altar, doing each of these steps, and then in the last verse that I read, verse 10, "And Abraham picked up the knife to slay his son," what would we see there? We would see simply his hand holding the knife. We are being moved to focus from the more general picture of Abraham down to the specific of his now holding the knife in his hand, as he prepares to slay his son. Of course, if this were staged on film, if this were done as a movie, the music would be becoming louder and louder with each of these actions, until we could not bear it anymore at which point, in verse 11, "Then an angel of the Lord called to him from heaven, 'Abraham! Abraham!' and he answered, 'Here I am!' And he said, 'Do not raise your hand against this boy or do anything to him, for now I know that you fear God since you have not withheld your son, your only one from Me.'" It's at that point where the story of the Aqedah comes to its dramatic conclusion and we, the readers, are able to breathe a sigh of relief because Abraham does not sacrifice Isaac. Of course, it's not quite the breath of relief that I have just suggested because, as we have indicated from the beginning, we have known all along that this is a test and how marvelously and how wondrously and how nobly Abraham passed that test.

So, what's the story all about? A simple comment first—the story illustrates the move from child sacrifice, which was practiced by the Canaanites and others in the ancient world, and we have evidence of this in particular from the site of Carthage. Carthage was a Canaanite or Phoenician outpost in the western Mediterranean in modern-day Tunisia. The archeologists there found hundreds of infant skeletons burnt, showing that they were indeed sacrificed to one of the gods.

Even though it's in the western Mediterranean, it reflects Canaanite culture because, as I repeat, Carthage was a Canaanite or Phoenician outpost. Not so with Israel. Israel will not engage in child sacrifice; it engaged only in animal sacrifice. So, right after God tells Abraham not to harm the child, he spots a ram with its horns caught in a thicket and he sacrifices the ram. So on the simple level, this story can be interpreted as a way of explaining why Israel does not engage in child sacrifice, but uses only animals in the sacrificial worship of God—in particular, rams, but also goats and cattle.

That's a simple comment, and now, a more complex analysis. This story is the culmination of Abraham's spiritual odyssey. We noted that it begins in chapter 12 and it ends here in chapter 22. The words of God's first speech to Abraham about how he will be blessed echo here in chapter 22, the first and last times that God speaks to Abraham. So we fit that in here once more. I call this Abraham's spiritual odyssey. One cannot imagine a more fitting narrative, one filled with such power and such ethos as this one, to serve as the conclusion to the life story of Abraham and his relationship with God. Genesis 22, the Aqedah, the binding of Isaac, is indeed the appropriate conclusion to Abraham's spiritual odyssey.

Lecture Twelve
Women in the Bible—Sarah and Hagar

Scope:

One of the new avenues of biblical scholarship during the last few decades has been an increased awareness of the many important female characters in the story. This lecture illustrates the point by paying attention to the roles of Sarah and Hagar in the Abraham narrative. The presence of these women in the story stands in contrast to other ancient Near Eastern literature, in which female characters typically do not play major roles. We will explore the reasons for the use of important female characters by Israelite literati in crafting their narratives. Our main conclusion will be that these women represented the people of Israel, a lowly nation, not among the major powers of the ancient world, for whom women, traditionally viewed as the weaker sex, served to exemplify Israel's self-definition.

Outline

I. Before getting to the heart of this lecture, we begin with a literary reading of another theme that appears in the Abraham cycle.

   A. Genesis 12:10–13:4: Abraham attempts to pass Sarah off as his sister, and thus, she is taken into the palace of the pharaoh in Egypt.

   B. Genesis 20: Again, Abraham attempts to pass Sarah off as his sister, and this time, she is taken into the palace of Abimelech, king of the city-state of Gerar (in southern Canaan).

      1. In verse 2, Abraham says *to* Sarah, "She is my sister," as if to say, "I am going to pass you off once more as my sister."

      2. God comes to Abimelech in a dream and warns him that he will die for having taken a married woman.

      3. Abimelech summons Abraham, and the literary device of "X said…X said…" appears in verses 9–10, indicating to the reader that a momentary silence, a pregnant pause,

occurs between the two speeches by Abimelech, with Abraham unable to respond to the charges.

C. A close reading of Genesis 20:12 in conjunction with Genesis 11:29 reveals the very real possibility that Abraham is telling the truth, that indeed, he and Sarah are half-siblings.

   1. In ancient Hebrew the same word (*'ahot*) was used for sister or half-sister or step-sister.

   2. Given that incest is prohibited in Leviticus 18 and 20, we may assume that the Genesis narrative is older than the law in Leviticus. That is to say, no later Israelite writer would have crafted a story in which Abraham and Sarah appear in such blatant violation of a prohibition in the Torah.

D. Although all English translations for verse 13 use the singular *God* to render "*Elohim,*" in this case the noun is actually in the plural (we know that because the verb, which is predicated, is in the plural). Thus the passage should be translated, "when the gods made me wander from my father's house."

   1. How could Abraham be speaking such language?

   2. Abraham uses the word *gods* in verse 13, because he is speaking to a (presumed) polytheist, Abimelech. This is an instance of style-switching, that is, adopting the speech of one's interlocutor.

E. The word *hesed* in verse 13 means "kindness" generally, and that is its surface meaning here, as Abraham describes how he asked Sarah to do a favor for him.

   1. But the word also means "shameful act" occasionally, and it is used in this fashion in Leviticus 20:17, specifically with reference to brother-sister marriage.

   2. As such, I believe that these texts are speaking to one another. Scholars call this "intertextuality."

F. The literary device used here is as follows: The characters know something that the reader does not know; there is a gap in the reader's knowledge, and that gap is filled at a later point in the story, when the reader learns what the characters knew all along.

II. In the above two stories, our sympathy lies with Sarah. Abraham, the male, is the dominator; Sarah, the female, is the passive one. Abraham speaks; Sarah never does—in both stories. She is objectified. Our hearts go out to her.

III. Note further that in the Ugaritic parallels to the childless hero motif (see Lecture Nine), the focus was on the male hero's quest for an heir, with little or no mention of the hero's wife. By contrast, in the Abraham cycle (and elsewhere, as we shall see in Lecture Fourteen), the focus is on the female. Recall the passage in Genesis 11:30 that Sarah was barren and childless (again, see Lecture Nine).

IV. When Hagar is introduced into the picture, however, Sarah becomes the dominator, and Hagar becomes the mistreated one. See Genesis 16 and Genesis 21. Now our sympathies lie with Hagar.

    A. Note that God speaks twice to Hagar in each of these stories, in loving and comforting fashion.

    B. Note that God never speaks to Sarah, except in Genesis 18:15, and then only in very curt language to chastise her.

V. These women represent Israel—the lowly, the marginal, the one in need of God's special protection. These women, whether Sarah vis-à-vis Abraham or Hagar vis-à-vis Sarah, are the lowly, and this is how Israel saw itself. We call this Israel's *self-definition*, and the ancient Hebrew writers used these women to great effect in creating the literature of ancient Israel, including the book of Genesis.

    A. Tamar in Genesis 38—we will read that story in detail in Lecture 21—has the moral upper hand as opposed to her father-in-law, Judah.

    B. In Exodus 2, a woman, Jochebed, hides Moses in the bulrushes, while the father of Moses is mentioned only in passing and is not seen as an active participant.

    C. In Joshua 2, a prostitute named Rahab becomes the heroic figure who helps Israel conquer the city of Jericho.

    D. In Judges 4 and 5, the great Israelite general Barak does not get the glory when the Israelites defeat the Canaanite army. Instead, the glory goes to Deborah, and even more importantly, to Jael (Hebrew: Ya'el), who kills the Canaanite general Sisera by hammering a tent peg into his temple after having deceived him.

E. Note that both times God speaks to Hagar, he finds her in the wilderness. This represents the larger picture of God finding Israel in the wilderness, the major storyline of the Torah.

F. As a later parallel to this idea, note the statement of the prophet in Jeremiah in 31:2, in a later context: "The people escaped from the sword, found favor in the wilderness."

Essential Reading:

Gary A. Rendsburg, "Unlikely Heroes: Women in the Bible," *Bible Review* 19:1 (February 2003), pp. 16–23, 52–53; available at: http://www.bib-arch.org/ bswb_BR/bswbbr1901feat1.html.

Tikva Frymer-Kensky, *Reading the Women of the Bible*, esp. pp. 93–98, 225–237.

Supplementary Reading:

Phyllis A. Bird, *Missing Persons and Mistaken Identities: Women and Gender in Ancient Israel.*

Peggy L. Day, ed., *Gender and Difference in Ancient Israel.*

Questions to Consider:

1. In Judges 9, the hero of Israel (even if aspects of his career are less than noble and stellar) is Abimelech, the son of a concubine (see Judges 8:31), while in 2 Kings 7, the heroes of Israel are four lepers. How do these stories relate to the main theme of this lecture?

2. Although one might "blame" Eve for eating the fruit in Genesis 3, she nevertheless appears in that story as more active than Adam. Identify specific elements in the text that underscore this point.

Lecture Twelve—Transcript
Women in the Bible—Sarah and Hagar

One of the new avenues of biblical scholarship during the last few decades has been an increased awareness of the many important female characters that occur in the story. This lecture will illustrate the point by paying close attention to the roles of Sarah and Hagar in the Abraham narrative. The presence of these women in the story in Genesis 12–22 stands in contrast to other ancient Near Eastern literature in which female characters typically do not play a major role. We will explore the reasons for the employment of important female characters by the Israelite authors in crafting their narratives.

Before we come to that part of our lecture however, I want to spend some time returning to a literary reading of two stories that appear in the Abraham cycle. Twice, once in Genesis 12 and again in Genesis 20, Abraham attempts to pass Sarah off as his sister. Let's look at those two narratives. In Genesis 12:10, soon after Abraham has arrived in the Land of Canaan, having made the trek from Ur in Mesopotamia, a famine strikes the Land of Canaan and this forces Abraham to go down to Egypt. In verse 11 we read:

> As he was about to enter Egypt, he said to his wife Sarai, 'I am well aware that you are a beautiful woman. When the Egyptians see you they will say, 'She is his wife,' and they will kill me, but they will let you live.'

That is to say, Sarah, who is so beautiful, the Egyptians will want to take her into their own homes and into their palaces, but, of course, they cannot do this if they are married. If Abraham and Sarah are married, that would be a case of adultery. So, Abraham fears for his life, that they will kill him in order to, therefore, allow Sarah to be taken because at that point, of course, she would no longer be married. Therefore, he asks her to pose as his sister. They are going to play the role of brother and sister as they go into Egypt, and it works because, yes, Sarah is beautiful and, therefore, the pharaoh takes Sarah into his palace and this is what we read in verses 14 and 15. Things don't go so well, however, in verse 17, "But the Lord afflicted Pharaoh and his household with mighty plagues on account of Sarai, the wife of Abraham." In verse 18:

> Pharaoh sends for Abram and he says, 'What is this that you have done to me? Why did you not tell me that she was your

wife? Why did you say, 'She is my sister,' so that I took her as my wife. Now here is your wife. Take her and be gone.'

Apparently, the plagues which God sent against Pharaoh at this point, was a message to him which he well recognized that somehow he was committing some sort of crime or sin and therefore he determined—although we don't have a lot of details here in this story—that he should return Sarah to Abraham, which is what he does. Then Abraham and Sarah leave Egypt at the beginning of Genesis 13 to return to the land of Canaan. An enigmatic story and a relatively short story, we don't have too much detail, but that is the way the Bible presents it in Genesis 12.

By contrast, as we move to Genesis 20 we have it in a much longer version, a much longer and more detailed story in a second instance where Abraham seeks to pass his wife, Sarah, off as his sister. This time, they don't go to Egypt. They make a shorter journey. They go to the city of Gerar. Gerar is a city in the southern or southwestern part of the land of Israel, or the land of Canaan and there they encounter the king of Gerar, a man who is called Abimelech. The pronunciation of his name is different depending on how one pronounces and how one speaks. In English, he is typically called Abimelech; sometimes in Hebrew, Abimelech; sometimes Abimelech. I'll use the last of those terms when I refer to him. Remember we spoke about how the land of Canaan was divided into a series of dozens of city-states. Here is a classic example of this in the Bible, where the city of Gerar has its own king. In verse 2, we read that Abraham said—and now at this point, we have a problem because the Hebrew text has a preposition, which has a variety of meanings—and it says, "He said to Sarah," or "of Sarah" or "about Sarah". It is a preposition that is hard to determine its meaning. It depends on the context. And what he said about Sarah was, "She is my sister." That, indeed, is how most translators handle verse 2, "Abraham said of Sarah, his wife, 'She is my sister.'" I am reading the Jewish Publication Society Version, but actually I would take the most literal meaning of that preposition there and that is, "to," "Abraham said to Sarah, his wife, 'She is my sister.'" Now the reason translators in fact translated it as "of" or "about" is because it is a little odd that Abraham should say to Sarah, "She is my sister," but I think that is exactly what he said and I think we should translate it that way. Abraham said to his wife, as an aside, almost, "She is my sister," that is to say, "Let's use that plot again. Let's use that ploy. I am going to pass you off once more as my sister," and the same thing happens in this case. Abimelech, the king of Gerar, takes Sarah into his palace.

Now, once again, God intervenes or interferes and this time he appears to Abimelech in a dream. Mind you, that the idea of adultery is mentioned here specifically in verse 3. God came to Abimelech in a dream by night and said to him, "You are to die because of the woman that you have taken, for she is a married woman." In verse 4, the narrator informs us that, in fact, Abimelech had not approached her yet. So indeed, no adultery has taken place in a legal sense but at least he has already taken her into his palace. And then, a long discussion between God and Abimelech in this dream where Abimelech realizes that he needs to return Sarah to Abraham. In verse 9, "Early next morning, Abimelech called all his servants and told them all that had happened," meaning about the dream, "and the men were greatly frightened." That is verse 9:

> Then Abimelech summoned Abraham and said to him, 'What have you done to us? What wrong have I done that you should bring so great a guilt upon me and upon my kingdom? You have done to me things that ought not to be done.'

In verse 10 "Abimelech said to Abraham, 'What, then, was your purpose in doing this thing?'" Abraham will now respond in verse 11 but I want to point out and emphasize again the reading of verses 9 and 10. Verse 9 begins with, "Abimelech said to Abraham," and then we have a quote. And then verse 10 begins again, "Abimelech said to Abraham," and another quote. So the question I pose here is why do we need to have "Abimelech said to Abraham," a second time at the beginning of verse 10? Why not just have the long quote that begins in verse 9 flow directly into verse 10? We have seen other examples of speech that goes more than one verse, two verses, three verses, sometimes even more than that. And this is a literary device which we scholars call, "X said, '…'", "X said, '…,'" that is to say, "Abimelech said" in verse 9 where he then says something to Abraham and then again, "Abimelech said," and then verse 10, where he says more to Abraham.

And the purpose of this literary device is that between verses 9 and 10, you are supposed to see a pregnant pause. That is to say, that

Abimelech asks Abraham in verse 9, "What wrong have I done to you that you should bring so great a guilt upon me and my kingdom? You have done to me things that ought not to be done." Abraham is silent at the end of verse 9. In between verses 9 and 10 in that pregnant pause indicated by this literary device, "X said, '…'", "X said, '…'", you are supposed to see Abraham dumbfounded, not knowing how to respond to Abimelech's question, which is why Abimelech then must continue in verse 10, "What then was your purpose in doing this thing?" If in fact, you had had one single quotation from the mouth of Abimelech to Abraham, that pregnant pause would not be felt. But indeed, it is present there in the text. That, again, is another one of the literary devices as we continue to build our collection of literary devices that the biblical authors utilize. You can add that one to the panoply of literary techniques that we have surveyed so far in this course. Only then, in verse 11, does Abraham respond and he says:

> I thought surely there was no fear of God in this place. And they will kill me because of my wife. And besides, (I am now in verse 12) she is, in truth, my sister, my father's daughter though not my mother's and she became my wife.—verse 13. [My translation reads as follows:] So when God made me wander from my father's house, I said to her, 'Let this be the kindness that you shall do me: Whatever place we come to, say there of me, 'He is my brother.''

Now I am going to come back and talk about the translation of verse 13, "So when God made me wander," in just a moment. But let's go back to verse 12 where we learn some information that is quite shocking and startling, a real surprise for us as the readers of this text. Abraham informs Abimelech and accordingly informs us, the readers, as well, "She is, in truth, my sister, my father's daughter, though not my mother's and she became my wife." Now let's recall that in the ancient world, including ancient Israel, polygamy was permissible, at least men were able to take more than one wife. Women could not have more than one husband but men could have more than one wife. And so, we know the name of Abraham's father. We have learned that earlier in our story, Terah, and we now learn that Terah must have had two wives, one of whom was the mother of Abraham and the other of whom was the mother of Sarah. Now this piece of information affects the way we read this particular story in Genesis 20 because it turns out—and we have no reason to doubt this information as I hope to show you right now—that Abraham, in fact, was telling the truth to Abimelech. When he passed Sarah off as his sister, he did not, in fact, lie. She was indeed his sister. And you may say, "Well, it's only a half-sister", but in Hebrew there is really no way of saying that. It is the same word for sister or half-sister or stepsister. There would be no distinctions as we have in the English language. You could only use the simple Hebrew word, *'ahot* which means, "sister," or, in this case specifically, "half-sister."

But then we, as readers, ask ourselves, "How come we didn't know this information? Why are we surprised here when we come to Genesis 20:12 and we learn this information? Now in the previous lecture, you will recall that at the beginning of the Aqedah in Genesis 22:1, we the readers were informed by the storyteller, by the narrator, that God was putting Abraham to the test, but that was information that we knew but that Abraham did not know. Remember the rules of storytelling and that the characters and the reader typically know the same information. But we saw a divergence from that norm in Genesis 22 at the beginning, where we, the readers, knew something but Abraham, the character, did not know. He did not know it was a test. Here in this particular passage, in this case, we have the opposite. The characters in this story, Abraham and obviously, Sarah, know something that we, the readers, do not know. This has been a gap in the readers' knowledge and that gap is filled only at this point in the story where the readers learn what the characters knew all along.

Then we go back and ask ourselves, "Where should I have known this information?" So we go back to Genesis 12 and we re-read the story of Abraham and Sarah in Egypt where Pharaoh takes Sarah into his palace and no, we did not learn that information there but we are forced to re-read our story because we now want to go back and look at that story in the new light of indeed, Abraham and Sarah, being siblings. Then we go further back to Genesis 11 because we say to ourselves, "Wait. The storyteller gave us genealogical information about Abraham and Sarah. Let's go back to the end of Genesis 11, indeed, before God even spoke to Abraham the first time and told him to go forth from his land to the new land of Canaan, and there we have a wealth of genealogical information.

You remember when we first started reading the story of Abraham in a previous lecture, we looked at the end of Genesis 11 and we learned that Abraham had two brothers and that one of his brothers, Nahor, had a wife named Milcah, and indeed, we learn at the end of Genesis 11, we learn who the father of Milcah was, and we learn a little bit about Milcah's family history. She is the wife of a brother in that family who is of very little consequence, Nahor. The main character, Sarah, or, as she is still called at the end of Genesis 11, Sarai, we are given no information whatsoever about her background. We are not given the name of her father. Why? Because if we had learned there at the end of Genesis 11 that her father was also Terah, that would have ruined the surprise for us that we are here in Genesis 20:12 when through the mouth of Abraham, we learn that indeed, they are half-brother and half-sister—children of the same father but through different mothers. Again, a gap in our knowledge; we never knew anything about Sarah's family, Sarah's origins, her father or anything until this point where the gap is filled, at this later point in the story. The reader learns what the characters knew all along.

This is a literary device that writers like to use, springing surprises on their readers. In film, we can point to a number of examples from recent movies. Two of my favorites are *The Sixth Sense* and *The Usual Suspects*. When you reach the end of those movies, you, the viewer of the movies, learn something that you never knew all along. And what do you have to do at that point? You are forced to re-watch the movie in light of the new information that you learned at the end of *The Sixth Sense* or *The Usual Suspects*. Similarly, here, I submit, here in Genesis 20, we, the readers, are invited to go back and re-read elements of the story, of not the whole narrative, in particular, Genesis 12 where Abraham and Sarah pass themselves off as siblings in Egypt in the palace of Pharaoh and earlier in Genesis 11 where information that we should have learned was, indeed, not given to us.

Now, the marriage between Abraham and Sarah means that, indeed, they are in violation of the laws of the Torah that appear later on in Leviticus 18 and 20. In those two chapters, we have a list of the laws of incest, and among the prohibited marriages are between brother and sister. This causes all sorts of problems, in particular, for later commentators. That is to say, Jewish and Christian interpreters of the later age will be bothered by the fact that Abraham and Sarah violated the laws of God that are presented in those two chapters in the book of Leviticus. There is another example of this in the book of

Genesis as well. Later on in Genesis 29—and we will look at that story in a future lecture in detail—we will read how Jacob marries two sisters. He marries Leah first and then Rachel and that also is in violation of the laws of incest in Leviticus 18 where one is not permitted to marry a woman and her sister. You cannot marry your sister-in-law. That is not a blood issue; nevertheless, it falls under the category of incest, according to the laws in Leviticus 18.

How do we resolve this difficulty? All we can say is that the stories of Genesis must be more ancient than the laws in Leviticus. We have talked about the dating of the biblical material, and in a future lecture, we will talk about the dating of Genesis in much greater detail. But what I would argue here is that if the laws of Leviticus 18 were already in place, and at whatever point they came to be part of Israelite society we cannot determine. I cannot give you explicit centuries here. But in a relative chronology, I can say that the stories of Genesis must be older than the laws in Leviticus. No later biblical writer would have invented a story about Abraham and Sarah being siblings in violation of Leviticus 18 if that were already in place. Similarly, no later writer would have invented a story about Jacob in violation of Leviticus 18 if that law were in place. So the stories in Genesis must antedate the laws in Leviticus. That is the main point I want to make here although, again, I can't pin a century on it. I can't tell you that the laws in Leviticus come from the 7th or 8th centuries and therefore, the stories in Genesis are from the 9th or 10th centuries. But in a relative basis, we can see the picture that I am presenting here.

Now let's go back to verse 13 which I said we would speak about in detail. My translation, and most English translations read, "So when God made me wander from my father's house," but the word there, and that's our word, "*Elohim*," is actually in the plural here and we know that because the verb, which is predicated is in the plural. It should read, "So when the gods made me wander from my father's house." How could Abraham be speaking such language? This is another literary device which we might call "style-switching" of a sort because he is speaking to a person who is presumably not a worshiper of the one God, but presumably someone who is a polytheist and therefore, uses the plural form, "So when the gods made me wander from my father's house." No English translation that I have consulted catches that or renders it in that fashion, but I wanted to point that out to you here. The Hebrew original is actually in the plural and that is a literary device unto itself. Abraham speaking to Abimelech will use the language that Abimelech will understand.

Finally in this passage we have the most delightful literary device that we can encounter, a wonderful wordplay. Abraham says in verse 13, informs Abimelech that he had said to Sarah, "Let this be the kindness that you shall do me" or "do for me" or "do to me". "Whatever place we come to, say there of me, 'He is my brother.'" "Let this be the kindness." This is the Hebrew word, "*hesed*". Now *hesed* means, literally, "kindness". But this is one of those examples in language of a word which means not only its own meaning but actually the opposite as well. We have examples of that in English where "cleave" means "to cut something in half" and it also means, "to cling to." Another example is "scan" which means, "to look at something carefully" and also, "to look at something quickly." And that is true of the word, *hesed* in Hebrew. Its meaning 99 per cent of the time is kindness but it sometimes also means the opposite and that is a negative thing, something that is negative and indeed, in Leviticus 20, that word is used there. Perhaps we should translate it as "disgrace" or something like that. In the laws of incest, it says specifically that the marriage between a brother and sister is an example of *hesed*, it is a *hesed*. It is a disgrace. One could not translate it in Leviticus 20 as "kindness." So somehow, I think these stories, these texts, are speaking to one another. Scholars call this, "intertextuality." The use of *hesed*, normally "kindness" here in Genesis 20:13, where clearly Abraham means it as kindness, also must mean "disgrace" because it was used that way in Leviticus 20 to refer to the marriage between a brother and a sister.

Okay, you have all sorts of examples of literary devices that appear here in these narratives of Genesis, specifically in Genesis 20, which is the longer of the two versions where Abraham tries to pass Sarah off as his sister. Now to the main point about these two stories. When we read these stories, our sympathy lies with Sarah. Abraham, who is the male character, obviously, is the dominator and Sarah, the female character, is the passive one. In these stories, Abraham speaks several times but Sarah never does. Sarah is objectified. She is the one who is taken into the palace of Pharaoh in Genesis 12 and Abimelech in Genesis 20 and our hearts go out to her. The only time we ever may hear any words coming out of Sarah's mouth is in

Genesis 20:5 but it is not from her mouth, it is actually Abimelech quoting Sarah, saying, indeed, "I heard her say that he is my brother," but we never hear Sarah actually speaking in these stories.

Note that in the Ugaritic parallels to the childless hero motif, which we spoke about in a previous lecture, the focus was on the male hero's quest for an heir, with little or no mention of the hero's wife. By contrast, in these stories about Abraham, the focus is on the female. Recall the passage in Genesis 11:30 that Sarah was barren and childless. Not Abraham, but Sarah, so we had that focus on Sarah there. So our attention in these stories is on Sarah and we feel for her. She is the lowly figure in these stories. She is the one who needs to give birth. She is the one who is objectified in these stories in Genesis 12 and Genesis 20.

Now, when Hagar is introduced into the picture, however, something different happens. Sarah, now, becomes the dominator, and Hagar becomes the mistreated one. If you look at Genesis 16 and Genesis 21, you will see that that happens in both stories. Now in these stories, our sympathies lie with Hagar. Not with Sarah who has the greater power over her maidservant, Hagar, but our sympathies now lie with Hagar. Note that God speaks twice to Hagar in these stories, both in Genesis 16 and Genesis 21. It is an angel of God that speaks in Genesis 16 to Hagar, and again, in Genesis 21 to Hagar, and an angel of God, remember, is a manifestation of the deity. We have talked about that earlier in our course. So you have a relatively long speech in Genesis 16. The angel of God, speaking to Hagar, Genesis 16:9-12, four verses, and Hagar speaking back to God in verse 13, and in Genesis 21:17-18, the angel of God again speaks to Hagar. In both situations, she is out in the desert. She fled in Genesis 16 to escape the harsh treatment of her mistress, Sarah and in Genesis 21, she was sent away from the household of Abraham with her son, Ishmael, the story we looked at in detail in a previous lecture, and in both of those cases in the desert, God speaks to her. By contrast, note that God never speaks to Sarah in these stories except in one place, Genesis 18:15 and then only in very curt language to chastise Sarah because she lied. She denied having laughed and indeed God said, "No, but you did laugh," in the story where God tells Abraham and Sarah that they will have a child. So Hagar is the one with whom our sympathies lie and Sarah is the one who dominates her, mistreats her and who never hears God speak in any kind fashion but the one very curt, chastising phrase from God to Sarah in Genesis 18:15.

Now, these women represent Israel. Israel is the lowly, the marginal, and the one in need of God's special protection. When we read about Sarah vis-à-vis Abraham, Abraham is the stronger, Sarah is the weaker and therefore, as I indicated, our sympathies lie with Sarah. When Hagar is introduced into the picture, now Sarah is the stronger and Hagar is the weaker, Hagar is the lowly and our sympathies now lie with Hagar, and this is how Israel saw itself. We call this Israel's self-definition and the ancient Hebrew writers used these women to great effect in creating the literature of ancient Israel, including the book of Genesis. Whenever there are characters in the story that are lowly, they always have our sympathies and they always rise to heroism in some fashion.

Examples: Tamar in Genesis 38—we will read that story in detail later on, and we will see that she has the moral upper hand as opposed to her father-in-law, Judah. In Exodus 2, another woman, Jochebed—Hebrew, Yochéved—she is the one who hides Moses in the bulrushes and the father of Moses is mentioned only in passing and is not seen as an active participant. She becomes the heroic figure who saves the baby, Moses, leading to the salvation of the people of Israel and the exodus from Egypt. In Joshua 2, we have a character named Rahab. She is a prostitute in the city of Jericho, and yet, she becomes the heroic figure, the one who helps Israel conquer the city of Jericho, and the first city they encounter as they entered the land of Canaan. A prostitute from a relatively small Canaanite city that is someone of low social status, somewhat on the social margins, she is the heroic figure in Joshua 2. In Judges 4 and 5, there is a great Israelite general named Barak, but he does not command the glory in that story, a story about how the Israelites defeat the Canaanite army. Indeed, the glory goes to Deborah, a woman, and even more importantly, Ya'el—in the English pronunciation, typically, Ja'el, or Jael, Ya'el in Hebrew, she becomes the heroine in that story and she is called "the most blessed of women". She is a tent-dwelling Bedouin type woman living on the social margins, the desert fringe, and she becomes the one who gains heroic status in that story by killing the Canaanite general by hammering a tent peg into his temple and killing him after having deceived him.

Always it is these lowly figures. Another story I have been focusing on the women here: Tamar, Jochebed, Rahab, Deborah, Ya'el, in our story, Sarah and Hagar. But lowly figures in general are given this kind of heroism. In Judges 8 and 9, we read of another person named Abimelech, no relationship to the person in our story of Genesis 20, Judges 8 and 9, one of the judges, the son of Gideon. Gideon has seventy sons, one of whom is born to a concubine, he is actually the seventy-first son, that's Abimelech and the one born to the concubine becomes the next judge of Israel, not any of Gideon's seventy sons, which, of course, may be an example of hyperbole. And in Second Kings 7, there is a story of four lepers who save the day. The lepers are on the social margins and the physical margins because they must live outside the city. Women, sons of concubines, lepers, always the lowly, Israel saw itself as the lowly. Israel was not among the great powers of the ancient Near East. Egypt was a dominant force, Assyria, Babylonia, the Hittites. By contrast, Israel was a lowly nation without great power. It understood that about itself. Its self-definition is the lowly marginal and it is these characters, which will always come to the fore in heroic fashion as one reads through the Bible.

The stories of God speaking to Hagar in the desert represent Israel, God speaking to Israel. God finds Israel in the desert and supplies water as we see in Genesis 21. To quote the later prophet, Jeremiah 31:2, "The people escaped from the sword found favor in the wilderness"—thus Israel, thus Hagar in Genesis 21.

Essay: The Hebrew Language

Hebrew is actually a dialect of the Canaanite language, along with the other neighboring dialects of Phoenician, Ammonite, Moabite, and Edomite, all attested during the 1st millennium B.C.E. This means that the Israelites could converse with their neighbors with relative ease, as is implied throughout the Bible. Canaanite, in turn, belongs to the Semitic family of languages, along with Arabic, Aramaic, Akkadian, and Ethiopian.

We also should mention here Ugaritic, because we have referred to the literature of Ugarit at several junctures during our course. Scholars debate how to classify Ugaritic: Some believe it to be a separate Semitic language unto itself, while others, myself included, believe it to be another Canaanite dialect, albeit one attested at a slightly earlier time, c. 1400–1200 B.C.E.

Hebrew, in turn, can be subdivided into two regional dialects: Judahite Hebrew, used in the south (the area of the kingdom of Judah), and Israelian Hebrew, used in the north (the area of the kingdom of Israel). Given that most of the Bible emanates from Judah in general and/or Jerusalem in particular, the standard dialect used in the biblical books is Judahite Hebrew. Significant portions of the Bible, however, especially material in Judges concerning the tribal leaders who were active in the north and material in Kings detailing the history of the northern kingdom of Israel, are composed in the Israelian dialect. Because the book of Genesis, as we discussed in Lecture Nineteen, is the product of scribes in Jerusalem, it is not surprising to find the standard Judahite Hebrew used throughout the book.

Hebrew is a relatively simple language. That is to say, for example, there are no case endings for nouns (nominative, genitive, accusative, and so on), as exist in such languages as Latin, German, and Arabic; and verb formation is rather standard and predictable, without the large number of anomalous forms and exceptions that occur in a language such as English.

There is grammatical gender, however, so that nouns are either masculine or feminine, and the corresponding verbs, adjectives, pronouns, and so on must agree. A sample Hebrew sentence, taken from the beginning of Genesis 1:21, reads as follows (in transliteration and with grammatical forms identified):

wayyibra'	*'elohim*	*'et*	*hattanninim*	*haggedolim*
and-created	God	DIR-OBJ	the-(sea)-serpents	the-great
(masc. sing.)	(masc. sing.)		(masc. pl.)	(masc. pl.)

"And God created the great sea-serpents"

we'et	*kol*	*nepesh*	*hahayya*	*haromeset*
and-DIR-OBJ	every	being	that-lives	that-crawls
		(fem. sg.)	(fem. sg.)	(fem. sg.)

"and every living being that crawls [about]."

From this short sample of Biblical Hebrew prose, we may note the following points:

- The standard word order in prose is verb-subject-object, or VSO, in linguistic shorthand.

- Because the subject *'elohim*, "God," is masculine singular, the verb *wayyibra'* must appear in the masculine singular form as well.

- The word order of an adjectival clause is noun + adjective.

- Because the noun *tanninim*, "(sea-)serpents," is masculine plural, the corresponding adjective *gedolim*, "great," must occur in the masculine plural form as well.

- The definite article *ha-*, "the," is prefixed to both the noun and the adjective, with the initial consonant of the word doubled, thus *hattanninim* and *haggedolim*.

- Because the noun *nepesh*, "being," is feminine singular, the corresponding modifiers *hahayya*, "that lives," and *haromeset*, "that crawls," must occur in the feminine singular form as well.

- The conjunction *and* is expressed by the consonant *w* with vowel following and is prefixed to the next word, as in *wayyibra'*, "and-created," and *we'et*, "and-DIR-OBJ."

- Hebrew has a special form, *'et*, that serves to mark the direct object, but this is not translated when rendered into English (indicated here by DIR-OBJ).

As in all languages, basic prose, as in the above and in almost all of the book of Genesis, is simpler than poetry. The latter, which occurs, for example, in Genesis 49 in Jacob's deathbed blessings to his sons, is typically more archaic, both in grammar and lexicon. We may illustrate the point with the use of the word *sut*, "garment," the last word in Genesis 49:11. This lexeme occurs only here in the entire Bible; presumably it was a very rare word, most likely an archaism retained in poetry only.

By and large, however, to emphasize what is intimated above, the prose of the book of Genesis is written in a very basic Hebrew. Almost all of the words used, both nouns and verbs, come from the core vocabulary of ancient Hebrew. Moreover, the same words repeat throughout the book: *man, woman, father, mother, son, daughter, brother, sister, God, covenant, earth, sky, garment, goat, donkey, city, mountain, rock, altar, create, say, go, come, eat, build, sacrifice*, and so on. For this reason, and because the stories in Genesis are so well known, most students of Biblical Hebrew begin their study of the language with material from this book.

The Hebrew language was written in a 22-letter alphabet, invented by the Phoenicians and borrowed almost immediately by all the peoples of Canaan. Note that all 22 letters are consonants (see below for a discussion of the vowels). The direction of writing was from right to left.

Note further that the forms of the letters have changed over time. The inscriptions from ancient Israel use the original letter forms, while the Dead Sea Scrolls and all Hebrew literature to the present day use letter forms that developed sometime in the 5th or 4th century B.C.E.

(The difference between the two alphabets is somewhat analogous to the difference between the Gothic script [also called Blackletter or Fraktur], used in Germany until the 1940s, and the Roman or Latin script, which became the norm in Germany since the 1940s and, of course, is used to write English, Romance languages, and hundreds of others.)

The following chart provides the forms of the Hebrew letters, both the original ones and the later ones; the names of the Hebrew letters;

and their consonantal values. Note that some of the consonantal sounds of Hebrew do not correspond to specific sounds in English.

Original and Later Hebrew Letters, Their Names, and Consonantal Values

Original letter form	Later letter form (incl. present-day)	Name	Value
𐤀	א	aleph	(glottal stop)
𐤁	ב	bet	/b/
𐤂	ג	gimel	/g/
𐤃	ד	dalet	/d/
𐤄	ה	he	/h/
𐤅	ו	waw	/w/
𐤆	ז	zayin	/z/
𐤇	ח	het	/ch/ as in German ich, Bach, etc.
𐤈	ט	tet	/t/
𐤉	י	yod	/y/
𐤊	כ	kaf	/k/
𐤋	ל	lamed	/l/
𐤌	מ	mem	/m/
𐤍	נ	nun	/n/
𐤎	ס	samekh	/s/
𐤏	ע	ayin	(a rough ejection of air from deep in the throat)
𐤐	פ	pe	/p/
𐤑	צ	tsade	/ts/ as in tse-tse or cats, boats, etc.
𐤒	ק	qof	/q/
𐤓	ר	resh	/r/
𐤔	ש	shin/sin	/sh/ or /s/
𐤕	ת	taw	/t/

- Most Jews today pronounce the *waw* as a /v/ sound, not a /w/.

- The letters *tet* and *taw* had distinct pronunciations in antiquity, though almost everyone today pronounces both as simple /t/.

- The letters *kaf* and *qof* had distinct pronunciations in antiquity, though almost everyone today pronounces both as simple /k/. However, because the Latin alphabet includes both <k> and <q>, we avail ourselves of both letters and transliterate *kaf* as *k* and *qof* as *q*.

- The letter ש (next-to-last one in the alphabet) carried two pronunciations, either /sh/ (the more common) or /s/ (the less common). The latter, however, which we call *sin*, was pronounced differently than *samekh* /s/.

As implied above, vowels were not indicated in the writing system. Thus, for example, a string of consonants, such as *samekh – pe – resh*, <spr>, could be pronounced in a variety of ways, including the following:

> *sapar*, "he counted" (past tense)
> *sepor*, "count!" (imperative)
> *sapor*, "to count" (infinitive)
> *sipper*, "he told, he recounted" (past tense)
> *sapper*, "tell! recount!" (imperative)
> *sapper*, "to tell, to recount" (infinitive)
> *suppar*, "was told, was recounted" (past tense passive)
> *seper*, "letter, scroll, written document" (noun)
> *soper*, "scribe" (noun)
> *separ*, "census" (noun)
> *separ*, "Sephar" (toponym; cf. Genesis 10:30)
> *sappir*, "sapphire" (noun)

Readers of texts knew how to pronounce individual words either because they were heirs to an oral reading tradition, passed down from generation to generation, or because the context demanded only one particular possible meaning. For example, in a sentence such as "and David wrote a <spr> to Joab" (2 Samuel 11:14), the word <spr> can only be *seper*, meaning "letter, scroll, written document."

With the passage of time, certain letters came to indicate vowels (though the practice was not carried out consistently), in particular, *waw*, <w>, for /o/ and /u/, especially when long; *yod*, <y>, for /i/, especially when long; and *he*, <h>, at the end of a word to indicate final /a/. Thus, for example, the spelling of the last word listed above was extended from <spr> to <spyr> because the /i/ vowel therein was pronounced long.

In the early Middle Ages, Jewish scribes invented a series of diacritical marks to be placed (mainly) below and (in one case) above the letters to indicate the vowel sounds consistently. At the same time, they created a complex system of additional marks to indicate the accented syllable on each word and the punctuation of a sentence into syntactic units and subunits (serving like our comma, semicolon, and other marks). Yet another symbol—a simple dot in the middle of a letter—was used to indicate the doubled pronunciation of the consonant, as is necessary in the forms *sipper*, *sapper*, and *suppar* cited above.

Finally, it is important to note the following: This system of markings (comprised of dots, dashes, and so on, in various alignments and arrangements) to indicate vowels, accents, and punctuation was simply a physical way of notating in writing a reading tradition that had been passed down orally by professionally (as it were) trained *tradents* (that is, transmitters of the oral reading tradition) for hundreds of years, stretching back to biblical times.

These tradents and scribes are called the Masoretes, from the Hebrew word *masora*, meaning "tradition," and the text they created is called the Masoretic Text, or the traditional text as transmitted within Jewish tradition for centuries. Our earliest exemplars of the text are the Aleppo Codex, written c. 900 C.E., housed for many years in the synagogue in Aleppo, Syria, and now on display in the Israel Museum, Jerusalem; and the Leningrad Codex, written 1009 C.E., housed in the Russian National Library, St. Petersburg (though still called the Leningrad Codex, because it was first studied by scholars and published in the 1920s, when the city was known by that name).

A website devoted to the former, with pictures of each page available for viewing, is: http://aleppocodex.org/ flashopen.html.

For information on the latter, including several photos, go to: http://www.usc.edu/dept/LAS/wsrp/educational_site/biblical_manusc ripts/LeningradCodex.shtml.

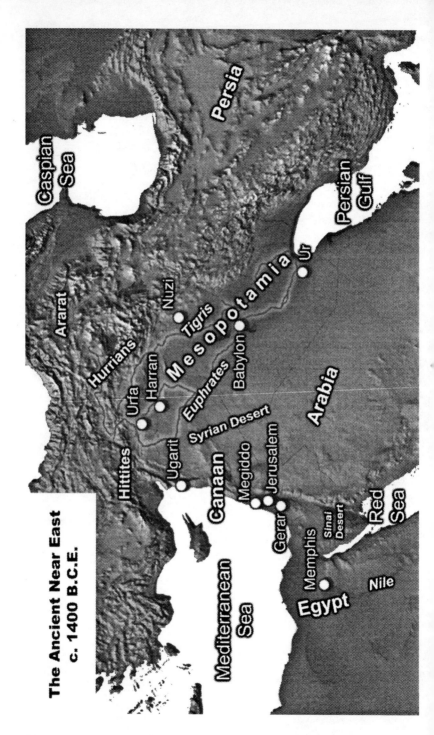

The Ancient Near East
c. 1400 B.C.E.

Timeline of Israelite History

c. 1400–1300 B.C.E.	Patriarchs
c. 1300–1275	Joseph as viceroy in Egypt
c. 1275–1175	Slavery
c. 1175	Exodus
c. 1175–1150	Wandering
c. 1150–1140	Joshua
c. 1140–1020	Judges
c. 1020–1000	Reign of King Saul
c. 1000–965	Reign of King David
c. 965–930	Reign of King Solomon
930–721	Kingdom of Israel
930–586	Kingdom of Judah
586–538	Babylonian Exile
538–333 B.C.E.*	Persian Rule

*Note: Alexander the Great's conquest of Persia in 333 B.C.E. and his rule over the entire Near East, including Israel, from 333–323 B.C.E. brings an end to the biblical period. The succeeding centuries are known as the post-biblical period, the Hellenistic period, the Greco-Roman period, or late antiquity.

Formation of the Canon

c. 450 B.C.E.	Books of the Torah become Jewish canon.
c. 250 B.C.E.	Books of the Prophets enter Jewish canon.
c. 100-150 C.E.	Books of the Writings (e.g., Psalms, Proverbs) enter Jewish canon.

c. 200-700 C.E. .... Christian canon formed, by different churches in the Near East and the Mediterranean, by accepting the books of the Jewish Bible, the books of the Apocrypha, and the New Testament as Scripture.

Biblical Names—People and Places

Note: All names in Hebrew mean something, and frequently, the biblical authors played upon these names and their meanings. In such cases, especially where they are relevant to our course, I have included the meaning of the Hebrew name in parentheses.

Aaron: Older brother of Moses; first high priest of Israel.

Abel: Second-born son of Adam and Eve; brother of Cain (see Genesis 4).

Abimelech: King of Gerar, visited by both Abraham (Genesis 20) and Isaac (Genesis 26).

Abimelech: Judge in ancient Israel, son of Gideon and his concubine (Judges 8–9).

Abraham ("great father"): First of the patriarchs; the originator of the Israelite tradition centered on the worship of one god.

Abram ("great father"): Original name of Abraham until it was changed in Genesis 17. The two names are dialectal variants of each other.

Absalom: Son of David; he led a popular rebellion against his father, which was squelched by David's general Joab, who then killed Absalom (see 2 Samuel 15–19).

Adam ("man"): First male human being according to the biblical tradition.

Adonijah: Son of David and apparently the leading contender to succeed his father, at least until David nominated Solomon as his successor (see 1 Kings 1–2).

Amnon: Firstborn son of David, presumably the one who would have succeeded his father under normal circumstances; killed by his brother Absalom (see 2 Samuel 13–14).

Arabia: Major region to the southeast of Canaan.

Aram: Country to the northeast of Canaan, more or less modern-day Syria.

Aram Naharaim: Literally "Aram of the two rivers," referring to that part of Aram along and beyond the Euphrates River.

Ararat: Mountainous region to the far north of Mesopotamia, in modern-day northeastern Turkey and Armenia.

Asenath: Joseph's Egyptian wife; daughter of Potiphera; our knowledge of ancient Egyptian allows us to explain the name as "the deity is Isis."

Babylon: Major city of ancient Mesopotamia, on the Euphrates River, in modern-day south-central Iraq.

Benjamin: Youngest son of Jacob.

Bethuel: Father of Rebekah, son of Nahor, and thus, a nephew of Abraham.

Bilhah: Handmaiden to Rachel; given to Jacob as a secondary wife.

Cain: Firstborn son of Adam and Eve; brother of Abel (see Genesis 4).

Canaan: Region between Egypt and Mesopotamia, with rather amorphous boundaries, but essentially the land bounded by the Mediterranean Sea to the west and the Syrian Desert to the east; it was in this land that the people of Israel were resident.

Cyrus the Great: First great ruler of ancient Persia; conquered Babylonia in 538 B.C.E., then permitted the Jews to return to Jerusalem and rebuild the Temple.

David: Second king of Israel, c. 1000–965 B.C.E.; son-in-law of Saul.

Dinah: Daughter of Jacob and Leah.

Dothan: City in northern Israel, north of Shechem, mentioned in Genesis 37:17.

Edom: Land bordering Israel to the south in the mountain region of Seir (straddling both sides of the modern-day Israeli-Jordanian border).

Egypt: Great culture of the Nile valley.

Eliezer: Servant of Abraham.

Ephraim: Second-born son of Joseph, who supersedes his older brother Manasseh when Jacob places him first in the blessing ceremony.

Esau: Twin brother of Jacob; son of Isaac.

Euphrates: One of the two great rivers of Mesopotamia, west of the Tigris.

Eve ("living"): First female human being according to the biblical tradition.

Garden of Eden: Legendary location that served as home to Adam and Eve before their expulsion.

Gerar: City-state in southern Canaan (see **Abimelech**).

Greece: Major culture of the Aegean Sea region.

Hagar: Handmaiden of Sarah who became Abraham's second wife; mother of Ishmael.

Hannah: Mother of Samuel.

Isaac ("he laughs"): Second of the patriarchs; son of Abraham.

Ishmael ("God hears"): First son of Abraham, born to Hagar.

Ishmaelites: Desert people living to the south and southwest of Israel; biblical tradition held them to be the descendants of Ishmael.

Israel: The people and culture, resident in the land of Canaan, that produced the Bible.

Israelites: People of ancient Canaan, unique in their religious position, characterized by the worship of one deity; the people responsible for the Bible.

Jacob ("heal-grabber," "deceiver"): Third of the patriarchs; son of Isaac.

Jerusalem: Capital city and religious center of ancient Israel, established by David c. 1000 B.C.E.; location of the Temple, built by Solomon c. 965 B.C.E., destroyed 586 B.C.E. by the Babylonians; location of the Second Temple, built by Jews who returned from exile and dedicated in 516 B.C.E., destroyed by the Romans in 70 C.E.

Joab: David's general (also his nephew), who quashed the rebellion by Absalom, then slew him.

Joseph ("add"): Eleventh and favorite son of Jacob; he rose to high station in the government of Egypt.

Joshua: Leader of the Israelites after Moses, c. 1150 B.C.E.

Judah: Fourth son of Jacob, who is very prominent in Genesis 37–50; the name of the leading tribe of ancient Israel, from which came such individuals as David and Solomon; the name of the southern kingdom from 930 B.C.E. onward, until its destruction in 586 B.C.E.

Laban: Brother of Rebekah, son of Bethuel, uncle and father-in-law of Jacob.

Leah (possibly "cow"): First wife of Jacob, daughter of Laban.

Levi: Third son of Jacob; progenitor of the priestly group of ancient Israel (see next entry).

Levites: Group of men who assisted the priests in the sacrificial cult in the Jerusalem Temple.

Lot: Nephew of Abraham.

Manasseh: Firstborn son of Joseph, who is superseded by his younger brother Ephraim.

Medanites: A semi-nomadic people who traversed the Sinai-Negev region south of Israel; mentioned in Genesis 25:2, 37:36 (though in the latter passage, most translations incorrectly read "Midianites").

Megiddo: Major city in northern Israel.

Midian: Land in the general region of Sinai.

Midianites: Desert people living to the south and southwest of Israel, in the general region of Sinai.

Moses: Leader of the Israelites during the Slavery period in Egypt, the Exodus, and the Wandering that followed, c. 1200–1150 B.C.E.

Mount Halaq (spelled "Halak" in most English Bibles): Mentioned in Joshua 11:17, 12:7 as the southernmost extreme of Israel before one crosses the border into the land of Edom.

Nahor: Brother of Abraham.

Noah: Flood hero according to Genesis 6–9.

Perez ("breach"): Son of Judah, younger twin brother of Zerah, who emerges first from the womb of his mother, Tamar.

Persia: Major empire of the ancient world, centered in ancient Iran, created by Cyrus the Great c. 550 B.C.E., who then conquered Babylon in 538 B.C.E.; eventually defeated by Alexander the Great in 333 B.C.E.

Pharaoh: Title of the king of Egypt.

Potiphar: Courtier of Pharaoh and master of Joseph (see Genesis 39).

Potiphar's wife: Wife of Potiphar who attempted to seduce Joseph, then falsely accused him of rape (see Genesis 39).

Potiphera: Egyptian priest; father-in-law of Joseph; our knowledge of ancient Egyptian allows us to explain the name as "he who is given by Ra," with reference to the sun-god; the name of Potiphar (see above) may be a variant form.

Rachel ("ewe"): Second and favorite wife of Jacob, daughter of Laban.

Rebekah: Wife of Isaac.

Reuben: Firstborn son of Jacob; he slept with his father's concubine, Bilhah, then later tried to save Joseph from the scheming of his brothers.

Samson: One of the Israelite judges, c. 1050 B.C.E.

Samuel: Leader of the Israelites during the transition from the period of the Judges to the period of the early monarchy, c. 1040–1010 B.C.E.

Sarah ("princess"): Wife of Abraham; originally called Sarai.

Sarai ("princess"): Original name of Sarah, until it was changed in Genesis 17. The two names are dialectal variants of each other.

Saul: First king of Israel, reigned c. 1020–1000 B.C.E.

Seir: Mountainous region south of Israel; homeland of Edom.

Simeon: Second son of Jacob.

Sinai: Tract of land separating Egypt and Canaan; the mountain in that region in which God revealed himself to Moses.

Solomon: Third king of Israel, c. 965–930 B.C.E.; son of David.

Tamar: Daughter-in-law of Judah (see Genesis 38); mother of Zerah and Perez.

Tigris: One of the two great rivers of Mesopotamia, east of the Euphrates.

Ur of the Chaldeans: Biblical term for the birthplace of Abraham; many scholars identify it with the major city by that name in southern Mesopotamia (modern-day southern Iraq); to my mind, however, it should be identified with Urfa in southern Turkey.

Zaphenath-paneah: Joseph's Egyptian name, given to him by Pharaoh, which translates as "the god has spoken, he has life."

Zerah ("shiny, brilliant"): Son of Judah, older twin brother of Perez, though the latter emerges first from the womb of their mother, Tamar.

Zilpah: Handmaiden to Leah; given to Jacob as a secondary wife.

Zipporah: Wife of Moses, originally from Midian.

Glossary

'abrek: Hebrew word appearing in Genesis 41:43, derived from Egyptian *ib-rek*, literally "heart to you," or more idiomatically, "hail."

Akhenaten (also **Akhenaton**): Pharaoh of the 18th Dynasty, who ruled Egypt for 18 years during the mid-14th century B.C.E. (suggested dates are 1353-1336 according to one chronological schema). He is most famous for having introduced the worship of only Aten (Aton), the god of light, into ancient Egypt, thereby establishing a short-lived monolatry; his name means "spirit of Aten."

Akkadian: Language of ancient Mesopotamia, known more popularly by the term *Babylonian*.

Alexander the Great: King of Macedon who ruled over Greece, then all of the ancient Near East and more; his victory over Persia in 333 B.C.E. marks the end of the biblical period and begins the period known as late antiquity.

alliteration: The repetition of the same sounds or similar sounds in words in close proximity to each other. In English usage, this usually implies that the *first* letter or sound of each word is the same. In Hebrew, however, the same sounds or like-sounding sounds can appear anywhere in the alliterative words, that is, in scrambled order, for example.

ancient Israelite literati: Collective term used for the writers of ancient Israel who produced the book of Genesis and the other books of the Bible.

ancient Near East: General term for the cultures of the Near East in antiquity, stretching from Egypt in the southwest to Mesopotamia in the east, from c. 3000 B.C.E. onward.

angel: In the earlier parts of the Bible, including Genesis, the term refers to a manifestation of God; later, especially in post-biblical times, the term refers to celestial beings who act as intermediaries between heaven and earth.

annunciation: The technical term for a scene in which a deity reveals to a woman the fact that she is pregnant and will bear a child.

Anteia: Wife of Proetus, king of Tiryns, who attempted to seduce Bellerophontes in the *Iliad*.

anthropocentric: Focused on man, as in the second creation account in Genesis 2.

Apocrypha: Group of eight works (five whole books and three additions to earlier biblical books) that are canonical in the Roman Catholic and Eastern Orthodox churches but are not included in the Protestant Bible; all of these works were written by Jews in the last few centuries B.C.E. but did not become part of the Jewish canon.

Aqedah: Literally "binding," referring to the story of Abraham and Isaac in Genesis 22.

Aqhat: Young hero of the Canaanite epic poem found at Ugarit.

Aramaic: Semitic language closely related to Hebrew.

archaeology: The study of the past, especially human culture, by the recovery and examination of remaining material evidence, such as pottery, tools, buildings, tombs, and so on.

Assyrians: Major people of northern Mesopotamia, centered on the Tigris River; they defeated the kingdom of Israel in 721 B.C.E.

B.C.E.: Before the Common Era; used in the study of religion to replace *B.C.*, "Before Christ," which reflects a Christian view of the world.

Babylonian Exile: The period from 586–538 B.C.E., during which the people of Judah were conquered by Babylonia and taken into exile, that is, resettled in Mesopotamia; the period came to an end when Cyrus the Great of Persia conquered Babylonia and permitted the Jews to return to Jerusalem and rebuild the Temple.

Babylonians: Major people of southern Mesopotamia who replaced the Sumerians as the dominant culture in the area; they exiled the people of Judah in 586 B.C.E. (see also **Babylon** in Biblical Names—People and Places).

Bellerophontes: Valiant and heroic young man in the *Iliad* who was falsely accused of rape by Anteia after she unsuccessfully tried to seduce him.

Bible: Canonical scriptures of Judaism, later adopted as canonical by Christianity (to which were added additional books, most importantly, the New Testament).

Biblical Hebrew: Language in which the Bible is written.

Bronze Age: Term used by archaeologists for the years 3000–1200 B.C.E., during which time bronze (an alloy of copper and tin) was the common metal in use for the production of tools and implements.

C.E.: The Common Era; used in the study of religion to replace *A.D.*, "Anno Domini" (= the year of our Lord), which reflects a Christian view of the world.

Canaanites: People of the land of Canaan, with whom the Israelites shared the region; they never achieved any sort of political unity but, rather, were organized into dozens of city-states, each with its own king.

canon: Books of the Bible officially accepted as Scripture; more generally, the works of a writer that have been accepted as authentic, for example, the Shakespearean canon.

canonization: Process by which the biblical books came to be considered sacred Scripture; this process occurred in stages and took several centuries.

Carthage: Major city in North Africa (near modern-day Tunis), founded by the Phoenicians c. 814 B.C.E. and destroyed by the Romans at the conclusion of the Third Punic War in 146 B.C.E. (though later, the city was rebuilt as a Roman urban center).

chiasm: A literary or rhetorical device in which the words in a sentence or verse, or the units in a larger chunk of text, are presented in one order in the first parallel half, then in inverted order in the second parallel half.

chiastic structure: See **chiasm**.

Christianity: Offshoot of Judaism that developed in the 1st and 2nd centuries C.E., eventually to become the most populous religion in the world.

Church of England: The official church of England since the time of Henry VIII and Elizabeth I, corresponding to the Episcopalian Church in the United States.

cosmocentric: Focused on the cosmos as a whole, as in the first creation account in Genesis 1.

countertext: A hypothesized alternative reading that the author could have utilized, instead of the actual wording of the text.

covenant: Term used by biblical scholars to refer to the bond between God and humanity in general (represented by Noah) and the bond between God and the people of Israel in particular (represented by Abraham).

creation *ex nihilo*: Belief that the world was created "from nothing."

cult: Formal means of religious worship, including ceremonies and rituals.

cycle: Term used by scholars to refer to a series of distinct (and, at times, unrelated) episodes in the life of an individual character that, together, create a narrative unit, such as the Abraham cycle or the Jacob cycle.

Dan'el: Legendary Canaanite king, father of Aqhat.

demythologizing: Conscious removal of mythological elements from a text or story that might have been present in the mind of the ancient reader. For example, Genesis demythologizes when it avoids the Hebrew word *Shabbat*, which meant both "Saturn," a non-Hebrew deity, and "Saturday" ("Saturn's Day").

Deuteronomist: Author of the third source of the Torah according to the JEDP theory, dated to the 7th century, abbreviated as D.

Diaspora: The dispersion of the Jews into lands outside the land of Israel.

documentary hypothesis: See **JEDP theory**.

Ea: Babylonian god who warns Utnapishtim of the flood in the Gilgamesh Epic.

Early Bronze Age: First subdivision of the Bronze Age, 3000–2200 B.C.E.

Elohim: One of the two common names of God in ancient Hebrew, the generic word for "god, deity."

Elohist: Author of the second oldest source of the Torah according to the JEDP theory, dated to the 9th century, abbreviated as E.

Enuma Elish: The Babylonian creation myth, meaning literally "when on high," the opening words of the text.

epic: A story about a human hero or human heroes, in which gods (or God, in the case of ancient Israel) may appear, but with the focus on the human character(s); examples mentioned in our course include the *Iliad* and the Gilgamesh Epic.

eschatology: Belief or doctrine in the end of days, the ultimate or final destiny of humankind and the world, the Messianic Age.

etiological story: A story that seeks to explain the origin of a peculiarity, such as why snakes have no legs but instead move on their stomach (see Genesis 3).

Exodus: Second book of the Bible, following Genesis; also the term used for the Israelites' collective leaving of Egypt according to the biblical tradition.

expressionism: Literary style characterized by exaggerating the reality to stress the point or to emphasize the emotions.

fiat: Literally "let it be done" (in Latin) referring to the method of creation by the spoken word in the first creation account in Genesis 1.

focal point: The centerpiece of a chiastic structure, on which the entire chiasm turns.

form follows content: Literary device in which the style and language of the narrative reflects the action and content of the narrative; for example, fast action may be narrated in snappish style, with the conjunction *and* omitted.

free will: Doctrine by which man's freedom to choose good and evil, and other such choices, governs one's destiny (in contrast, for example, to predetermination or predestination).

Gilgamesh Epic: Great literary classic of ancient Mesopotamia whose main theme is the legendary King Gilgamesh's quest for immortality; its most famous scene is Gilgamesh's visit to Utnapishtim, the survivor of the flood in Mesopotamian tradition.

Greco-Roman period: Period immediately following the biblical period, when first, the Greeks, and then, the Romans held political and cultural sway over Israel and much of the Near East (see also **late antiquity**).

Hebrew: Semitic language used in ancient Israel; actually a dialect of Canaanite. For additional information, see **Essay: Hebrew Language**, which follows Lecture Twenty-Four.

Hebrews: Term used by the Bible to refer to the Israelites; the term is used especially in international contexts, either when the Israelites identify themselves to non-Israelites or when non-Israelites (Egyptians and others) refer to the Israelites.

Histories: Second part of the biblical canon according to the Christian tradition; it includes such books as Samuel and Kings.

Hittite: Indo-European language of ancient Anatolia (modern-day Turkey).

Hittites: Major people of Anatolia in antiquity.

holistic: Emphasizing or concerned with the whole, rather than with the component parts; in our course I take a holistic approach to the book of Genesis, emphasizing its literary unity, instead of concerning myself with hypothesized earlier sources.

Homer: Ancient Greek poet, author of the epics the *Iliad* and the *Odyssey*; his exact date is unknown, but most likely, he lived in the period of the 10th–8th centuries B.C.E.

Hurrian: Non-Semitic language of far northern Mesopotamia.

Hurrians: Major people of far northern Mesopotamia who flourished in the 2nd millennium B.C.E. (see also **Nuzi**).

Iliad: Epic poem of ancient Greece, written by Homer, detailing the war between the Achaeans and the Trojans.

intertextuality: The process by which one text needs to be read in the light of its allusions to another related text.

Iron Age: Term used by archaeologists for the period beginning c. 1200 B.C.E., when iron tools and implements became more and more common.

JEDP theory: Theory that posits four separate sources for the Torah or Pentateuch, which were later redacted into a single work; also known as the *documentary hypothesis*.

Jerome: Church father of the late 4th and early 5th centuries C.E.; translated the Bible into Latin (see **Vulgate**).

Judaism: Religion that sprung from ancient Israel.

Judges: Term used to refer to the leaders of Israel in the period between their arrival in the land of Canaan c. 1150 B.C.E. and the establishment of the monarchy c. 1020 B.C.E.; the term is a misnomer, because essentially, these individuals were military (not judicial) leaders.

Ketuvim: Literally "writings," that is, miscellaneous writings, referring to the third part of the biblical canon in the Jewish tradition.

King James I: King of England during the years 1603–1625 (also reigned as King James VI of Scotland from 1567 onward); commissioned an authorized English translation of the Bible, which was published in 1611.

King James Version (1611): First authorized translation of the Bible into English (see **King James I**).

Kingdom of Israel: Northern kingdom comprised of nine northern tribes, established upon the death of Solomon; existed from 930–721 B.C.E.

Kingdom of Judah: Southern kingdom comprised of three southern tribes, continuing the kingdom established by David and Solomon and ruled by their descendants, though now over a much smaller territory; existed from 930–586 B.C.E.

Kret (also Keret): Legendary king and hero of the Canaanite epic poem found at Ugarit.

late antiquity: Period of history commencing with the conquest of Alexander the Great over Persia in 333 B.C.E.; the setting for the development of post-biblical Judaism and early Christianity (see also **Greco-Roman period**).

Late Biblical Hebrew: Latest stage of the Hebrew language during the biblical period, in use from c. 550 B.C.E. onward.

Late Bronze Age: Third subdivision of the Bronze Age, 1550–1200 B.C.E.

Leitwort: Literally "leading word," a common feature in biblical prose, whereby the same word is used over and over again to unite the various scenes of an extended story or narrative.

levirate marriage: Marriage custom of the ancient Near East (attested to in Israel and elsewhere), whereby the brother of a man who dies childless must impregnate his brother's wife in order to produce offspring for his deceased brother, so that the deceased's lineage will not die out; from Latin *levir* "brother-in-law."

literary foreshadowing: Literary device in which an author drops subtle hints about plot developments to appear later in the story.

Marduk: Storm god of the Babylonians, head of the pantheon, and creator-deity in the *Enuma Elish*.

maximalists: Scholars who believe that the biblical account is essentially historical, even when evidence is lacking from the ancient Near East to confirm a particular point.

merism: Literary device by which two opposites are placed together to indicate the totality; thus, for example, *good and bad* means "all," so that *the tree of knowledge of good and evil* means "the tree of all knowledge."

Mesopotamia: Region of the Tigris and Euphrates Rivers, essentially, all of modern Iraq and parts of northern Syria and southern Turkey.

Middle Bronze Age: Second subdivision of the Bronze Age, 2200–1550 B.C.E.

minimalists: Scholars who believe that the biblical account is essentially fictional unless specific evidence is available from the ancient Near East to confirm a particular datum.

monolatry: Worship of one God, without necessarily denying the existence of other gods.

monotheism: Belief in one God, with a denial of the existence of other gods.

mummification: Ancient Egyptian funerary ritual, characterized by embalming the deceased before the body is placed in a tomb. For additional information, see **Essay: Mummification**, which follows Lecture Twenty-Three.

myth: A story about the gods, in which no human characters appear; such stories were told by all of the ancient peoples, with the exception of ancient Israel, due to their unique understanding of the deity; an example mentioned in our course is the *Enuma Elish*, the Babylonian creation account.

naming technique: Term used to describe the manner in which characters are referred to in the narrative, whether by their names, by various terms, or by pronouns.

Nevi'im: Literally "prophets," referring to the second part of the biblical canon in the Jewish tradition.

Nuzi: Hurrian city in Mesopotamia (near modern-day Kirkuk in northern Iraq); the archives found there date to c. 1350 B.C.E. and provide social and economic parallels to practices mentioned in the book of Genesis.

Old Testament: Term used by Christians to refer to those books of the Bible canonized by Judaism, to which were added the New Testament books to create the Christian Bible.

pagan: Polytheistic.

patriarchs: Common term used for the three individuals Abraham, Isaac, and Jacob, whom biblical tradition consistently saw as the originators of the people and religion of Israel.

Pentateuch: Greek for "five books" (more literally, "five scrolls"), equivalent to Torah.

Peshitta: Syriac translation of the Bible, accomplished by Christian scholars in the 4th-5th centuries C.E. This text is still used today by various Christian communities in the Middle East.

polytheism: Belief in many gods.

Priestly: Author of the fourth and latest source of the Torah according to the JEDP theory, dated to the 5th century, abbreviated as P.

priests: Group of men who officiated in the Jerusalem Temple (or any ancient temple), with their main responsibility being the offering of animals and other food items in the sacrificial cult.

Primeval History: Term used to describe Genesis 1–11, that is, the stories from creation through Abraham.

primogeniture: Inheritance by the firstborn.

prooftext: A clearer passage in the Bible that allows us to prove the meaning of a more obscure passage in the Bible.

prophet: Spokesperson for God, endowed with the dual gift of receiving the divine word and transmitting it to the people of Israel; prominent ones in the biblical tradition include Moses, Samuel, Isaiah, Jeremiah, Ezekiel, and others.

Prophets: Fourth and final part of the biblical canon according to the Christian tradition.

Ptolemy II: King of Egypt; reigned 281–246 B.C.E. in Alexandria; he commissioned the translation of the Bible into Greek known as the Septuagint.

redactional structuring: Literary device by which the individual units in an extended narrative are structured into a unified whole; see also **chiasm**.

redactor: Term used by biblical scholars to refer to the individual who compiled the Torah into its final form; adherents of the JEDP theory date this person to the 5th century B.C.E.

refrain: Phrase or verse repeated at intervals throughout a literary composition, especially at the end of each stanza or section.

royal *we*: The use of first-person plural forms even when the speaker is an individual; used especially by monarchs and similar figures.

Sabbath: Seventh day of the week in Judaism, marked as a holy day.

Satan: Evil adversary of God and humanity, also known as the Devil, the belief in which developed in the very late biblical and post-biblical periods.

self-definition: Term used by scholars for the manner in which a people or culture defines and understands itself.

Septuagint: Greek translation of the Bible, accomplished in the 3rd century B.C.E. by the Jews of Alexandria.

style-switching: The literary device by which an author of a text adjusts his or her language to reflect the specific conditions of a scene. In the Bible, for example, the author incorporates Aramaic words, phrases, and grammatical forms in Genesis 24 and Genesis 30–31, because these chapters are set in the land of Aram.

Sumerians: Major people of southern Mesopotamia who flourished in the 3rd millennium B.C.E. and developed the oldest known writing system; by the time ancient Israel appeared on the scene of history, the Sumerians had long disappeared from the historical record.

Syriac: Dialect of Aramaic used by Christians in the general region of Syria, Iraq, and Lebanon.

Syrian Desert: Large tract of empty land to the east of the land of Canaan; the northern extension of the Arabian Desert.

Tale of Two Brothers: Egyptian story from the 13th century B.C.E., with a striking parallel to the story of Joseph and Potiphar's wife.

Tanakh: Hebrew for "Bible"; the term is an acronym created by the first letters of the words *Torah*, *Nevi'im*, and *Ketuvim*, that is, the three parts of the canon.

Targum: An Aramaic translation of a biblical book or set of books (plural: Targumim), accomplished by Jewish scholars in the 2nd–7th centuries C.E.; there are three Targumim of the Torah, one for the Prophets, and single Targumim for each of the Writings (except for Esther, for which there are two Targumim; and for Daniel, Ezra, and Nehemiah, for which we possess no Aramaic renderings).

Targumim: See **Targum**.

temple: Center of worship in the ancient world, usually through the means of animal sacrifice; the Temple in Jerusalem was built by Solomon c. 965 B.C.E.; the Second Temple was dedicated in 516 B.C.E. early in the Persian period (see also **Jerusalem** in Biblical Names—People and Places).

theology: System or school of opinions concerning God and religious questions.

tithe: A tenth of one's income or wealth given to a religious authority or institution; see Genesis 14:20.

Torah: Literally "teaching," referring to the first five books of the Bible, also called the Pentateuch and traditionally referred to as the Five Books of Moses; the first part of the biblical canon.

Tree of Knowledge: One of the two trees in the Garden of Eden, whose fruit God prohibited Adam and Eve to eat.

Tree of Life: One of the two trees in the Garden of Eden; its fruit was not explicitly prohibited.

Trinity: Christian doctrine that developed in the first two centuries C.E. concerning the three aspects of God (Father, Son, Holy Spirit).

typescene: Literary device in which the same theme or story is narrated over and over again, only with different characters or under different circumstances.

Ugarit: Major city in far northern Canaan, on the Mediterranean coast, in modern-day northwestern Syria.

ultimogeniture: Inheritance by the lastborn.

United Kingdom: See **United Monarchy**.

United Monarchy: The relatively short period of Israel's history when all 12 tribes were united under a single king, c. 1020–930 B.C.E.

Urfa: City in modern-day southern Turkey; traditional birthplace of Abraham according to the local Jewish, Christian, and Muslim traditions.

Uruk: City in southern Mesopotamia (modern-day southern Iraq), home of the legendary King Gilgamesh; it is mentioned in the Bible as Erech.

Utnapishtim: Flood hero in the Mesopotamian epic tradition.

Vulgate: Latin translation of the Bible, accomplished by Jerome c. 400 C.E.

we-hinne: Hebrew word for "and behold," used to change the perspective from looking at the scene from the outside to experiencing the scene through the eyes of one of the characters.

Wisdom: Third part of the biblical canon according to the Christian tradition; it includes such books as Psalms, Proverbs, and Job.

wordplay: Umbrella term used for a variety of literary devices in which the multiple meanings of words are played upon, for example, through double entendre.

Xenophon: Ancient Greek historian, c. 427–355 B.C.E.

Yahweh: One of the two commonest names of God in ancient Hebrew, the specific name of the God of Israel; in origin meaning, most likely, "the one who is" or "the one who causes things to be" but traditionally rendered as LORD (in all caps) in English.

Yahwist: Author of the earliest source of the Torah according to the JEDP theory (see **JEDP theory**), dated to the 10th century, abbreviated as J.

ziggurat: Tower-like temple complex of ancient Mesopotamia, having the form of a terraced pyramid with successively receding stories.

Biblical Scholars

Alter, Robert (b. 1935): Professor of comparative literature at the University of California at Berkeley and a major figure in the literary approach to the Bible. His translation of Genesis was published in 1996, and his translation of the entire Torah appeared in 2004.

Astruc, Jean (1684–1766): French professor of medicine who also worked in the field of biblical studies. In 1753, he proposed that the book of Genesis was composed of two separate sources used by Moses to compile the book, thus laying the groundwork for the documentary hypothesis.

Buber, Martin (1878–1965): Jewish philosopher and biblical scholar, active in Germany through 1938, then in Israel until his death. He developed a unique style of translating the Bible (together with his colleague Franz Rosenzweig) based on the sounds, rhythms, and syntax of the Hebrew original, which he attempted to capture into German.

Cassuto, Umberto (1883–1951): Jewish biblical scholar, active in Italy through 1938, then in Israel until his death. He was one of the first scholars to integrate the study of the Ugaritic literary texts and the study of the Bible. His major publications include commentaries on Genesis and Exodus.

Fishbane, Michael (b. 1943): Professor of biblical studies at the University of Chicago (and previously for many years at Brandeis University). He has written major studies on the literary style of biblical narratives, on intertextuality within the Bible, and on post-biblical Jewish interpretation of the Bible.

Fox, Everett (b.1947): Professor of biblical studies at Clark University, Worcester, MA; translator of the Torah and Samuel (other books are in progress), using a unique translation method borrowed from his spiritual mentors, Martin Buber and Franz Rosenzweig.

Gordon, Cyrus (1908–2001): One of the leading scholars of the Bible and the ancient Near East in the 20th century. He was active in the field for about seven decades, teaching at Dropsie College, Brandeis University, and New York University (where I studied with him during the years 1975–1980). His autobiography, *A Scholar's Odyssey* (2000), is a delightful read.

Langton, Stephen (c. 1150–1228): Archbishop of Canterbury (head of the Catholic Church in England) who created the system of chapter and verse divisions in the Bible. He also is famous for his role in siding with the English barons in their successful attempt to get King John to sign the Magna Carta.

Rosenzweig, Frank (1886–1929): Jewish philosopher and biblical scholar in Germany. He collaborated with Martin Buber on a unique translation of the Bible into German based on the sounds, syntax, and rhythms of the Hebrew original.

Sasson, Jack (b. 1941): Contemporary biblical scholar, who has made major contributions to the study of the literature of the Bible and the society of the ancient Near East. He taught for many years at the University of North Carolina and now teaches at Vanderbilt University.

Smith, George (1840–1876): British amateur Assyriologist (that is, one expert in the study of ancient Mesopotamia), who first discovered the Babylonian flood account on a tablet in the British Museum in 1872.

Tyndale, William (1484–1536): Early translator of the Bible into English. He was condemned as a heretic, both by the Catholic Church and by the newly established Church of England. Tyndale fled England for the Continent; eventually, he was burned at the stake in Belgium.

Wellhausen, Julius (1844–1918): German biblical scholar who created the classical and most widely accepted version of the JEDP theory in 1878.

Woolley, Leonard (1880–1960): Excavator of major ancient Near Eastern sites, most famously, the great Sumerian city of Ur in southern Mesopotamia.

Wycliffe, John (1320–1384): Early translator of the Bible into English. The Church condemned him for this action and ordered that his books be burned.

Bibliography

Translations:

Alter, Robert. *The Five Books of Moses*. New York: W.W. Norton, 2004. A superb translation of the Torah by a master reader of ancient Hebrew prose, replete with notes explicating the literary devices used by the ancient Israelite literati.

―――. *Genesis*. New York: W.W. Norton, 1996. The first book of the Bible translated by Alter, which later was incorporated into *The Five Books of Moses*, described above.

Fox, Everett. *The Five Books of Moses*. New York: Schocken, 1995. A unique translation of the Bible that attempts to replicate as closely as possible the sounds, syntax, and cadence of the Hebrew original. Often, this results in an odd-sounding English, but for readers who want to know exactly how the biblical text is worded, this is the best guide available.

The Jewish Study Bible. New York: Oxford University Press, 2004. A recent volume, gaining popularity in college classrooms today. The translation used is the New Jewish Publication Society Version, produced in the 1960s and 1970s, which takes an idiomatic (and, therefore, less literal) approach to the biblical text. The volume includes detailed notes and fine essays, two of which are included below (one under Essential Reading and one under Supplementary Reading).

King James Version. The first authorized translation of the Bible into English, accomplished by a committee of scholars sponsored by King James I of England and completed in 1611. The work is available in a variety of editions, and free access is available on a number of Web sites, including, for example, http://etext.virginia.edu/kjv.browse.html, http://www.hti.umich.edu/k/kjv/ and http://www.bartleby.com/108/.

The New American Bible. Grand Rapids, MI: Catholic World Press, 1997. The standard translation of the Bible in use by North American Catholics. It first appeared in 1970, and it has appeared in a variety of editions since then. The text is available online at http://www.usccb.org/nab/bible/index.htm.

The New Oxford Annotated Bible. New York: Oxford University Press, 1982. An edition of the Bible commonly used in college classrooms today, incorporating the Revised Standard Version, the translation used by most Protestant mainline churches in the United States, along with useful notes, maps, and other material.

Oxford Study Bible. New York: Oxford University Press, 1992. An edition of the Bible commonly used in college classrooms today, incorporating the Revised English Version, a translation produced by scholars from the British Isles representing different denominations, along with useful notes, maps, and other material.

Zondervan NIV Study Bible. Grand Rapids, MI: Zondervan, 2002. This volume includes the New International Version, a translation sponsored by the International Bible Society and widely used by Evangelical Christians. The text of the NIV is available online at http://www.ibs.org/niv/.

Essential Reading:

Alter, Robert. *The Art of Biblical Narrative*. New York: Basic Books, 1981. A masterful guide to the Bible as literature, with a particular emphasis on the prose material. This volume includes treatments of several stories in the book of Genesis.

Berlin, Adele. *Poetics and Interpretation of Biblical Narrative*. Winona Lake, IN: Eisenbrauns, 1994. A readable guide to the workings of biblical prose, describing the many techniques present in the text, including, for example, the naming technique and the use of the term *we-hinne*, "and behold."

Friedman, Richard E. *Who Wrote the Bible?* New York: Summit, 1987. The best introduction to the JEDP theory, or documentary hypothesis, available. The author presents the theory in its classic formulation, along with a few of his own original insights and contributions. A very readable work.

Frymer-Kensky, Tikva. *Reading the Women of the Bible*. New York: Schocken, 2002. The definitive work on biblical stories centered on female characters. Because so many of the stories in Genesis focus on women, Frymer-Kensky's book makes for essential reading. As a bonus, the author offers her own translations of the biblical texts scrutinized.

Goldin, Judah. "The Youngest Son, or Where Does Genesis 38 Belong?" *Journal of Biblical Literature*, vol. 96 (1977), pp. 27–44. A seminal article in a scholarly journal on one of the dominant motifs in the book of Genesis: the vaulting of the younger brother over the firstborn.

Gordon, Cyrus H. "The Patriarchal Narratives." *Journal of Near Eastern Studies*, vol. 13 (1954), pp. 56–59. A short, scholarly article situating the patriarchs in time and place, with the dual conclusion that the main characters in Genesis date to the Late Bronze Age and that Ur of the Chaldeans, the birthplace of Abraham, is to be identified with Urfa in northern Mesopotamia.

Gordon, Cyrus H., and Gary A. Rendsburg. *The Bible and the Ancient Near East*. New York: W.W. Norton, 1997. A basic introduction to the Bible set against the backdrop of ancient Near Eastern history, society, law, and religion.

Greenspahn, Frederick. *When Brothers Dwell Together: The Preeminence of Younger Siblings in the Hebrew Bible*. New York: Oxford University Press, 1994. A detailed investigation into one of the dominant motifs in the book of Genesis and the Bible as a whole, that of the younger son, as discussed in our course.

Greenspoon, Leonard. "Jewish Translations of the Bible," in A. Berlin and M. Z. Brettler, eds., *The Jewish Study Bible*. New York: Oxford University Press, 2004, pp. 2005–2020. A fine survey of the many translations of the Bible produced under Jewish auspices, spanning more than 2,000 years, from the Septuagint in the 3rd century B.C.E. to the most recent effort of Everett Fox. The volume as a whole, incidentally, is an outstanding reference work, with introductions to each of the biblical books, a running commentary, and excellent essays at the back of the volume (including this one, for example).

Heidel, Alexander. *The Gilgamesh Epic and Old Testament Parallels*. Chicago: University of Chicago Press, 1963. This work is dated, but it nevertheless remains as a serviceable introduction to a comparison between the Babylonian and biblical flood traditions.

Hoffmeier, James K. *Israel in Egypt: The Evidence for the Authenticity of the Exodus Tradition*. New York: Oxford University Press, 1997. A fine treatment of all the Egyptological data relevant to the biblical traditions recorded in the end of Genesis and the beginning of Exodus. Although the emphasis in this book is on the latter material (that is, the Slavery, the Plagues, and the Exodus), the work includes a fine chapter on the Joseph story as well.

Rendsburg, Gary A. "Confused Language as a Deliberate Literary Device in Biblical Hebrew Narrative." *Journal of Hebrew Scriptures*, vol. 2 (1998–1999), available on the Web at http://www.arts.ualberta.ca/JHS/. A scholarly article in an online journal treating the literary device of confused language to reflect the confusion or bewilderment of the moment. Two examples from Genesis 37 are included in this article.

———. "An Essay on Israelite Religion," in Jacob Neusner, ed., *Approaches to Ancient Judaism*, New Series, vol. 8. Atlanta: Scholars Press, 1995, pp. 1–17. A basic introduction to the official religion of ancient Israel, that is, the worship of God as espoused by the authors of the biblical books (with occasional side comments about popular trends in ancient Israel).

———. "The Genesis of the Bible," in *The Blanche and Irving Laurie Chair in Jewish History*, Separatum published by the Allen and Joan Bildner Center for the Study of Jewish Life, Rutgers, 2005, pp. 11–30; available at: http://jewishstudies.rutgers.edu/faculty/grendsburg/genesis.pdf. The inaugural lecture delivered by the professor of this course upon assuming his position at Rutgers University in 2004. The article presents in detail the arguments for dating the book of Genesis to the 10th century B.C.E., along with the author's theory for assuming that an earlier poetic account underlies the large prose narrative that extends from Exodus through Samuel. (See also the next entry.)

———. "Reading David in Genesis: How We Know the Torah Was Written in the Tenth Century B.C.E." *Bible Review* 17:1 (February 2001), pp. 20–33, 46; available at: http://www.bib-arch.org/bswb_BR/brf01reading_david.html. A more popular version of the author's theory that the book of Genesis dates to the 10th century B.C.E. This article also includes a basic critique of the JEDP theory.

———. *The Redaction of Genesis*. Winona Lake, IN: Eisenbrauns, 1986. A detailed presentation of the literary structure of the entire book of Genesis. This monograph demonstrates the patterns inherent in the four major cycles (Primeval, Abraham, Jacob, Joseph), along with the linking material, then discusses how the redactional structuring militates against the division of Genesis into the postulated sources J, E, and P.

————. "Unlikely Heroes: Women in the Bible." *Bible Review* 19:1 (February 2003), pp. 16–23, 52–53; available at: http://www.bib-arch.org/bswb_BR/ bswbbr1901feat1.html. A basic article on the use of women in the Bible as reflections of Israel's self-definition, that is, women (and Israel) as the lowly and marginal.

Roaf, Michael. *The Cultural Atlas of Mesopotamia and the Ancient Near East.* New York: Facts on File, 1990. An excellent survey of the culture and history of the various peoples of Mesopotamia and environs, including the Sumerians, Babylonians, Assyrians, Hurrians, and Hittites.

Sarna, Nahum. *Understanding Genesis.* New York: Schocken, 1970. A first-rate survey of the book of Genesis, with full control of all the scholarly material yet presented in a very readable fashion.

Shanks, Hershel, ed. *Ancient Israel*, 2nd ed. Washington, DC: Biblical Archaeology Society, 1999. An excellent survey of the history of ancient Israel, extending from Israel's origins through the Roman period. The first chapter in the book, by P. Kyle McCarter (with Ronald S. Hendel), surveys the patriarchal narratives.

Sternberg, Meir. *The Poetics of Biblical Narrative.* Bloomington, IN: Indiana University Press, 1985. The gold standard of scholarly books on the Bible as literature, in particular the prose material of Genesis through Kings. This volume does not make for easy reading, but it pays major dividends to all who are willing to mine its nuggets.

Supplementary Reading:

Arnold, Bill T., and Bryan Beyer. *Readings from the Ancient Near East: Primary Sources for Old Testament Study.* Grand Rapids, MI: Baker, 2002. A fine collection of ancient Near Eastern documents relevant to the study of the Bible, including translations of many of the texts discussed in our course (such as the *Enuma Elish*, the flood story incorporated into the Gilgamesh Epic, the Ugaritic epics of Aqhat and Kret, and the Egyptian Tale of Two Brothers. For a second such work, see the source by Victor H. Matthews and Don C. Benjamin, below.

Bar-Efrat, Shimon. *Narrative Art in the Bible.* Sheffield: Almond Press, 1989. The most detailed book available on the panoply of literary devices utilized by the biblical authors. Examples abound on every page, and a comprehensive index allows the reader to look up individual passages, such as the texts that we read from the book of Genesis.

Bird, Phyllis A. *Missing Persons and Mistaken Identities: Women and Gender in Ancient Israel*. Minneapolis: Fortress, 1997. An excellent volume on women in the Bible, with special attention to the various roles they play, including, for example, prostitute (or in the case of Tamar in Genesis 38, a woman disguised as a prostitute).

Brettler, Marc Z. "The Canonization of the Bible," in A. Berlin and M. Z. Brettler, eds., *The Jewish Study Bible*. New York: Oxford University Press, 2004, pp. 2072–2077. An introductory survey of the process that led to the canonization of the biblical books. The volume as a whole, incidentally, is an outstanding reference work, with introductions to each of the biblical books, a running commentary, and excellent essays at the back of the volume (including this one, for example).

Callaway, Mary. *Sing, O Barren One: A Study in Comparative Midrash*. Atlanta: Scholars Press, 1986. A study of the barren woman motif, which we examined in Lecture Fourteen. This book focuses more on post-biblical interpretations, however, than on the biblical material itself.

Day, Peggy L., ed. *Gender and Difference in Ancient Israel*. Minneapolis: Fortress, 1989. A fine collection of original essays treating various female characters in the Bible.

Fishbane, Michael. *Text and Texture: Close Readings of Selected Biblical Texts*. New York: Schocken, 1979. A collection of close readings of selected biblical texts (as per the subtitle of the book), including, for example, Genesis 1–11 (the Primeval cycle) and Genesis 25–35 (the Jacob cycle).

Fokkelman, J. P. *Reading Biblical Narrative: A Practical Guide*. Louisville, KY: Westminster John Knox Press, 1999. Another of the many excellent guides aiming to introduce the reader to the workings of biblical narrative prose. This volume is very user-friendly, as its subtitle indicates, directing the reader with questions for consideration and self-study at every turn.

Foster, Benjamin R. *The Epic of Gilgamesh*. New York: W.W. Norton, 2001. One of the two recent translations of the Gilgamesh Epic, including plenty of background material about the world's first great narrative epic poem. (See the source by Andrew George below for the second volume.)

Fox, Everett, "Stalking the Younger Brother: Some Models for Understanding a Biblical Motif." *Journal for the Study of the Old Testament* 60 (1993), pp. 45–68. A scholarly article (though quite accessible) devoted to one of the main literary motifs of the book of Genesis and the Bible in general, that of the younger brother superseding his older brother(s).

Friedman, Richard E. *The Bible with Sources Revealed.* San Francisco: HarperCollins, 2003. A polychrome poly-font edition of the Torah, allowing the reader to see with ease the postulated sources of the Pentateuch (J, E, D, and P—along with, at times, their various presumed subdivisions).

George, Andrew. *The Epic of Gilgamesh.* New York: Penguin, 2000. One of the two recent translations of the Gilgamesh Epic, including plenty of background material about the world's first great narrative epic poem. (See the source by Benjamin R. Foster above for the second volume.)

Licht, Jacob. *Storytelling in the Bible.* Jerusalem: Magnes, 1978. Another of the many excellent guides aiming to introduce the reader to the workings of biblical narrative prose. The author deals with certain techniques not treated in other works, such as ways of indicating the passage of time.

Matthews, Victor H., and Don C. Benjamin. *Old Testament Parallels: Laws and Stories from the Ancient Near East.* New York: Paulist, 1997. A fine collection of ancient Near Eastern documents relevant to the study of the Bible, including translations of many of the texts discussed in our course (such as the *Enuma Elish*, the flood story incorporated into the Gilgamesh Epic, the Ugaritic epics of Aqhat and Kret, and the Egyptian Tale of Two Brothers). For a second such work, see the source by Bill T. Arnold and Bryan Beyer above.

McCarter, P. Kyle (with Ronald S. Hendel). "The Patriarchal Age," in H. Shanks, ed., *Ancient Israel*, 2nd ed. Washington, DC: Biblical Archaeology Society, 1999, pp. 1–31. This article was referred to above under the source by Hershel Shanks in the Essential Reading section.

McGrath, Alister. *In the Beginning: The Story of the King James Bible and How It Changed a Nation, a Language, and a Culture.* New York: Doubleday, 2001. One of two recent books describing the making of the King James Version of the Bible. This book is must reading for anyone interested in the early history of the Bible in English. The world of early-modern Britain comes alive in McGrath's lively prose. Ditto for Adam Nicolson's book (see next entry).

Nicolson, Adam. *God's Secretaries: The Making of the King James Bible*. New York: HarperCollins, 2003. One of two recent books describing the making of the King James Version of the Bible. This book is must reading for anyone interested in the early history of the Bible in English. The world of early-modern Britain comes alive in Nicolson's lively prose. Ditto for Alister McGrath's book above.

Rabin, Elliot. *Understanding the Hebrew Bible: A Reader's Guide*. Hoboken, NJ: Ktav, 2005. A readable guide to the Bible as a whole, with individual chapters devoted to each of the Bible's main genres (narrative prose, law, poetry, prophecy, and so on).

Redford, Donald B. *A Study of the Biblical Story of Joseph*. Leiden: E. J. Brill,1970. A study of Genesis 37-50 in the light of the Egyptian evidence that sheds light on the narrative. Note, however, that the author seeks to demonstrate that the Joseph story dates to the Persian period, which runs contrary to the approach taken in our course.

Reis, Pamela T. *Reading the Lines: A Fresh Look at the Hebrew Bible*. Peabody, MA: Hendrickson, 2002. A series of original readings of selected biblical texts by an independent scholar. Among the best essays in this volume is the first one on the two creation stories, arguing for an integrated reading of the two accounts.

Rendsburg, Gary A. "The Vegetarian Ideal in the Bible," in L. J. Greenspoon, R. A. Simkins, and G. Shapiro, eds., *Food and Judaism, Studies in Jewish Civilization*, vol. 15. Omaha: Creighton University Press, 2005, pp. 319–334. An article dealing with the vegetarian ideal in the Bible, incorporating an array of texts, such as Genesis 1, Genesis 9, Leviticus 11 ($\approx$ Deuteronomy 14), and Isaiah 11.

Schniedewind, William M. *How the Bible Became a Book*. New York: Cambridge University Press, 2004. A scholarly yet accessible book about writing in ancient Israel, the production of literature, the social dimensions of reading and writing, and eventually, the creation and canonization of the biblical books.

Sperling, S. David. *The Original Torah*. New York: New York University Press, 1998. An original scholarly investigation into the political background of selected biblical stories, including, for example, the 10th-century-B.C.E. background of the Abraham material.

Walsh, Jerome T. *Style and Structure in Biblical Hebrew Narrative*. Collegeville, MN: Liturgical Press, 2001. Yet another of the many works intended to introduce the reader to the workings of biblical narrative prose. This book pays special attention to the patterns inherent in individual stories and to the structures observable in larger chunks of material.

Additional Internet Resources [also see the Translations section above]:

http://jewishstudies.rutgers.edu/faculty/grendsburg/index.shtml
This is the personal website of Professor Gary Rendsburg. One can find here a variety of articles written by Professor Rendsburg, which are available on the web; along with a complete list of his publications. Note further that one can access from here his non-credit online mini-course "The Bible and History," offered by Rutgers University.

http://www.bib-arch.org/
This is the website of the Biblical Archaeology Society, headquartered in Washington, D.C. The Society's main goal is to bring the scholarship of expert archaeologists and biblical scholars to educated lay people. It does so most importantly through its semi-monthly magazine *Biblical Archaeology Review*, but also through weekend and week-long seminars and through study tours of Israel, Egypt, and other lands.

http://www.bibleinterp.com/
The website of Bible and Interpretation, which, in its own words, is "dedicated to delivering the latest news, features, editorials, commentary, archaeological interpretation and excavations relevant to the study of the Bible for the public and biblical scholars." One can find a host of interesting essays at this website.

http://www.hope.edu/academic/religion/bandstra/RTOT/RTOT.HTM
This website contains the online version of Barry Bandstra's (Hope College) excellent textbook, *Reading the Old Testament: An Introduction to the Hebrew Bible*. Chapters 1 and 2, entitled "Genesis 1-11: The Primeval Story" and "Genesis 12-50: The Ancestral Story," are the most relevant for our course on the Book of Genesis.